IRVING FINE *An American Composer in His Time*

# Irving Fine

## An American Composer in His Time

### PHILLIP RAMEY

LIVES IN MUSIC SERIES No. 8

PENDRAGON PRESS
*in association with*
THE LIBRARY OF CONGRESS

*For the Library of Congress:*
*W. Ralph Eubanks*, Director of Publishing
*Iris B. Newsom*, Editor
*Stephen Kraft*, Designer

**Library of Congress Cataloging-in-Publication Data**

Ramey, Phillip.
  Irving Fine : an American composer in his time / Phillip Ramey.
      p. cm.
  Includes bibliographical references (p.   ), a list of Irving Fine's works (p.
), and index.
  ISBN 1-57647-116-0
  1. Fine, Irving, 1914-1962. 2. Composers--United States--Biography. I.
Title.
  ML410.F4488 2005
  780'.92--dc22

                        2005019260

Cover and frontispiece: Irving Fine, 1948.
Photo courtesy of the author.

*In Memory of*

*Verna Fine and Paul Bowles*

# Contents

# *Prefatory Note*

■ THERE ARE MUSICAL FIGURES OF THE RECENT PAST about whom I might perhaps justifiably speculate concerning character and motivation, among them, Aaron Copland, Samuel Barber, Virgil Thomson, Leonard Bernstein and Paul Bowles. These are people I knew well. I did not, however, know Irving Fine. Thus, even if I happened to be psychoanalytically oriented, I would feel obligated, out of professionalism and common sense, to let those close to him, whether family, friends or colleagues, reminisce here; and to refrain almost entirely from subjective interpretation.

In this study of the life and music of Irving Fine, I have been careful to assure that the portrait of the composer which emerges is sketched only by those who spoke from first-hand knowledge.

Phillip Ramey

# Foreword *(in the Form of a Reminiscence)* by Richard Wernick

■ ON A SNOWY DECEMBER NIGHT in 1950 (it might even have been Beethoven's birthday), I was permitted to use the family car. The importance of the trip was strong enough to overcome the trepidation of my nervous parents. Despite the fact that I had never driven in snow, and that there were already six inches on the ground, I had an appointment to meet Irving Fine for the first time, and I was determined not to miss it.

Having made up my mind, at the age of sixteen, that I wanted to be a composer, and having demonstrated sufficient will, I had begun to be taken seriously by my high-school music teacher as well as my parents. The latter could offer little guidance, but my teacher, a quite remarkable man by the name of Henry Lasker, insisted that the person I must seek out and try to study with was Irving Fine. Henry was my high-school theory teacher, my piano teacher and my mentor. He had guided me through my first serious, but feeble, attempts at composing, and now that college was approaching he wanted the best for me and went to great pains to arrange a meeting with Irving Fine.

But there was a complication. I not only wanted to compose, but had ambitions to do so at Harvard and had my application filled out and ready to go into the mail. Irving Fine, however, had just moved from the venerable hills of Harvard to join the faculty of Brandeis, a brand-spanking-new university, still in its earliest stages, and a totally unknown quantity. Built on the site of Middlesex College in Waltham, Massachusetts, a defunct establishment of higher education complete with a faux medieval castle, Brandeis was originally intended to be a haven for the large numbers of Jewish students who, subject to an insidious quota system, were denied entry to the country's most prestigious medical schools. There were lots of risks in going to a school that had not yet produced its first graduating class, let alone the fact

*xi*

that its raison d'être was a medical school (it is interesting that fifty-three years later there is still no medical school at Brandeis. But that is another story altogether). Henry Lasker, however, was insistent that I should study with Irving Fine.

So I got into the family Olds and ventured out in a storm, fishtailed all over the place and eventually arrived at a warmly lit house at the end of a small dark exurban road in Natick, Massachusetts. I had little idea that the results of that evening would continue to reverberate in my life for the next fifty-three years. It is hard to believe that this man, in whom I was putting so much trust, had just celebrated only his thirty-sixth birthday.

I was warmly welcomed by Irving and his wife Verna, served some warm libation, after which Irving and I retired to his studio, a comfortable room with two formidable Steinway grand pianos. We talked about music, although I must admit that most of what he had to say was well beyond my comprehension. He then gently, but thoroughly, put me through a series of tests: sightreading, clefs that were totally unfamiliar, identification of intervals and chords, repertoire, and so on. He let me talk about my goals and aspirations, and by the time another half-foot of snow had accumulated I was totally smitten. He, in turn, was obviously sufficiently impressed with my enthusiasm (it couldn't have been my skills) to promise to do what he could for me.

And so at the great age of seventeen I entered the world of Irving Fine and his family, at the approximate midpoint of Phillip Ramey's excellent book. I was witness to the remarkable growth and evolution of Fine's compositional style and esthetic, all the way from the *Notturno for Strings and Harp* (1950-1951) to the *Symphony (1962)*.

As the tale of Fine's life and career unfolds we are not only drawn into the artistic growth of a single composer, but also into the rather remarkable relationship, personal and professional, that existed among a group of six composers. This group was centered around a Harvard/Tanglewood/Brandeis junction, led by its senior member Aaron Copland (1900-1990). They were, aside from Fine, Arthur Berger (1912-2003), Leonard Bernstein (1918-1990), Harold Shapero (1920-) and Lukas Foss (1922-). I came to know them all during my 1951-1955 years at Brandeis and Tanglewood, and beyond. Their Harvard connection was the result of education and affiliation, and started in the student days of several of them, who, like Irving, worked with the great French pedagogue Nadia Boulanger. At Tanglewood under the tutelage of Serge Koussevitzky, whose dedication to new music was visionary, they not only worked together, but also shared living quarters under the watchful eye of their den-mother Verna. The Brandeis connection came about because Fine not only brought in Bernstein, Shapero and Berger as faculty, but created a strong presence at the university for Copland as well. They came to comprise what could almost be referred to as "The Boston School," that city being one of the country's strongest neoclassical centers.

In the days before direct long-distance dialing they were in constant touch with each other by mail, and a vast amount of that correspondence has been preserved. It's hard to imagine today, even with the proliferation of e-mail, that, at the time when these men were building careers as composers, conductors and teachers, they found not just the time but obviously had the need to stay in communication to such a degree. They commented in absolutely direct terms about each other's work. The numerous letters are at one and the same time full of praise, admiration and, above all, criticism; the exchange of views was often two or more times per week. They never seemed to feel uncomfortable about saying what was on their minds. If anything it made them closer. Yes, they had their quarrels, but who didn't? They also shared adventures of all sorts and descriptions, as Ramey vividly portrays. It is hard to imagine this from the perspective of the early twenty-first century, when composers seem to be so envious of one another, when one composer's success is often felt to come at the expense of another's. It appears too few of us today appreciate that what is good for one composer is good for the profession, and what is good for the profession is good for all composers. Ramey keenly defines how Fine's personal development was the result of not only his own probing musical and creative intellect, but also of his involvement with his American "Les Six."

Fine was onto something completely original in his search for a musical language and style that combined the elegance of neoclassicism with the rigor and toughness of twelve-tone technique. Copland had gone off in one twelve-tone direction, as did Stravinsky. But Fine did it somewhat differently, and perhaps more successfully. We will simply never know where this path would have taken him, but it is intriguing to imagine. Twelve-tone technique was the extension of nineteenth-century German romanticism and chromaticism, and grew from the seeds of early-twentieth-century German expressionism. That Fine, particularly in his *Fantasia for String Trio* (1956-1957) and *Symphony (1962)*, turned it into the modality of a highly personal mid-century neoclassicism was a remarkable musical accomplishment.

The story ends where it began, at the Fine house in Natick, a mere twelve years after that first trip in the snow. My family and I were in the midst of what had become an annual ritual, looking after the Natick house while the Fine family was at Tanglewood. Irving, feeling unwell, phoned and asked if it was all right for them to return home a few days early. We spent a wonderful couple of hours together, just the two of us, in his studio, a place that had become very much home for me. We talked about the Tanglewood performance of the symphony that he had conducted not much more than a week earlier, and for one last time the use of twelve-tone techniques in neoclassical composition.

Two days later Irving Fine died, in the hospital, of a massive coronary.

July 2003
Wolcott, Vermont

# Introduction

■ DURING HIS HIGH SCHOOL YEARS, Irving Fine would often hang from the lintels of doors. He was not quite five feet, eight inches tall and hoped to stretch himself. That adolescent activity can stand as a metaphor for Fine's development as a composer. In the last decade of his life, before his untimely death at the age of forty-seven, he managed to stretch himself out of the attractive but essentially lightweight generic neo-classicism that had nurtured him and, with a free adaptation of Arnold Schoenberg's twelve-tone method, to expand and lend *gravitas* to an increasingly romantic musical idiom. Two cornerstones of his legacy, the string quartet of 1952 and the symphony of 1962, were the result.

Personally, Fine, a Bostonian born and bred, was urbane, intellectual, witty, charming and generous. There was an innate shyness in his makeup, and a feeling of insecurity, for he never thought of himself as being as accomplished a composer as in fact he was. A dedicated family man, he loved his wife and was devoted to his three daughters. He was a good comrade. No one with whom I have talked had anything but respect and affection for him. I remember Aaron Copland's once calling him "simpatico"—Copland's highest accolade.

Fine's composer friend Harold Shapero described him as "a good academic." Consequently, he led the somewhat sequestered life of a college professor, initially on the Harvard faculty, then as an instructor at Tanglewood's Berkshire Music Center and finally as a teacher and innovative administrator at Brandeis University. He was an essayist of some distinction. He was also an excellent pianist and a capable conductor, although his range of activity and reputation as a performer were mainly limited to the Boston area. His compositional career spanned only two decades: 1942 to 1962.

From childhood, music was Fine's obsession, and even more than with most composers, his life *was* his music. As this biography will show.

Fine displayed a remarkable gift for melody throughout his career, even in his late serial-inflected scores. This singing quality is easily heard in early pieces such as the *Three Choruses from "Alice in Wonderland"* of 1942 and the *Sonata for Violin and Piano* of 1946, where the tunes are diatonic and direct. With the bittersweet *Notturno for Strings and Harp* of 1951 and the elegaic *Serious Song: Lament for String Orchestra* of 1955, Fine proved himself capable of writing sustained melody, which, as he once noted admiringly of Sir William Walton, "gives real pleasure to lots of people without being commonplace." A telling lyricism also informs his later works, for instance the *Fantasia for String Trio* of 1956 and the *Symphony (1962)*, where it is more chromatic and subtle.

Another essential element in Fine's music is rhythm. His preoccupation was generated early on by the intense influence of Igor Stravinsky's neoclassic style in 1940s works such as the *Symphony in Three Movements*, which also stimulated Fine's preference for clean-sounding instrumental textures. One of his major orchestral scores, the *Toccata Concertante* of 1947, is founded on ostinato rhythm. Sonata form is employed, but the piece is literally held together by constant underlying rhythm. The effect is that of a brilliant tour-de-force, impressive both for the quality of its syncopated and lyric themes and for the sheer energy that ultimately leads to a climactic minor-ninth chord in the full orchestra near the end. The *Toccata*, along with the *Partita for Wind Quintet* (1948), stands as one of Fine's neoclassic masterpieces.

Copland observed that Fine's music "wins us over through its keenly conceived sonorities and its fully realized expressive content," and praised it for its "elegance, style, finish and convincing continuity." Fine may have been an academic, but there is nothing academic sounding about his work, for he was a thoroughly "musical" composer in the old-fashioned sense. An examination of his small but notable output reveals a perfectionism on the order of Copland (whom he considered America's greatest composer) and akin to that of his idol Stravinsky. Fine was decidedly assimilative, yet possessed his own recognizable voice. He had an inborn sense of harmony, which at first was tonal and then bitonal, gradually became more dissonant and ended up complex though tonally anchored. His scores are carefully calculated and detailed, their increasing emphasis on melody allied with effective structuring, supple rhythm, clear textures and unobtrusive but integral polyphony. Fine's rhetoric is always appropriate to his materials and can range from childlike naivety to dramatic gesture. When, as the final development of his esthetic, he made use of serial technique, he subordinated it to his particular musical ideals, tonalizing serialism on his own terms and thus creating some of his most profound and moving works. Upon hearing Fine's last piece, *Symphony (1962)*, his colleague Leon Kirchner was amazed: "I thought, here's a whole new composer."

Leonard Bernstein once described Irving Fine as "a beautiful spirit in the world of music [who] brought honor to everything he touched." In the mid-twentieth-century American pantheon, Fine can be seen in retrospect as a musical aristocrat, an unusually refined artist well on his way to major status. That this gifted composer should die in middle age, just as a personal style consolidating seemingly contradictory elements was finally in his grasp, is not only tragic but deeply ironic.

June 2000
Tangier

# PART ONE

# Chapter 1

■ ON A SUMMER AFTERNOON during the late 1920s at the Fine home in Winthrop, Massachusetts, the family maid marched into the kitchen holding her hands over her ears. "I can't stand it anymore," she announced indignantly to Charlotte Fine. "He never stops!"

"He" was the teenaged Irving Fine, "it" the sound of his piano. The boy had been fixated on music since his early years and now practiced five or six hours a day at the Steinway grand in the living room. His sister Audrey recalled: "That's all you heard. I remember thinking, my God, he's at that piano again. Because he really worked at it. It wasn't something he just dreamed about."

From childhood, Irving was not a dreamer but a doer. He had to struggle for a long period to have a career in music, the opposing force being a father hostile to the idea. He grew up in what today would be described as a dysfunctional family. "Irving told me it was a very unhappy marriage and that it had scarred him," his widow Verna remembered. Both parents were Jews of Eastern-European extraction who had done their best to assimilate. His father, George, was an educated but unsuccessful lawyer who came to know the ins and outs of the stock market: "a bright but difficult man," said Verna. He had little if any sympathy for the arts. Physically, he was tall and domineering. Irving's mother, Charlotte, or Lottie, was short, buxom and plump: "a very pretty, sweet, weak but manipulative lady, blonde with blue eyes—a housewife."

The parents were relatively uncultured, though Lottie did try to be supportive of Irving's emerging talent. But George and Lottie often fought, and Lottie had to endure occasional beatings. Verna remembered: "Irving told me many times that one day, when he was eight or nine years old, he came home from grammar school and found his mother with all the gas jets on." Lottie was still conscious, and Irving rushed about opening windows. "He said it was a real shocker for him, a horrible sensation, because he was close to his mother. He had a love-hate relationship with his father, who was a big bully." Many years later, Irving would take note of his "constant sympathy" with his mother. "I would like to have identified with my father," he wrote, "but I identified really with my mother." Harold Shapero summed up George and Lotte Fine thus: "He was macho, a sort of old-fashioned martinet. She was a short, fat Jewish person."

All of Irving's grandparents had their origins in Latvia and all of them arrived in the United States sometime in the 1880s, to settle eventually in Hartford, Connecticut. There, the two grandfathers, still single, became friends and worked together peddling "anything they could get hold of," as Audrey put it. The paternal grandfather, Nathan Fine, married Annie Goldman and the maternal grandfather, David Friedman (formerly Greenburg), married Frances (Fannie) Siegel, both weddings occurring in Hartford. Irving's father, George Fine, was born there on April 16, 1891, part of a large family consisting of seven brothers and one sister. His mother, Charlotte Friedman, also was born in Hartford, in 1894, one of three sisters and two brothers. The maternal grandparents, the Friedmans, remained in Hartford, while the paternal grandparents moved to East Boston, Massachusetts, where Nathan Fine set up as a haberdasher. The Fines of Boston prospered, the Friedmans of Hartford did not.

Assimilation began early. Audrey remembered that "Grandma and Grandpa Fine would speak nothing but English to us, and my mother and father couldn't speak a word of Yiddish." According to Irving's younger sister Barbara, there had been musicians in their mother's family: "I think there were relatives who played in an orchestra in New York." There was no trace of musicality on their father's side.

George Fine and Charlotte Friedman were married in Boston, where they had met. George was a self-made man who peddled newspapers on the wharf in East Boston when he was ten years old and subsequently graduated from the Boston University Law School. "My dad got his education through his own hard work," said Audrey. George established himself as a lawyer in Boston, where he had mostly Italian clients. He was a distant man who didn't much like the law business and, perhaps as a result, wasn't very successful. "I remember Irving's telling me how he would come home, have supper and then have to go back to the office," recalled Verna. "On Sunday he never talked, but buried his head in the *New York Times*. He was interested in world economic conditions." George didn't practice law for long, instead becoming involved in stock-market investment, in which he did well.

Irving Fine was born on December 3, 1914, delivered by a doctor at home at 404 Meridian Street in East Boston, then a lower-middle-class area located near what is now Logan Airport. He was originally named Irving (the anglicized version of Isaac) Gabriel. But when his father's sister Louise picked up the birth certificate, she decided that Gabriel sounded too Jewish and had it changed to Gifford, after one of her brothers. Irving Gifford, she felt, might be an English name.

The first of three children (Audrey was born in 1916, Barbara in 1922), Irving had perfect pitch, and at age five began piano lessons at the East Boston Music Center, on White Street. His mother was surprised that he was enthusiastic about them and that he wanted to sit at the keyboard practicing for long hours. His father, known as Papa George, also thought it remarkable, until, much later on, Irving announced that he wanted to be a musician. "Then he didn't think it was so remarkable," said Audrey. When Irving's first piano teacher died, it took his parents four or five years to find another.

Irving, nicknamed "Golem" (monster or zombie) by his parents, was his mother's favorite. "She adored him," Audrey remembered. "My sister and I used to say, 'Well, Mother's got her love-child.' Everything he did was perfect. He was her golden boy." At a certain point, however, the boy's obsession with the piano became too much even for his doting mother. Barbara recalled Lotte's pleading, "Stop, already!"

For the most part, Irving practiced classical music, but there were forays into pop songs and jazz. Barbara, also, played the piano and had the same teacher. She adored her big brother and was impressed when he would take a piece of popular music "and play it in the style of Bach or Beethoven or Brahms. I thought it was pretty unique that he could do

3

that." Despite this early facility, he does not seem to have begun composing until he was in college. "I was a late bloomer," he told Verna.

Young Irving was mischievous, and Audrey, with whom he had a sometimes antagonistic relationship, was often the butt of his teasing. One time, Irving drove the family car to meet her at a bus stop. As she prepared to get in, he put his foot on the gas so that she had to run after the car. "So you see, he wasn't all music and seriousness," Audrey declared. He tended to criticize her choice of boyfriends. "If I mentioned I was going out with somebody, he would say, 'I don't like him. He isn't right for you.' That I remember clearly." He was also fond of grabbing Audrey by the back of the neck and propelling her along at an uncomfortably brisk pace. When Irving's friends would visit, they annoyed her by ruffling her hair and pinching her shoulders—"torturing me."

Both sisters stressed that Irving was not given to peculiar "artistic" behavior. "Even though he was a genius, there was a lot of him that was normal," stated Audrey. "He was not weird. He was a nice, decent guy who, naturally, drank, smoked and had girlfriends." Still, his friends and the girls he dated were "nothing like him intellectually." Barbara noted that Irving was "very sweet but strong, no marshmallow. He wouldn't take baloney from anybody." Nevertheless, Verna thought Irving "inherited a lot of his mother's soft side. He was very gentle."

Although Irving was affectionate and protective toward his younger sister Barbara, he had mixed feelings about Audrey. He would discuss this in later years with his wife. "He felt pity toward her because she grew up rather unattractive. He also resented her, because he felt his parents doted on her. There was a jealousy of that sibling." Irving was blond and blue-eyed and took after his mother's side, while Audrey had black hair, black eyes and took after her father's.

Any jealousy could only have been aggravated when Papa George bought a baby-grand piano for Audrey during Irving's early teens, for the piano at which he spent so much time was only an upright. Audrey did not play well and, by her own admission, was the untalented sister. But she had developed a serious ear infection and was running a high temperature. She remembered that "my father came into my room and said I must get better, and when I did he was going to buy me a Steinway. I wondered, why me? The abscess burst and was drained, and I did get the piano. But of course it was Irving who played it." Audrey was under the impression that the Steinway went with Irving when he left home, but Verna had another story. "Years later, when we were married and Irving wanted a grand piano, his parents said no, it's Audrey's. I was ready to scream. I'm giving that as an example: he did not come from supportive parents." To Audrey, the piano was just an attractive piece of furniture. Eventually, though, the disputed instrument did go to her brother.

Short, fair complected, with a rather husky build, Irving walked with his feet out and had a bouncy, slightly waddling gait. There was a large gap between his two upper front teeth, in which he would sometimes insert a quarter coin as a joke. His hands were not as big as he would have liked, and Audrey remembered him complaining about having to stretch to reach octaves. He was not particularly athletic in high school, although in later life he played golf and enjoyed swimming. Football and baseball didn't interest him. When he wasn't at school he wanted to be home at the piano. "He was a serious musician from the time he was a young boy," said Audrey. Occasionally he went out on weekends and got drunk with his friends. Audrey recalled one afternoon during Prohibition when their parents were away. She came into the kitchen and found Irving and another boy standing over the stove. "They were boiling something, and I asked, 'What are you doing?' I was the little sister who knows too much." Irving took her by the neck, yelled "Get out of here!", gave her a great push and slammed the door. An outraged Audrey screamed, "I know what you're up to and I'm going to tell Daddy!" Papa George had some 100-proof alcohol and Irving was "boiling it up, probably to mix it with something. They were going out on a date and wanted to have a cocktail party."

Audrey ultimately decided not to "rat."

Even as a child, Irving was a hearty eater, and in later years he would have to watch his weight. Audrey remembered: "Our mother was a great cook. Irving would come into the kitchen and smell something and get all excited about it. I don't think it made any difference whether it was raw herring or French cuisine. He just genuinely loved food." Barbara had fond memories of nights when she and Irving would make "egg trilby" sandwiches: a fried-egg concoction with a slice of onion on top. He had a sweet tooth, especially for chocolate, to which he was allergic. It took only a couple of chocolates to send him into a sneezing fit. Verna recalled his getting up in the middle of the night, sneaking out and taking chocolates from the dining room cabinet. Awakened by the violent reaction, she would yell, "Irving, are you snitching chocolates again?" "Oh, no, no, no," he would reply, laughing through his sneezes. "He didn't sleep well, was a slight insomniac, and loved to eat in the middle of the night," she remembered.

Irving's sisters noted that Papa George was physically protective of all his children and frowned upon sports. His attitude stemmed from an incident involving Irving when he was about fifteen. Irving was playing ice-hockey, probably acting as a goalie, when another player rammed into him with his mouth open. The boy's teeth pierced Irving's forehead, and he had to have a tetanus shot that made him violently ill. A small scar provided him with a lifelong memento of the accident. The post-collision status of the aggressor's oral cavity has gone unrecorded.

A couple of years later, Irving suffered a far worse injury. Throughout his high school years his parents insisted that he find summer jobs, mainly to keep him occupied during the day and the piano silent. One was at a delicatessen in Winthrop, "sweeping up and doing all the dirty work, like lugging corned beef," said Audrey. Another was in Hartford at the Merritt Blue Print Company, a firm that made documents for architects and was partly owned by Lotte's brother Joe. Irving stayed with his grandparents that summer, and his job was to make deliveries. One day, as he approached the shop car with a packet under his arm, he was struck by a passing automobile. The impact lifted him into the air and he landed on the car's hood, hitting his head. Irving ended up in a Hartford hospital with a severe concussion. According to Verna, "he left the hospital too soon, because he wanted to go home to Boston." For the rest of his life, he would suffer from periodic headaches, which he attributed to the accident. "By the time I met him," Verna recalled, "they were coming every month—bad headaches similar to migraines."

Although Irving's sisters frequently used the word "normal" to describe their brother, his first sexual experience was anything but that. He told Verna, who confided it to her daughters many years later, that at age six he had been molested by a twelve-year-old neighborhood girl who was acting as his babysitter. He was sexually active early on, and in his teens sometimes frequented whorehouses in Boston with a friend named Stanley. He also liked to write smutty limericks.

Verna recalled that Irving appreciated women with large breasts, theorizing that this might be because his mother and sisters were thus endowed. One summer in the late 1940s, while sitting on the lawn with his wife and Aaron Copland, Irving gave a quiet wolf whistle as an extremely busty female in a revealing halter passed by. Verna, who had average-sized breasts and was used to his ways, said, "Oh, Irving, act your age." Copland, puzzled, asked: "Can you explain to us why you like those ghastly things?" Irving just smiled. All his life he was a bit of a flirt, charming both sexes, although Verna insisted that he had no homosexual inclinations, even in adolescence.

# Chapter 2

■ IRVING'S EARLY EDUCATION was at the Chapman School in East Boston and at Winthrop Grammar School and Winthrop High School. Audrey said he was an outstanding student. Verna thought he was "very bright and very well read" but poorly trained in high school. He took German as his elective language but failed to pass the College Board German exam. He had applied to Harvard University and Amherst College and was rejected by the former and accepted by the latter. "I have never seen anyone so devastated," Audrey remembered. "I think there were two boys who applied to Harvard from Winthrop High and Irving's grades were better, but the other boy was not Jewish so that young man got in." True or not, the issue of anti-Semitism at Harvard would recur in later years. Irving was, said Audrey, "very much a Jew, though he wasn't an observant Jew who went to synagogue all the time. But the holidays meant a lot to him." He read Hebrew and was knowledgeable about Jewish history. At thirteen he had been initiated into the Jewish faith with a *bar mitzvah* ceremony.

Beginning in grade school and lasting into college, from 1924 to 1935, Irving had the good fortune to study piano in Boston with Frances L. Grover, an elderly woman who had been the teacher of the well-known composer and Harvard faculty member Randall Thompson. "She was a fantastic teacher," recalled Verna. "It was Mrs. Grover who said, 'Don't go to Amherst, go to Harvard. They have a fabulous music department'." At her suggestion, he enrolled at the prestigious Boys' Latin School in Boston for a postgraduate course in German, in effect his fifth year of high school. There, he met two lifelong friends: Leonard Bernstein, who became one of the world's most celebrated orchestra conductors, and Saul Cohen, who had a distinguished career as a scientist. Irving subsequently passed the College Board German exam and in 1933, at the age of eighteen, he was admitted to Harvard Col-

9

lege. That same year, the Fine family left Winthrop and moved to Chestnut Hill in Brookline, a suburb of Boston. At 154 Wallis Road, Papa George had built what Verna described as "a large and beautiful home."

When Irving entered Harvard in the fall of 1933, his father told him that, despite his music studies, he expected him eventually to go into medicine. Music, to Papa George, was not a proper field of endeavor, especially during the harsh economic climate of the Depression. He wanted his son to emerge from college with a useful profession, one that had a future. Barbara remembered that "Dad thought, who is going to be able to make a living out of being a musician? What was he going to be, a piano teacher? He was so negative about what Irving was doing." Said Verna: "The desire to be a musician seemed very strange to him."

So it was that, along with his music courses, Irving enrolled in a few science courses. He was mildly interested in zoology but not at all in medicine. Still, as Audrey recalled, he went to Harvard "with the understanding that he would at least try to be a doctor." As it turned out, Irving couldn't stand the sight of blood and the instruction in zoology bored him. "It was more a passive than active course," Verna said. "I remember he told me that all you did was look in a microscope and draw pictures of feathers. It turned him off the whole subject of science, and he didn't take any science courses in his last two years at Harvard." He did, however, take a course in Russian.

Despite the cross purposes of father and son, Papa George paid for Irving to live on campus when he could easily have lived at home in Brookline. He also made sure he had his own room, with his spinet piano in it. "He was not a generous man," Verna noted, "but he wanted Irving to have the real college experience."

One of only two letters that survive from Irving to his parents in his college years is dated March 8, 1934, written from Stoughton Hall at Harvard during his second semester. Lottie and George were vacationing in Florida and the letter begins with a description of the dreary winter weather in Cambridge that "weakened Mrs. Grover for a while." Irving is looking forward to singing in the Bach *B Minor Mass*, with the Harvard Glee Club and the Boston Symphony Orchestra, in

Symphony Hall, Boston. The conductor was to be the orchestra's famed music director, Serge Koussevitzky, who had failed to appear for a chorus rehearsal at the school because of "an outburst of artistic temperament or something like that." Already, Irving is clearly planning to become a composer: "I am certain now that solitude and solitude only is conducive to any productiveness. One must have friends but not see them too much—at least when one is trying to develop himself. I have been amazed lately to find out the number of fellows concentrating in music. Naturally I often compare myself to these budding musicians and I find that I have nothing to [be] ashamed of in comparison with them." He cites his "natural talent" and addresses his father: "I have found out much truth in what you have said to me since I have been away. But I am still determined to study music."

According to Audrey, during his sophomore year, after sitting dutifully through zoology and other science courses, Irving wrote his father "and told him that he was sorry and he hoped he wasn't disappointing him, but music was his only life. That was the end of anything that resembled what our father wanted. He was pretty upset." For Papa George, a man used to having his way, it was a major defeat, and one he would never fully accept, even in later years when Irving achieved recognition as a composer.

Home for the summer in June 1935, not long after defying his father, Irving wrote what was perhaps intended as a placatory poem. Titled "To Daddy on Father's Day," it bears quoting in full, if only because of the subtle barb in the second stanza.

> The mind's astrain, the hand a-twerp.
> The pen refuses aught but burp
> most wretched rhymes expressing naught.
> Yet in our hearts there strains full hot,
> a note that wills its way to light.
>
> O pen, wilt thou let gastric wrong
> stop thee from praising loud—full strong—
> a man whose outward mien reveals
> not even near all which he feels
> toward his dear own—his grateful brood.
>
> Then quill, forget thine ills and woes
> (Sodium bicarb' will quell *thy* foes)

and turn to laud our cherished père.
Where find ye better—where more fair?

The music department at Harvard was relatively small, and not a conservatory. Consequently, music theory and history, rather than performance, were emphasized. The only PhD.s given were in musicology. Composer Daniel Pinkham, an alumnus, noted the prevailing attitude: "At Harvard, music should be seen but not heard." The outlet Irving found as an undergraduate for his by-now considerable ability as a pianist was as accompanist for the Harvard Glee Club. Performances by the Glee Club were an honored tradition, but any other participation in live music-making was frowned upon. Sometimes, to make extra spending money and because he enjoyed it, Irving played pop music for silent films, in Cambridge movie houses.

His principal teachers were all distinguished. He studied theory and composition with the renowned composer Walter Piston (1894-1976); orchestration with Edward Burlingame Hill (1872-1960), also a composer of reputation; choral conducting with Archibald T. Davison (1883-1961), who had great influence on the teaching of that craft throughout the country; counterpoint with Arthur Tillman Merritt (1902-1998), author of a well-regarded treatise on the subject who would later become chairman of the music department.

Irving's initial efforts at serious composition date from the middle 1930s, his undergraduate years. There are several unfinished piano pieces (including one marked "for Prof. Piston"), six pages of an orchestral piece, two pages of a suite for brass instruments, and sketches for an *Intermezzo for Small Orchestra*, a string quartet and a sonata for violin and piano. One completed work is the *Prelude and Fugue* for piano (the title-page bears the notation "Submitted for Bohemian Club Prize Competition," but there is no record of its winning a prize), which is determinedly Bachlike, the *Allegro* prelude a contrary-motion canon in two voices, with running triplets, the *Andante* fugue a correct exercise in the usual four voices. Emphasizing the Baroque association is the fact that the neatly copied score contains no dynamics or phrasing.

Another finished piece, the *Passacaglia* for piano, is of more interest, if only because of the resolute chromaticism of its theme. No note is repeated for the first ten, lending a row-like aspect. Years later, in a 1945 letter to Aaron Copland, Irving would mock the work: "Have just been playing over [your early] passacaglia. You were pretty good in those days too. Someday I must play mine for you. As Evelyn Waugh would say, 'It is too-too vomit-making'." Still, although Irving's passacaglia shows no personality whatsoever, it is a perfectly respectable, if rather turgid, academic endeavor. The same can be said about the chorale "That we may worship Thee," a brief, ultra-conventional piece in F major perhaps intended for the Glee Club. From this period also date several piano pieces that seem to be lost, all with neobaroque titles: *canzona, ricercar, suite, pastorale.* A parodistic bagatelle, entitled *After Stravinsky* and scored for an ensemble of piccolo, horn, trumpet, violin and doublebass, exists only in instrumental parts and a sketchy preliminary score. Whether it was ever performed is unknown.

The most intriguing of Irving's extant student works is a near-atonal (beginning with an eleven-note row but cadencing firmly in A, with the third absent from the chord) piano piece (tempo: *Allegro con brio*) amusingly titled *"Thing" for Composition Seminar.* This may date from his undergraduate years or a little later, possibly 1938 or 1939. Although the chromatically meandering *Thing* is mildly bizarre and surprisingly unpianistic, it demonstrates fluency rather than individuality. Harold Shapero, who met Irving at Harvard in 1939 and became a close friend, might have been referring to *Thing* when he recalled: "The kind of music he was writing then was expressionistic and pretty ugly, nasty-sounding things he'd play on the piano. He had a dark streak. They were not in the light, dapper later style that everyone thought was so gay and charming."

In a different category entirely was Irving's incidental music, dating from 1936, to "A Musical Comedy on the Age that is Past," *The Christmas Sparrow or Double or Nothin',* by his classmate John Horne Burns. This was performed at Harvard at Dunster House on December 16, 1936, with singers, chorus and a small student orchestra conducted by Irving and another student. The setting was Dunster House and Harvard Square, and the cast included Sink the Strinker, Harassed Harvard Student, Lady in Red and Salvation Army Sally (all female roles played by boys). Among the songs were "I don't mind if I do," "Scrub it and rub it," "I am the queen of the biddies" and "Lonely little heart." One writer described Irving's score as "Gilbert and Sullivanish." Burns published three novels before his suicide in 1953 at the age of thirty-six, and it is probable that Irving was the prototype for the hero of *A Cry of Children* of 1952: a composer-pianist who plays Stravinsky, Scriabin, Bach and Jerome Kern.

Irving got considerable pleasure from accompanying the Harvard Glee Club, especially on tour. On one occasion, when they gave a concert at the Academy of Music in Philadelphia under their conductor, G. Wallace Woodworth, he reported to his parents that the critic Olin Downes "said that we were the finest choral body in the country." There were at least three thousand people in the audience, and Irving wrote: "I am getting so now that even I take a kind of delight in all of the fuss. I have lost all traces of nervousness." (In a cryptic postscript he asked, "Why in hell do my letters sound so formal?")

In his junior year, he was elected vice-president of the Glee Club. Verna said he "was quite Marxist in college" and an incident in June 1937 that stemmed from his election deeply shocked him and outraged his liberal instincts. It involved the elitist Harvard Club of Boston, which had no direct connection with the University but had a policy that every student who became an officer of any Harvard organization got an invitation to join. Irving received such a letter and was delighted. But when he went for an interview, the gentleman behind the desk kept looking at his watch. Finally he said: "I think, sir, that you got the invitation by mistake. This is embarrassing, but we really don't take your kind." Irving was advised to "go out in the world and make a reputation for yourself, come back in about ten years, and then we'll consider you for membership." It was a bitter experience, and perhaps Irving's first encounter with blatant anti-Semitism. Verna remembered that "even years later when he told me that story, he was *so* angry, absolutely enraged." A quarter of a century on, barely a month before his death, he would admit to "a secret dread of being turned down" upon applying for membership in the New York Harvard Club. "This happened in Boston many, many years ago when I was proposed for membership in the Boston Harvard Club," he wrote to a friend. Although he never returned to the Harvard Club of Boston, he would continue his happy association with the Harvard Glee Club: assistant conductor and choirmaster, 1938-1940 and 1942-1945; acting conductor and choirmaster, summer of 1944. "He loved choral conducting," said Verna, "and when you work with choruses you gain a feeling for words and rhythms."

In the spring of 1937, Irving graduated from Harvard, receiving a B.A. in music, *cum laude*. That fall, he enrolled in the graduate school to continue composition studies with Piston, who seemed to have become the first of his father figures. "Irving adored him and admired him tremendously," Verna recalled. "He liked the clarity of his music and thought his ballet *The Incredible Flutist* was wonderful." Piston was a model for Irving as far as elegant craftsmanship was concerned, and he envied his facility as a composer. But he was not, evidently, overly impressed by him as a teacher. Composer Richard Wernick remembered that many years later "Irving described some of his composition lessons with Piston. He apparently didn't do much teaching. He would look at a score for an hour and then say something like, 'Oh, maybe that should be a B-flat'."

From the beginning, Irving was a slow worker, much given to tinkering and revision. Composition was painful. "He used to joke: 'When I stew on a piece and work hard on it, it never comes out as good as my first rush of ideas.' He always doubted himself and wanted to get better," said Verna. In later years, he wished he had studied orchestration with Piston rather than Hill, who had imposed Debussy-like scoring. "Irving never thought he got a good enough, solid training in orchestration."

As his last assignment from Piston, Irving produced the *Fugue in F Minor* for string quartet, his most ambitious student work. The score is dated June 1, 1938. 106 bars long, cast in 3/2 meter at a slow tempo, this piece—at one point marked "altered form of subj. inverted" in the second violin and "subjected in retrograde measure by measure" in the cello—is a flawless academic exercise in fugal technique. Although the style is conventional, if mildly dissonant, the music is not dull and is clearly from the pen of a talented young man who has learned his craft. That same month, Irving was awarded an M.A. in musical composition.

In February 1939, the distinguished French pedagogue Nadia Boulanger came to Cambridge for her second residency as a visiting professor at Radcliffe College, an institution solely for women as, in those days, Harvard was for men. Boulanger (1887-1979) was a twentieth-century musical Renaissance Woman: organist, pianist, conductor; composer of cantatas, a piece for piano and orchestra, chamber music and songs. She came from an ultra-musical background. Her paternal grandparents were both musicians, he a cellist and teacher at the Paris Conservatoire, she a singer at the Opéra-Comique. Her father was a teacher at the Conservatoire, a composer of operas and choral music who was awarded a Prix de Rome, while her mother (whose Russian origins are obscure and who may or may not have been a princess) studied singing in her youth. Boulanger's younger sister Lili, a composer dead in her early twenties, had won a Prix de Rome.

Boulanger had studied organ with Félix Guilmant and Louis Vierne and composition with Gabriel Fauré. The first woman to conduct the Boston Symphony and the New York Philharmonic, she was a friend and colleague of some of the most famous musicians of the time, above all Igor Stravinsky, whose *Dumbarton Oaks Concerto* she conducted in its world premiere in Washington, D.C. in 1938. Innumerable American composers had studied with her in France, among them Piston, Virgil Thomson, Aaron Copland and David Diamond.

By most accounts, Boulanger was a brilliant and inspiring teacher. Copland wrote that "she knew everything about music—what came before Bach, Stravinsky's latest works, what came after Stravinsky, and everything in between. Technical skills—counterpoint, orchestration, sight-reading—were second nature to her." He noted that "she was profoundly committed to music [and] believed in strict discipline." Her critical faculty was "unerring." "Mademoiselle could always find the weak spot in a piece you suspected was weak, but had hoped she would not notice. She could also tell you *why* it was weak." Further, "she felt it her duty to be brutally honest and uncompromising." Technical mastery "was to be rigorously pursued and absorbed, and essentials implanted early." Copland remembered one of her favorite sayings: "To study music, we must learn the rules. To create music, we must forget them." He described her as "a superior person, knowledgeable about literature and other arts [and] a first-class intellect." Ned Rorem, who was not a Boulanger student but knew her well, recalled her "contagious enthusiasm," and went so far as to cite her as "our century's greatest pedagogue" and "arguably the greatest teacher since Socrates, certainly the greatest *music* teacher."

Some of Boulanger's quoted pronouncements give a vivid impression of her character. "The art of music is so deep and profound that to approach it very seriously only is not enough. One must approach music with a serious rigor and, at the same time, with a great affectionate joy." "Great art likes chains. The greatest artists have created art within bounds." "The more engrossed you become in the history of music and strict academic form, the more free you will be as you compose later on." "Life is denied by lack of attention, whether it be to cleaning windows or trying to write a masterpiece." "More the student is gifted, more you must be careful not to invade his self. The teacher must respect the personality of the student and the student must submit to what makes life possible: order, rigor and freedom." "It is the life of the spirit that counts."

Boulanger was a stringent taskmaster who had a durable influence on several generations of composers from several countries. Virgil Thomson wrote that "a certain maternal warmth was part of her charm for all young men; but what endeared her most to Americans was her conviction that American music was about to 'take off'." To her students, she was "furiously loyal" and "deeply affectionate." Oddly, though Boulanger held great reputation and authority in France, she had the most influence on foreign composers, especially Americans. Thomson whimsically noted that every town in the United States seemed to contain both a five-and-ten-cent store and a student of Nadia Boulanger.

Copland, who always gave her credit for his early technical proficiency, felt that, nevertheless, Boulanger's "insistence on discipline and reliance on traditional formulae was not right for everyone. Roy Harris said that except for the strongest musicians it was dangerous to study with Boulanger, because her *own* personality and talents were so strong." One of her standard notations on students' exercises was "Very musical, but forbidden." If a pupil protested that the violation of rules could be found in Bach or Beethoven or even Stravinsky, she would reply acidly, "He may, but you may not."

In addition to being formidable, Boulanger was indefatigable. At various French institutions and privately, she gave instruction in sight-reading, harmony, counterpoint, orchestration, analysis, piano and composition. She taught not only composers, but also conductors, teachers and performers.

Boulanger aggressively promoted the neoclassic ideals of Stravinsky. His music, she said, "satisfied the mental capabilities while at the same time touching the heart."[1] She admired his extraordinary sense of rhythm and, above all, the accuracy of his ear. Rorem wrote that, to her, Stravinsky was "he-who-can-do-no-wrong," while Jean Cocteau reportedly criticized her for administering "not the school of Stravinsky, but the church of Stravinsky." Irving had no such reservations. In 1949 he would refer to Boulanger as "a kind of fairy godmother of American music," approvingly citing her role as a "propagandist for Stravinsky's music."[2]

Her presence at Radcliffe College in early 1939 excited a good deal of interest at the Harvard music department. Verna recalled that "Boulanger couldn't teach at Harvard because she was a woman, so all the Harvard boys had to go to Radcliffe to take composition with her. That's where Irving met her." At the time, he was a tutor at Radcliffe, and he attended Boulanger's lectures with fascination.

For Irving, it was a momentous encounter, and not only because Boulanger was to be his most significant teacher. Through his studies with her he would become involved in

---

1. Not everyone was enthusiastic about Stravinsky's neoclassicism. Sergei Prokofiev once derided it as digging down into the graves of long-dead composers for inspiration.

2. On an ironic note: the Slav Stravinsky, who had discovered American ragtime and jazz at second hand in 1918 through sheet music, in effect codified in his *L'Histoire du Soldat* of the same year many elements of what came to be considered, from the 1920s into the 1940s, as quintessentially American rhythmic life and would be so employed by a whole school of serious composers in the United States.

what composer David Diamond termed "the Stravinsky-via-Nadia Problem," a matter of influence that somewhat bedeviled him later in life. "He had a thing about Stravinsky," Diamond remembered. "We once talked about it. I said, 'You know, Irving, I think that's where Nadia had a not-too-good influence on you.' Whenever there was a new Stravinsky work, she would make a point of analyzing it bar by bar with her students. The Stravinsky style, no matter what the period, is so potent that it is very dangerous, especially to a young composer."

Aaron Copland observed that "Fine grew up musically during the ascendancy of the neoclassic movement. This style, as developed by Stravinsky and his followers during the thirties and forties, had a profound influence on the younger composers. It satisfied a deep need in Fine's creative psyche—the need for an emotive world that includes imaginative freedom along with a sense of order and control."

Irving studied with Boulanger during the spring of 1939, at Radcliffe and also privately at the Forbes mansion in Cambridge, where she was staying. "She lived with the fancy Forbes," said Verna. "She worked around the clock and he sometimes had a 2 a.m. lesson with her. She was very good to him." So intrigued was Boulanger by Irving that she arranged for him to continue his work with her in France on a Wyman Foundation grant, during the summer.

# Chapter 3

■ ON JUNE 29, 1939, IRVING SAILED for France, traveling third class aboard the French Line ship *S.S. De Grasse*. It seems unlikely, but according to Verna his parents gave him no money. "I don't think Irving's father was at all pleased with him going to Europe to study with Nadia Boulanger. Irving always felt that Boulanger had probably paid for his trip."

On the first day out, he wrote to his mother and father that his cabin steward spoke nothing but French so he was trying "quite unsuccessfully" but "out of sheer necessity" to do likewise. "The sea has been relatively calm although a few people have been rather mal de meerish [sic]. So far I have been alright. It is now eleven o'clock in the evening and there is a strong or rather heavy mist and the sea is kicking up a bit." He has given the "maître d'hôtel" a dollar bribe to have a single stateroom, in which he is "quite alone and very comfortable." His accommodating steward has received a pack of cigarettes and a glass of whiskey. A heavy smoker from his youth, Irving describes himself as being "practically swamped with tobacco," having brought along ten packages of cigarettes and being given five packages of "flat fifties" by a Mrs. Tatel.

He has received telegrams from his Friedman relatives in Hartford, and also from two young ladies, one of them named Verna Rudnick: "the latter two were indeed a surprise." He is blissfully unaware that Miss Rudnick, whom he hardly knows, will become Mrs. Irving Fine two years later, almost to the day.

A Mr. De Angelis has called on him, and Irving, ever food-conscious, hopes to be invited to the first-class dining room for dinner, "which should be quite an experience as the food on third class is excellent. By the time I land I should be fatter than a hippo."

Several days later, on July 6, the ship reached Ireland, and Irving wrote a long letter to his parents describing life on board and giving vivid cameo descriptions of some of his fellow passengers. The third-class salon, he says, is "monopolized from morning to evening" by "swarms of students" traveling under the patronage of the American Youth Hostel Association and the Experiment in International Living. Many teachers accompany them, "mostly French instructors."

A Mr. D., who is acquainted with Papa George, meets with Irving's stern disapproval. "A more exasperating four-flusher [that is, humbug] I have never seen. Every noun he uses has a price tag. As he says, he has been successful in everything he has touched—a great stock-market operator, a great bond investor, a successful real-estate operator, and a fabulously fortunate rain-coat manufacturer. He is so thick-skinned he is not even aware of the iciness with which people treat [him] on board." The dreadful Mr. D. invites Irving up to the first-class lounge and importunes a girl to join them. "Then he began to ply her with the most stupid crude remarks, and I finally asked her to dance so as to relieve the general embarrassment. Both she and her cousin regard Mr. D. as a kind of freak."

Back in third class, Irving meets a "princess," "She is quite popular and is known as princess Harriet. She is rather stocky, has a remarkably fine face and is quite black. Formerly a Harlem laundress, she met some African potentate at the World's Fair. He asked her to be his Parisian wife (he has four others in Africa) and she consented." The "flamboyant" Harriet had been given sufficient money to travel cabin class on the luxury liner *Normandie*, but was informed by snooty French Line officials that she would "feel more comfortable" in the third-class section of the *De Grasse*. "Already two itinerant artists have attached themselves to her and have appointed themselves as her publicity agents."

Also in third class is Becky Merrick, "an extraordinary person who is quite naive and goes around telling everybody that she is. Her face always seems to have a look of amazement on it; she is always discovering new and wonderful things and yet she has a prescience of death (the nuns on board accentuate the feeling)." Becky is given to hero-worship, and Irving is on her list. "She decided this upon hearing me improvise. I think she is slightly mad." Irving is pleased, however, to find a piano student from Amherst College with whom he can read through four-hand music on the lounge piano. "We have played Schubert sonatinas [?] and had some fun at it although the results were meagre enough." And there is a Stanford boy who writes lyrics for popular songs. "I have helped him with some of his stuff and he considers me quite a genius because I can make up or string together a bunch of musical clichés."

Every night his tablemates at dinner are two female high-school teachers. "One of them is rather fat and good-natured and rather alert. The other is lean and more intense." The lean lady is the daughter of the president of the New York State Women's Christian Temperance Union, but "may be persuaded into a glass of wine occasionally." She expresses herself oddly while dining. "For example, she might say, 'Could I interest you in a few olives,' or 'would you consider a piece of Camembert'." She is somewhat flirtatious. "A few days ago she got a little kittenish on the subject of love. It seems that she has some fish nibbling at the line but hasn't hooked him yet." Later at night comes the real thing, a young couple who occupy the stateroom next to his. "They stay most of the time in their cabin out of sheer boredom with the food, the ship and the trip in general. They are exceptionally witty people who are always having wrestling bouts or something at night and then apologize to me for it in the morning." One can easily imagine the sensual young musician with his ear to the wall.

On July 7, at five in the morning, the *De Grasse* arrived at Plymouth, England, and at seven that evening reached France, docking at Le Havre. Irving took a train to Paris, where he settled temporarily into the Hotel Mont-Joli in the picturesque Montmartre district. Permanent accommodations for Irving and several other students had been arranged in the village of Hanneucourt par Gargenville, the site of Boulanger's family estate, in northern France some thirty miles from Paris, near the city of Mantes. On July 13, Irving wrote: "I went to Gargenville on Monday and found that the place was not ready for students and would not be ready until the end of the week. Boulanger has been in a kind of turmoil and doesn't know when she will go."

Meanwhile, Irving was enjoying sightseeing in his first foreign city: "The public buildings of Paris are undoubtedly the most beautiful I have ever seen," although he was not entranced with the area in which he found himself: "The central part of the Montmartre and other sections are rather ugly—though some people might call them quaint." One evening he had couscous at an Algerian restaurant on the Left Bank and then went on to the Opéra Comique to see Mozart's *The Marriage of Figaro*. "My French stinks," he wrote. "So does Paris (literally), but it disguises its odor with perfume." He visited Versailles and was unimpressed: "The Palace is boring." He cited soaring living costs: "This is, I suppose, due to the armament boom. People seem to be less hysterical about war here than at home. You see soldiers and war preparedness bulletins everywhere." Nevertheless, "it is a wonderful country, this France, and Paris is a marvelous city." It was the beginning of a lifelong love affair with all things French.

The village of Gargenville, however, did not particularly appeal to him. "Gargenville, or more properly, Hanancourt [*sic*] par Gargenville, is not very much of a place [although] it has a beautiful view from the top of its one hill and a very fine *allée* of magnificent trees. As far as I can see, these are its only attractions, and practically any French village has more to offer than this."

Gargenville was about halfway between Paris and Fontainebleau where, at the American School of Music, Boulanger had taught for decades. She also taught at Gargenville during the summers, commuting to Fontainebleau by automobile. (Her student David Diamond noted that "she was sort of an Italian driver, a crazy driver. I often wondered if I'd get home alive.") Boulanger's property in Gargenville, in French rustic style, was called Les Maisonettes and consisted of a main house in which she lived and gave lessons and a smaller house with several rooms where students could lodge. Diamond recalled that the little estate was entered by a gate and "surrounded by crumbling concrete walls, with wildflowers around the borders and a big tree in the back." In 1938, the year before Irving arrived, Boulanger had added a new room at the rear of the main house, an annex whose modern architecture warred with the rural atmosphere of the rest of the enclave. Large enough for two grand pianos and a couple dozen students, it functioned as her music salon.

Irving was assigned to the small house, La Petite Maison, which was in the charge of Madame Markevitch, the mother of the celebrated composer and conductor Igor Markevitch.

Irving described her as having "extraordinary culture and ability," and said he intended to study French with her at forty cents a lesson. The situation was somewhat chaotic. "When we arrived on Saturday, nobody seemed to know anything about anything. The best room in the house had been grabbed by Mrs. Dickens. I discovered later that I was to live in the next best one (a room which had the advantage of being next to the bath) but by mistake it was given to another man. Finally I was placed in a chamber on the top floor. The room is small but is exceptionally private." In the downstairs salon there was "a pretty horrible piano" for the residents' use.

Irving was the youngest, "by about ten years," of the newly arrived students. There was the aforementioned Mrs. Dickens, "a cocky little N.Y. woman [who] is trying to write a manual of musical instruction for adults—something to be used in popular mass education. In her first encounter [with Boulanger] she or her project was greeted by a most frigid response, for Boulg is almost violently opposed to short cuts to education." Other housemates included Miss Florence Shute, "an awfully nice gray-haired woman who teaches school in Pittsburgh," and Mr. Frost, another Pittsburgh teacher, a distant relation of the poet Robert Frost, who "is here to go through the whole business—harmony, counterpoint, etc." Additionally at La Petite Maison there were Mme. Markevitch's "gifted younger son Dimitri, an Englishman named "Bill something [Bardwell], who is supposed to be an exceptionally talented composer" and a Bostonian named "Hervey" (Hervé Armington, who became a documentary-film producer), who had "lots of money and I don't know how much talent." Other students living at Gargenville that summer were the Americans Elliot Forbes (scion of the Cambridge Forbes, later a choral conductor, Harvard professor and author of a history of music at Harvard), Barbara Trask and Katherine Wolff and the Englishman Peter Pope.

In his letters home, Irving never mentions the location of his lessons. Although Boulanger's famous summer classes were given at Fontainebleau, Verna Fine thought that he had commuted by train to Paris. There, Boulanger had a spacious apartment on the fourth floor at 36 rue Ballu, reached, Aaron Copland remembered, by a "small shaky elevator." Her living room contained two grand pianos and a large organ. Copland noted Boulanger's "imposing presence"—her severe black nunlike attire and pince-nez glasses—and was amused by the thought that twentieth-century music had been "nurtured in her old-fashioned salon." He noted that the ambiance in her studio suggested that one was "at the center of what was going on in the artistic life of Paris," that "it was all alive, and being created around you." Copland first met Stravinsky there, and once Camille Saint-Saëns came and played for Boulanger's students. "Imagine," said Copland, "a kid from Brooklyn shaking hands with Saint-Saëns!"

In summer, however, Boulanger normally closed her Paris flat and moved to Gargenville. As it is clear from one of Irving's letters that he did not visit Fontainebleau until August, and as David Diamond, who studied there in the summer of 1939, never encountered him, the most likely scenario involves lessons at Gargenville, at least until mid-August, possibly shifting to Fontainebleau after that (Irving is present in an undated group photograph taken at Fontainebleau).

Wherever it was held, Irving's first composition lesson with Boulanger was "a rather exciting affair." He had brought fragmentary sketches for a cello sonata, and "after offering some corrections or suggestions, she practically indicated the shape these fragments were to assume. (In other words practically composed the exposition for me.)" She felt his sketches were "steps in the right direction." Irving was studying not only composition but harmony and counterpoint, and he settled into a routine in which, aside from classes, his day was divided into three or four hours of composition, two hours of theory and two hours of piano practice.

His next lesson was even more stimulating, and it brought on a crisis. On July 23, he wrote to his parents: "Last night I had another lesson with her during which I showed her an entirely new beginning to a suite for cello and piano. She said that she liked it very much, that she felt it was just right, and that for the first time she could say unreservedly that I had a definite gift for composition. This in itself was wonderful but then she went on with the following suggestions the gist of which is that she wants me to stay on for a year. What in the world am I to do?"

The problem was that he had accepted three part-time

teaching jobs in the Boston area during the fall and winter of 1939-1940, at the Roxbury Latin School, Chamberlayne Junior College and the Beaver Country Day School; and money from his Wyman grant would end with the summer term. Despite the looming war clouds, he wished to stay on in France, but to do so he would have to "borrow or get some financial aid." Boulanger, he said, "wants me to see if I can get out of my commitments for the next year." He informed his parents that he intended to inquire whether the Wyman grant could be extended and pointedly asked his father to give his advice, but only after "careful deliberation": "Send me your answer as soon as possible by transatlantic plane." Then: "In an environment like this—among fellow musicians—work becomes pleasure and above all one gets to learn so much by the exchange of ideas. I played my sonata for violin and piano [an incomplete work from the Harvard years] today with Priscilla Thierry [a Radcliffe graduate and fellow student] and discovered spots in it which were better than I expected. That's the sort of thing that Boulanger says is so wonderful about working here and in Paris. There is the wonderful association with people who are creating and there are the multitudes of concerts which are inexpensive beyond belief—concerts where the emphasis is on music and not on the performance."

In the same letter, Irving praises the French. "You live with a people in whose life art is all pervasive. Somebody told of receiving a basket of beans from the market arranged so as to form a number of rosebuds. I have seen workmen [who] are artisans in the old sense of the word, men who take a great deal of pride in their jobs. I don't think there are many of the same sort in America." He betrays some unease about the ominous political situation. "What is rather strange is that along with this almost medieval concept plus the famous French individualism, France also has a proletariat which is amazingly well organized and highly militant. Dangerously so, because it has succeeded in coalescing Fascist opposition."

The eloquence of the July 23rd letter evidently won over Papa George, and on August 14 Irving gratefully responded to two cablegrams from his father. "When I received the first one from Dad, I felt the most awful wave of homesickness come over me. I couldn't help thinking of how generous a nature he has to continue to support an ambition of mine in which he himself has no faith." He was waiting for a response about the Wyman grant but there is no record of one. It is more likely that Papa George agreed to send money and that Boulanger, also, helped Irving, for he had become one of her favorites. He mentioned that if he could raise a certain amount, "she felt sure she could get me an additional $150 to $200, and perhaps more." In any event, Irving was still in France when war broke out in September, which must have worried his parents.

In mid-August Boulanger had driven Irving to Fontainebleau, a town in northern France that was the site of the American School of Music. The famous palace there was surrounded by forest and had long been a favorite residence of the French kings. Boulanger was a staunch monarchist and, according to Verna, had promoted royalty to him on a previous trip to Versailles. "She said: 'I hope the King comes back.' She also tried to interest him in Catholicism." Irving found Fontainebleau delightful. "I walked around the palace grounds, saw all the royal apartments and watched the carp in the pool jump for bread. These carp are the most extraordinary fish. They are large, quite fat, and many are almost completely blind. Some are reputed to be at least two centuries old."

Irving's intensive studies with Boulanger in the summer and fall of 1939 were crucial, and provided him with a solid technique. She insisted on clarity in music, an element that would strongly manifest itself in all of his mature scores. She also instilled confidence in him about having a career as a composer. Verna noted that "he always doubted, and felt he was a lesser talent. He had modest expectations. I think Boulanger was probably the most influential of his teachers. She was very supportive."

On August 14, Irving was in a cheerful mood. "The cello sonata progresses nicely, there are sketches for 3 movements, and the first and third movements are half done. Friday we had Boulg over for dinner. Towards the end she sent out for some champagne to celebrate my good luck." The reference was to his plans for an extended stay in France. But the letter ends forebodingly: "Cross your fingers for the international situation."

The promising cello sonata, rhythmic and neoclassic in

manner, was never to be finished. By October, with the Nazi blitzkrieg threatening much of Europe, the situation seemed so menacing that Irving decided he must abandon his studies and return home (Boulanger herself would spend the war years as a refugee in the United States, first in California, then Boston). He did this at the end of the month, passing through Belgium and finally arriving back in Boston in a depressed state.

He was able to reclaim the part-time teaching jobs he had been offered and thus spend the winter gainfully employed. G. Wallace Woodworth, with whom he was friendly, had become chairman of the Harvard music department the year before, and that spring Irving was invited to join the faculty as a teaching fellow, starting in September 1940. It was the beginning of a decade-long association with Harvard. If Irving was pleased, Papa George was thrilled. Verna remembered: "He started to brag about his son, to go around and tell people, 'My son is on the faculty of Harvard University!' But he didn't say he taught in the music department." Irving's academic career, begun auspiciously, would last for the rest of his life.

Meanwhile, during the winter and spring of 1939-1940, Igor Stravinsky gave the prestigious Charles Eliot Norton Lectures (the first musician to do so), six talks delivered in French that were subsequently published under the title *Poetics of Music* (translated by Arthur Knodel and Ingolf Dahl). Probably through Woodworth's influence, Irving was delegated to accompany the eminent composer around the campus and to make the initial English translation of the lectures, though he had taken only one year of French in college. As Irving had recently been immersed in Stravinsky's music and come to revere it during his studies with Boulanger, he was delighted with the assignment. Cordial terms were quickly established with Stravinsky. Verna recalled that "Irving worked with him, chauffeured him and got to know him quite well."

On March 8, 1940, Stravinsky himself conducted and was a pianist in a concert of his chamber music presented by the Harvard music department at Sanders Theater. The evening was almost entirely devoted to neoclassic pieces and the program notes were by "I.G.F." Analytic mind to the fore, Irving wrote perceptively about the music, noting a relationship between Stravinsky's *Concerto for Two Pianos* and Liszt's *Concerto Pathétique* for the same forces: "This is especially noticeable in the thematic linking of the last two movements and in the employment of the Lisztian device of theme transformation. Thus the subject of the final fugue is a rhythmic variant of one of the chief motives found in the variation. The fugue itself is a veritable contrapuntal tour de force, marked by numerous *stretti* and concluding with a section using the material in inversion." The association between Fine and Stravinsky would prove extremely salutary to the younger man, both on a personal and musical level. As Irving would later write: "Stravinsky's music has probably influenced more young composers than that of any other man alive."

# Chapter 4

■ DURING THE YEAR BEFORE HE BEGAN TO TEACH at Harvard, Irving had met a Radcliffe student named Marsha. He was twenty-four and she was several years younger. She came from a wealthy, non-Jewish family and was, by all accounts, extremely beautiful. Harold Shapero recalled: "I was crazy about that girl. I saw her only once or twice but I thought she was lovely, a killer." Irving was smitten and soon asked Marsha to marry him. Although she agreed, it turned out that both families were dead set against the idea. Verna remembered Irving telling her that Marsha's parents objected to her marrying a Jew while his parents did not want him to marry a Gentile. His sister Barbara said: "It was a religious matter. My folks just didn't think it was the right thing." Since Marsha was underage, there was no question of an elopement. Sadly they went their separate ways.

Not long after this unhappy affair, in late 1939, Audrey coaxed her brother into accompanying her to a party. There, he ran into Verna Rudnick, who had sent him a surprise telegram the previous spring as he embarked for Europe. A nineteen-year-old mathematics major at Wellesley College, she had come with her brother Spencer. She was five years younger than Irving. The two had met only a few times before, the first occasion years ago in the hallway of Mrs. Grover's Boston studio, where they both had piano lessons—"a funny coincidence," Verna thought. The day after the fateful party, Irving called her to ask for the telephone number of one of her girlfriends. Verna, who found Irving handsome and interesting, was not pleased. She angrily told him off, with the unexpected result that he asked her out. They began dating, and during her senior year, 1940-1941, they got engaged.

This time, there was no objection, either from Verna's widowed mother or Irving's parents. Verna Louise Rudnick was Jewish, rich, intelligent (though not intellectual), attractive and lively—a vivid if somewhat hard-edged personality.

Lottie and George both liked her, especially George, who sensed a kindred spirit in her down-to-earth practicality.

Verna's mother, Florence Rudnick, was originally from New York. She came from a wealthy family that owned considerable real estate in the Boston area, including the swanky Kenmore Hotel. When her lawyer husband Carl died at the age of thirty-nine, his brothers had tried to cheat the widow and her two children out of their inheritance. Florence engaged a famous attorney from Boston University to fight them in court during 1929-1930, a celebrated lawsuit that she won.

Irving and Florence took to each other immediately. In fact, Irving had a better relationship with Florence than Verna did. Florence was elegant and cultivated, and she considered her daughter too brash, aggressive and independent for her own good. She appreciated Irving's gentleness, restraint and good manners. To her, and to all who knew them, the romance of Verna and Irving seemed a clear illustration of the axiom that opposites attract.

Decades later, one of the Fine daughters noted that Verna, in her youth, wanted to be an actress. She had performed in summer stock, but her mother vetoed her choice of career. Verna "used to play male parts. She was very masculine; even her voice was masculine, gruff." She was a heavy smoker and used a cigarette holder. As a young girl she had been full of high spirits and something of a prankster. "She hated a neighbor, and one day when she was home, sick, from school, she called a funeral parlor and said: 'So-and-so next door has died. Please come and pick up the body'."

Audrey remembered Verna as "a strong woman, a determined woman. If she made up her mind to do something she did it, and thoroughly. She was good at managing and could be very tough. I think she and Irving loved each other tremendously, but I also think he must have gotten angry with her at times, that their life together was a little volatile." Barbara thought Verna "a very pretty girl and a toughie." Irving himself noted that "my wife Verna has more than enough vivacity and charm to pull me out of the torpor that I occasionally find myself in, usually as a result of the sheer contemplation of hard work—especially creative work. She is also very practical and orderly, has a positive genius for figures and accounts and taxes [and] adores luxurious living, but chiefly away from home."

Harold Shapero was curious when Irving announced that he was going to get married. "I said, what's her last name? Rudnick, he replied. I said, that's not so good, you don't want to marry a girl named Rudnick. I was anti-Semitic and liked *shiksas*, blue-eyed blondes. I asked, what's her first name? Verna, he said. Oh, that's better, I replied. Then she showed up at the Harvard music department wearing high heels. She was a pretty girl with a good-looking figure, so I told him: she's all right."

Composer Arthur Berger, a friend from Irving's under-graduate years, said that "they were very different, the two of them. I wondered how Irving could stand Verna, with that raucous voice. She was very dominating." Shapero had mixed feelings about Verna. "She was bossy to the end, hard to take for a lot of people. But she was very generous, too. We got along fine, though she could be a pest. I used to call her a composer's wife, meaning pushy. Early on, if one of my works would be performed, she'd be a little jealous and say something very aggressive to me. But she took care of Irving, and he needed her. She was a solid girl who did the taxes." Shapero's wife, the painter Esther Geller, reflected that "Verna was very practical and Irving was naturally elegant. I think it was a comfortable marriage."

Other friends and colleagues of Irving recalled the different sides of Verna. Lukas Foss thought she "could be a little bossy, but in a sweet kind of way. She was herself all the time. I never felt Irving was being treated badly. I think they were a good couple." Leon Kirchner remembered that "when I first met Irving and Verna I thought they were mismatched. He seemed cool and aloof, alert and somehow splendid. But I really didn't get Verna. I thought she was terribly vulgar, a real tough girl, cold as hell. Then I began to see what an intelligence was there. Not only that, but her response to music was wonderful in later years. She had a good ear for the false and honest assumptions in a musical work. As I got to know her, I realized she was actually a very generous person. But it took me a long time to put the two of them together." Richard French said: "I always felt there was a certain distance between them, that each one was a personality and cultivated their own personality." In Martin Bookspan's recollection, "Verna was gorgeous as a young woman. In social situations she was the person to whom people would turn. In some respects she overshadowed Irving."

All three of the Fine daughters had strong memories of their mother. Claudia noted that Verna "came from this aristocratic, Jewish-Waspy background. I think that was part of what attracted my father to her: marrying a beautiful and smart Jewish woman and a *shiksa* at the same time." Emily recalled that "my mother always bastardized my father's name. She had this horrible Boston accent and just couldn't say the word Irving, but called him 'Yarving'." Joanna thought that Verna and Papa George had similar personalities: "tough, pragmatic, no-nonsense, intolerant of anything metaphoric. He was a curmudgeon and she was a bit of one too. They were both rigid characters. So, in a sense, my father married his father."

Irving was far more sensitive and adaptable than Verna. Joanna remembered that, though he had a temper, "he was always worried about how you felt. He very much wanted to be loved." Verna, she said, "could be quite cruel to people and not intend to be. She lacked a certain sort of empathy. She had a way of speaking without much screening. Sometimes, when she would say something inappropriate, my father would kick her gently under the table, and she would laugh about it and cry, 'Oh-oh, Irving just kicked me!' She was like that all her life." Verna agreed that Irving had a temper: "He wasn't a saint, but we very rarely had fights. When we did, they were over his inaction—he didn't do something I asked him to do. He was very soft-spoken. I was the loud one."

Verna and Irving had set a June 1941 wedding date. On January 3, he was in New York and his dependence on her is already apparent in a letter, for he addresses her as "My dear little pillar of strength, my rod, my staff, my darling," and, later, "my little mainstay." Verna was still a virgin, and he drolly regrets that she had not been allowed to accompany him on the trip. "Through the wisdom of your Aunt Liz and your mother you have been spared the temptation of Satan and the bitter remorse that follows the yielding to that temptation; you have been spared the anxieties of driving in a snow storm and staying over night in a strange city with a wicked young man." The letter is signed, "Love, Gifford (the young man)" and a postscript reads: "The young man really loves you."

In February, Verna and Florence took a brief vacation in the sun, probably in Florida. On the third, he writes to her that he is busy correcting test papers at Harvard. "The Music 1 papers creep along at a snail's pace—about three an hour. They must be done by Thursday, which means that some students are going to have their examinations corrected in the early hours of the morning—psychologically, certainly, a most inopportune time for the exercise of the instructor's judgement." He reports the warm reception accorded Piston's new violin concerto (No. 1) at the Boston Symphony concerts: "a very fine piece of music—one of his best [which] seems to be, with the exception of *The Incredible Flutist*, the nearest thing to a popular success that he has written." On February 5 he writes again, noting that he is suffering "a splitting headache" from the long hours spent correcting exams. Living at home, he is bored. "I have done very little lately except go to classes and correct papers. Last night, at about 9:30, I got so completely fed up that I got my father to go down to the bowling alleys with me. He trimmed me properly. As you know, I am a wonderful arm-chair athlete." He hopes that Verna is not corrupted by her "plutocratic surroundings" (perhaps The Breakers in Palm Beach?), so that she forgets her "little, lower-middle-class boyfriend." He concludes: "Although he's not six-feet-two, he has eyes of blue (sometimes they're green), and he kind of goes for you—even when you misspell anti-semitism."

March 14 was Verna's birthday, and he sent her a mushy note: "Strong and sweet music for the sweetest and the strongest little pillar of strength, who, on her twenty-first birthday has theoretically attained her full strength, but who, according to some, was born with a surfeit of sweetness."

The happy couple were married on June 25, 1941, in a religious ceremony that took place at Boston's Kenmore Hotel—ironically, the same hotel that had been involved in Florence Rudnick's legal battle with her in-laws. At Jewish weddings, it is traditional for the groom to step on a glass and break it, and when the time came Irving was so nervous that he repeatedly failed the task. His sister Barbara remembered the day well and may have thought this a bad omen. "At the ceremony I was sitting in the audience and suddenly I heard this loud weeping. It was awful—and it was me! It had nothing to do with Verna. He certainly went out with girls prior to going out with her, and I knew he would eventually get married. But he was my big brother and I was crazy about him and he was leaving. Such emotion. It was pathetic." Years later, however, Barbara confided to one of her nieces that the real reason she had been upset was that she felt Verna wasn't right for Irving. It took her a long time finally to accept her. Verna and Irving enjoyed a brief honeymoon in Quebec, where they stayed at the ritzy Chateau Frontenac.

That spring, upon graduating from Wellesley, Verna took a job as a statistician for the State of Massachusetts. Although she was now married to a budding composer, she knew little about music. One semester at college, she had signed up for a music appreciation course, but was so afraid of flunking it that she withdrew just as it began. Verna recalled: "I had a very intelligent mother. I was dragged to the opera when I was five and she had a subscription to the Boston Symphony. She went every Friday, and if there was something worthwhile she would take me on a Saturday night." She remembered spraining her wrist dancing in her dormitory to the Mendelssohn violin concerto.

Irving did what he could to expand Verna's musical horizons. "He bought me a gift of the Prokofiev violin concerto, the lyric one. We had a record machine that you wound up." He also took her to concerts, and she remembered "having a hard time" with the Bartók string quartets. "I told Irving that my ears weren't ready for them, and he was understanding." Little by little, she began to comprehend and appreciate serious music, thanks to Irving's unfailing patience and his pleasure in educating her. Many years later, at a Kennedy Center concert in Washington, D.C., she would reply to an inquiry from First Lady Rosalynn Carter: "Madame President, I got into music the way you got into politics. I married into it."

# Chapter 5

■ FINE WAS A TEACHING FELLOW IN THE HARVARD music department for two years, from 1940 to 1942, and an instructor and tutor and assistant conductor of the Harvard Glee Club from 1942 to 1945. He settled quickly into a routine at the apartment he had rented at 15 Everett Street in Cambridge. "When we were first married," said Verna, "he liked to get up early in the morning and work when it was quiet. He would get a lot done in the morning, before he had a ten o'clock class." Harold Shapero was always encouraging him to compose, for he thought Fine rather lazy. "When Irving was young, he would spend weeks, months without composing. Verna used to say that without me he would never have written a note." The two musicians developed a mutually dependent friendship, "a close association," recalled Esther Shapero. They had long telephone conversations: "Irving would be consulting Harold on what to do, every little note." Shapero noted that "Irving lived in Cambridge and we lived in Newton. We'd often call each other, and I'd say, how do you like this tune? Should I go to A or to D?"

Music was not the only subject that interested them. "We talked endlessly about sex," said Shapero. "I got married, and he said: 'When you're first married you don't hunt anymore. But married sex is much duller than non-married sex.' I think Verna was probably quite good at sex, but in a sort of direct way. Too direct for him, not artistic enough."

In addition to composing sporadically, Fine kept honing his considerable skills as a pianist. Just prior to his marriage, he had given the premiere of the *Piano Sonata No. 1* by Allen Sapp (1922-1999), his first tutorial student at Eliot House, Harvard, with whom he was friendly. Fine had overseen the composition of this piece and even revised some of the passagework to make it more pianistic. (Several years later, Sapp would inscribe one of his scores: "To Irving Fine—from whom I learned how to be a musician.") The eighteen-year-

*37*

old Sapp wrote to his parents: "This sonata of mine is fiendishly difficult. The performance was magnificent! Mr. Fine played it so brilliantly I could hardly keep from crying." Shapero, who often read through Schubert and Mozart duets with Fine, remembered him as "a very good pianist who played cleanly. He was not a virtuoso, didn't have big power or technique, but it was very accurate playing. He never made a mistake." The pianist and composer Noël Lee studied harmony with Fine at Harvard in 1942, and noted that he was "quite agile at the keyboard. Maybe he was virtuosic at times but I didn't hear that. I can imagine him playing a Mozart concerto but not one by Tchaikovsky. I don't think he had the character for that." Later on, when Lee heard Fine perform his own works, he had the impression that "that's the real music, coming from the source. I didn't think about him, then, as a performer." Caldwell Titcomb, a musicologist, pianist and Harvard alumnus, said that Fine was "no slouch as a pianist, but really superb. In classes, we'd do analyses of the Chopin preludes, and he could play them all." Composer Richard Wernick, who studied with Fine at Brandeis University in the early 1950s, had vivid memories of him as a pianist. "His piano playing was always very controlled, everything was absolutely clean. I don't remember him playing with much *rubato*, but when the music needed a *ritard* he would make an elegant one. Gershwin used a word about American pianism. It was different from European, he said, because Americans played with 'crackle.' Very little pedal. That's how Irving played. It was not romantic but it was very very elegant. His Mozart was really beautiful."

Despite Fine's facility as a pianist, the piano as a solo instrument evidently did not exert strong appeal for him as a composer, for he would write but little keyboard music. Verna reflected that "for some reason, he never got around to writing a piano concerto. He used to joke about it, saying, 'All those notes!'" He planned to compose a piano sonata in 1949, but never got around to that, either.

In December 1941, the United States entered the war and, not long after, the war came to Harvard in the form of the U.S. Naval Training School established there. In early 1942, Fine was appointed conductor of the School's glee club. The naval cadets were taking communications courses but were allowed one elective, so Fine was additionally assigned to give a course on the history of music.

The military presence on campus gave him the idea of applying for a Naval commission. "It wouldn't have occurred to him if the Navy wasn't parked outside his front door," Verna recalled. "He was like every human being and didn't want to fight or get killed in a war. But all of a sudden he wanted to serve his country." Fine passed all the tests and then received a letter announcing he had been awarded an ensignship and would be called for active service in three months. Evidently, the Army and Navy did not coordinate their enlistment efforts, for not long after, his number came up for the Draft. When Fine went for the Army's physical examination, an electro-encephalogram showed irregular brainwaves, and it was discovered that he had almost no reflexes on his right side. "That meant he had a poor trigger finger," said Verna. "This was a man who played fantastic piano, who could have been a concert pianist. Whatever it was didn't affect that." Fine was rejected for Army service and classified 4F. When the Navy was informed, it withdrew his commission. Verna noted that "he was very depressed, but it made me happy." Subsequently, Fine consulted a brain specialist, who determined that the concussion he had suffered years before in Hartford was responsible for his dulled reflexes. "Irving hit the right side of his head, and the brain is enclosed, so the damage was to the left side of the brain—scar tissue. He felt guilty, because the fingers of his right hand were stronger than normal due to his being a pianist. He would have been perfectly able to shoot a gun."

Fine resumed teaching at Harvard's Navy school and wrote a short, patriotic choral piece in unison titled "It's the Navy!" for the Naval Glee Club. The marchlike music in popular style is set to words by a friend, Maynard Kaplan (using the pseudonym "Dick Maynard"), and a note on the score states that the project was "suggested by Warrant Officer Edgar C. Bibeault, U.S.N.R." The text begins, "It's the Navy! The Navy!/Our ships on the sea/With the flag of the Free/Waving high," and continues in the same spirit. Additionally, Fine began a never-completed item, "When men of war roll ashore in Cambridge Town," and wrote another song, "My Name is Mussolini," with jeering lyrics by Kaplan ("Benito is our hero/He fiddles just like Nero/But his fiddle is a diff'rent sort/for second fiddle is his forte/He plays in Hitler's court"). Two years later, in 1944, Fine's arrangement of "Battle Hymn of the Republic," titled "Voices of Freedom," was presented in Symphony Hall, Boston at a concert grandly billed as "Let Freedom Ring." The scoring is for baritone solo and chorus with organ and piano accompaniment, and the soloist was one Waldemar Johnson, intriguingly described in the program as "Norwegian baritone, fugitive from the Gestapo."

In early 1942, Fine and Kaplan collaborated on several pop songs. "I introduced them the first year we were married," Verna recalled. "Maynard Kaplan had married a friend of mine from Wellesley and was a lawyer who went into the travel business. Irving and he wanted to get rich by writing pop songs. It was the first flush of youth, I guess." The songs included "A Kiss from Mr. Liszt," with a melody borrowed from Franz Liszt's symphonic poem *Les Préludes* ("very strange, cute and funny," thought Verna); "What Is this Warm Feeling?"; "It's Funny, Honey"; "Springtime Is Ringtime"; "This Is Heaven—I Don't Have to Hear Music" and "A Letter from Paris." The music is consistently light, sometimes dashing, sometimes jazzy and bluesy. There are Gershwinesque harmonic touches, and one writer has aptly cited the tradition of Rodgers and Hart and the songs of Vernon Duke. The lyrics are often amusingly, and contemporaneously, corny: "I don't have to see angels to know this is heaven"; "You're maybe not smart, you're maybe not handsome. For you in my arms I'd pay a king's ransom." "You're fresh from the farms, can't tell Gershwin from Brahms." None of these songs ever reached print, though two were submitted to a publisher in March 1942 and were politely rejected. Fine seems to have understood that they did not have what it took for commercial success, for he inscribed one song to his mother-in-law, "who was sure this was good, even when I wasn't."[1]

---

1. Another pop song from 1942, "There'll Come a Day," with words by one Michael Lynde, is a simple ballad in C major and especially pretty. In this gentle war lament, a girl awaits the return of her boyfriend from the battlefields: "There'll come a day, Johnny, when there'll be love and laughter once more; a happier world than ever before"—echoing the sentiments of the famous English hit song, "The White Cliffs of Dover."

Although the rejection letter signaled the end of Fine's flirtation with the popular-music medium, he would enjoy musical comedies all his life. "Irving really liked good tunes," said Verna. "He was very conscious of melody, even in his serious music." Two of his favorite shows were *Carousel* and *Kismet*. "I remember that we went to *Carousel* and when he heard the song 'If I Loved You' he said, 'That's a great tune, an inspired tune. Oh God, what I would give to write that tune!' He was always envious of people who could write tunes." Harold Shapero confirmed Fine's interest in musical comedy. "He was well aware of it and had dreams of writing tunes and doing a Broadway musical. The only way to get ahead in America is with a musical. Lenny Bernstein said the American public doesn't give one shit about symphonies, and he was right."

Sometime in 1941, a score by Fine called *Music for Modern Dance* had been performed in Boston at the Erskine School. This is probably an untitled manuscript in the Fine archive at the Library of Congress listed as "Ballet, early (1940-1941)," consisting of three pages of piano music in 6/8 meter, a total of fifty-three bars, repeats indicated. It begins *fortissimo*, with dramatic bass tremolos and sweeping treble glissandos that lead to an assertively accented, somewhat discordant *pavane*. Material that is more lyric, marked *dolce*, follows: a simple tune set against a running accompaniment with mild dissonances. Choreographed, this might be an effective set-piece. In purely musical terms, it conveys foremost a desire to create an impression, and in an impersonal style.

The following year, 1942, marked Fine's real debut as a professional composer, although he could not have been aware of it at that time. Again, he was involved with the Erskine School, now with incidental music to a theatrical production of Lewis Carroll's classic children's books *Alice's Adventures in Wonderland* (published in 1865) and *Through the Looking Glass* (1872). These had been adapted for the stage by Eva Le Gallienne, a celebrated actress and director, and Florida Friebus, under the omnibus title *Alice in Wonderland*. Worried about meeting the deadline, Fine enlisted the help of Allen Sapp. Directed by Phyllis Stohl, *Alice in Wonderland* was performed on May 22 and 23 at John Hancock Hall in

Boston, and the program listed music by Fine and Sapp, both men "at the piano," each, one assumes, playing his own contributions. *Alice* was an unusually musical undertaking, and for it Fine composed no less than twenty-seven numbers consisting of songs and incidental pieces.[2]

There seem to have been no newspaper reviews, but Verna remembered that the production was successful. Most importantly for Fine, G. Wallace Woodworth attended one of the performances and was so taken with the deceptively simple music that he suggested Fine arrange some of the songs for chorus. It was a congenial idea, especially as Woodworth offered to introduce them with the Harvard Glee Club the following season. From his long experience with the group, Fine felt he knew the medium well. During the summer he chose three of the solo songs, "The Lobster Quadrille," "Lullaby of the Duchess" and "Father William," for arrangement as a choral set with piano accompaniment. The first two songs presented no problem, but, said Verna, "when he got to the Father William song he'd written for the theater, he decided it wouldn't make a good choral piece." Instead, he wrote a new and longer (134 bars as opposed to the theater song's 46 bars) "Father William," based in part on his patriotic song "It's the Navy!" from earlier that year.

*Three Choruses from "Alice in Wonderland"* had a tryout performance by the Glee Club, with Fine at the piano, on February 19, 1943, at Harvard. The official premiere was given on March 4, on campus at the Sanders Theater. The brief, witty and ironic, sophisticated yet spontaneous-sounding choruses, with their expert, sonorous, not-too-difficult choral writing and elegant word settings, were an immediate success, not only with the audience but with the critics. The *Boston Globe* reported that "it has a fantastic humor that nicely suits those piquant verses. The piano accompaniment [is] jazzy without affectation," and the *Christian Science Monitor* stated: "College singing, Harvard manner, has become immensely solemn since back somewhere in the 'twenties. Mr.

---

2. Two piano pieces, "Flamingo Dance" and "Measuring Music," would later be orchestrated and renamed as part of a suite titled *Diversions*.

Fine has done something to break the spell."[3] Perhaps the best capsule appraisal would come from the composer and critic Arthur Cohn, who wrote that Fine's *Alice* pieces are "choral probity at its best, with dancing light counterpoint, exuberant rhythmic dash [and] neoclassic harmonic spice." Looking back many years later, Harold Shapero reflected that "Irving knew what inspiration was: the early *Alice in Wonderland* set is, I think, a really deep inspiration."

That summer the *Alice* choruses became the first of Fine's scores to be issued in print, by M. Witmark and Sons of New York. Witmark's advertisement, adorned with four of John Tenniel's famous *Alice* illustrations, announced the new publication "with pride and pardonable whimsy," the whimsy comprising an arch paraphrase of the text of the "Lobster Quadrille": "Will you sing a little brisker! said a leader to a group/There's a purpose close behind you, but you sound like a baby's croup!/Hear how eagerly the tenors and the altos chant it wrong!/They are waiting for the downbeat—will you come and join the song?" The publisher made the three choruses available separately (at eighteen cents, sixteen cents and eighteen cents), and one review of the scores in a music magazine noted that the composer "must have enjoyed the original text thoroughly, for he seems very sympathetic in his settings."

The key to the great attractiveness of these *Alice* choruses lies in their vital rhythms—chantlike in "The Lobster Quadrille," marchlike in "Father William"—and their naïve, almost childlike tunes. Diatonic harmonies and ostinatos radiate straightforward simplicity, as do certain droll pictorial touches: for instance, in "Lullaby of the Duchess," bluesy left-hand piano octaves and piano chords with falling minor seconds that evoke, along with choral interjections on the word "Wow!" a caterwauling infant; and in "Father William," hints of a mocking children's cry contrasted with a centrally placed,

---

3. According to a blurb in a 1946 Boston Symphony program book, Archibald T. Davison, as conductor of the Harvard Glee Club, had initiated this choral gravity by "quietly plant[ing] a challenging idea—that there is more all-around enjoyment to be had in Palestrina or Byrd or Bach than in jolly jingles at undergraduate 'smokers.' A feeble cry of 'highbrow' was raised but soon spent itself as the idea proved to be not only good but indestructible."

sparkling little keyboard *fugato* à la Hindemith. Fine made occasional minor text adjustments throughout, always for the sake of the music's rhythm; and "Lullaby of the Duchess" contains one invented line: "Cry! cry! you ugly ugly baby, you ugly pig baby, cry! cry!" (which is based on the fact that in Lewis Carroll's tale the Duchess yells "Pig!" at her howling child and subsequently the brat is transformed into one).

*Alice in Wonderland* became a staple of the Harvard Glee Club and a choral best-seller quickly taken up by choruses nationwide. The ebullient, satirical "Father William" was especially popular and would often be programmed on its own in the future. In the spring of 1943, the Glee Club performed *Alice* at Harvard on April 6 during "Harvard Night" (a concert broadcast live in Boston and subsequently heard on radio in New York), and also in Rhode Island and Pennsylvania. Several years later, in 1949, Fine orchestrated the piano accompaniment, and in 1953 he would make three further settings of *Alice* poems.

Early in 1943, Fine provided two songs for the American premiere of a play by the Spanish poet and playwright Federico García Lorca, who had been executed by Fascists seven years before during the Spanish civil war. Although the play was listed on the program simply as *Doña Rosita, or the Language of the Flowers*, its full title was quite elaborate: *Doña Rosita, the Spinster, or the Language of the Flowers, a Poem of 1900 Grenada, Divided into Various Gardens, with Scenes of Song and Dance*. The Harvard Dramatic Club and the Radcliffe Idler produced *Doña Rosita* at Radcliffe College on April 28, 1943. Fine's songs—"Because I Caught a Glimpse of You" and "What the Flowers Say"—used an English translation by Richard L. O'Connell and James Graham-Lujan which contained lines that were romantically poetic ("Your languor sweet perceived was reason for my sighs") and bittersweet ("The whitest flowers wedding mean, the scarlet stand for ire, the blue ones mean a winding sheet, as we in chill expire").

Fine's music straightforwardly suggests the Spanish manner, folklike and Fallaesque. But where the recent *Alice* settings show the beginnings of a genuine musical personality, the *Doña Rosita* songs, effective in their way, are decidedly—and deliberately—artificial in style. Posthumously issued in

1998 (with the second song's title changed to "Song of the Flowers"), and evoking, in the words of editor Leo Smit, "the austere sensuality and spicy fragrance of old Moorish Spain," the *Two Songs from "Doña Rosita"* add little to an appreciation of Fine as composer. That he never attempted to publish them and didn't use any of their material elsewhere suggests he was aware of the fact.

During the war years, Fine, always a slow and meticulous worker, still had not found his stride as a composer. He thought of himself as a busy musician who sometimes composed, and he wrote but little music, most of it for chorus. His academic duties and Verna's social agenda accounted for large tracts of his time, along with his work as assistant conductor of the Harvard Glee Club and piano practice. Harmony was his forte as a teacher. Harold Shapero remembered that "he was good at harmony and very skilled at teaching it." Caldwell Titcomb recalled: "He was my instructor in advanced harmony and the best teacher I ever had. I just idolized him." "We used the Piston harmony book, and I thought Irving was an absolutely fantastic teacher," said Noël Lee.

In the 1943-1944 academic year, Fine introduced a new course at Harvard, one primarily for undergraduates, called "Introduction to Musical Masterpieces." At that time, Martin Bookspan had Fine as his "section man" in another course, Music 1. "It was enormous, perhaps 200 of us in the class, divided into twenty or so groups. Each group had an assistant or associate professor who supplemented the lectures, and I was fortunate to have Irving Fine." Bookspan described Fine as an academic type, but not forbidding. "He was a good listener. He had an orderly mind and used the English language brilliantly. He spoke rapid-fire, in complete sentences and paragraphs. Irving was a terrific teacher, articulate and perceptive. He also was witty, had a great sense of humor and an outgoing personality, although he could seem a little shy until you got to know him." Bookspan remembered a class where Fine and a violinist played the Stravinsky *Duo Concertant.* "The piano part is not easy and Irving tossed it off. That piece can be acerbic, but his playing was very sensual and he brought out all sorts of colors in it."

Verna stressed that Fine was dedicated to the undergraduates. "They usually got very little attention from the full professors. Most of the fancy ones—the Randall Thompsons and Walter Pistons—spent their time with the graduate students. Irving wasn't the kind of instructor who only saw the kids in class. He started the Harvard-Radcliffe music clubs." Caldwell Titcomb remembered that the Fines occasionally hosted parties for the students at their Cambridge apartment. He would encourage student composers he thought especially talented— for instance, Allen Sapp, Noël Lee and, later, Claudio Spies— become friendly with them and invite them home. "There was a whole roster of freshmen and sophomores who would come to our house," said Verna. "We liked people and enjoyed the life at Harvard. Irving was very popular with the students."

Verna and Irving both drank at parties, but in moderation. Verna recalled that "when we first got married, because during the war you couldn't get scotch or bourbon, we drank rum—*cuba libres*, rum and Coca-Cola." Fine, however, did not hold liquor well, a fact he attributed to his early head injury. "He always said at parties that he couldn't drink too much because his fingers got rubbery. One drink and he could get high. Then he would stop. There would be weeks when we didn't drink. Alcohol was always associated with our social life." Harold Shapero noted that he never saw either of them drunk, "not even tipsy," but that "Irving liked to have his cocktails, especially martinis."[4]

Fine's Harvard affiliation had already brought him into personal contact with Stravinsky, and now, in the winter of 1943-1944, Aaron Copland came to Cambridge to teach, replacing Walter Piston who was on sabbatical, and to give the Horace Appleton Lamb lectures in the spring. It was the beginning of a close and lasting friendship for both of the Fines. Copland would become, as Verna put it, "family." Fine had invited him to their apartment for dinner one evening early in 1944, and "it was love at first sight, just as if we had known him all our lives." Copland was "like an older brother

---

4. An undated nine-bar ditty, in manuscript, has a single-note harmonic accompaniment and is set to words by Fine: "Verna dear, your notions are so queer. You toss in bed the whole night long because you drink no beer" (the first two words are set to a rising tritone—C, E, F-sharp—and the latter note returns wittily on the word "queer").

*46*

to Irving" and the two spoke constantly about music. For the rest of his life, Fine would rely on Copland's advice and opinions. Noël Lee remembered once visiting Copland just after Fine had left. "Irving often went up to see Aaron, and Aaron made this very interesting remark to me. He said that Irving needed a father-figure."

Several years later, Fine himself would write: "Aaron's serenity, his never flagging interest in things of all kinds, his childlike curiosity in the news, all of those things are wonderful to watch, and to watch him gives one a sense of real security. Aaron's [personal] austerity adds to his fatherliness, of course." And in 1952, after Copland's departure from the MacDowell Colony, where both had been in residence, Fine informed him that another colonist, the genial Russian-born composer Nikolai Lopatnikoff, "does not quite fill the 'big brother' or 'father-confessor' role that you seem to carry off so admirably."

Harvard in the middle 1940s was "a pretty stuffy place," recalled Verna. "Aaron was an informal sort of person and he felt entirely comfortable with Irving. They were both soft-spoken [and] gave the impression of being calm and unruffled. They also had in common the fact that they were good listeners, and they listened closely to each other. I would say that Irving was probably Aaron's closest composer friend." Copland came to trust Fine as he trusted few others. He told him: "I can count on one hand the people who call me just out of friendship, who aren't after a letter of recommendation for something or other. In fact, maybe I can count them on one finger—you." Copland also trusted Fine's musical aptitude. Once, when a student asked him about the accuracy of a published analysis of his *Piano Variations*, he replied: "I'm not sure. Ask Mr. Fine." Another time, worried about the rehearsals of his *Third Symphony* in Mexico City, Copland wrote that he wished he "had the benefit of the Fine critical mind." On April 25, 1944, during a concert of music by Copland and Piston at Sanders Theater, Fine and Copland played the latter's *Danzon Cubano* on two pianos.

Fine's composer friends Harold Shapero and Lukas Foss ("The Three Musketeers," Verna called the group) lived in the Boston area in 1944, and they often met with Copland at Fine's apartment, where Verna cooked for them. Fine was fascinated by Shapero's talent and near-bizarre personality and awed by Foss's facility. He told Copland about two brief, highly eclectic, neoclassic piano sonatas of "the Newton genius, Karl Philip Emmanuel Domenico Igor Shapero" by which he was "terribly impressed"; and, after hearing Foss play the scherzo of his *Symphony in G*, he admitted that he "came away feeling that I ought to go into the rag business: what a natural!"

Copland was working on his populist ballet *Appalachian Spring* at the time and would sometimes play through his sketches for his Musketeer friends. That November, months after the end of Copland's Harvard stint, Irving and Verna attended the premiere in Washington, D.C., as his guests. The score's nostalgia, Fine said, "is almost overwhelming; yet it is always under control, and the music as a whole possesses a formal integrity that is all too rare in music for the dance." Upon returning to Cambridge, he wrote: "You were awfully kind to us in Washington. If we did not seem to be particularly effusive chalk it up to my diffidence—or is it gaucherie. I shan't ask when [*Appalachian Spring*] will be published, since I'd be afraid to look at the music—its charm is too insidious." Fine had been impressed with the score and its, as he wrote much later, "spirit of youthfulness and freshness." Verna remembered that "we stayed at the same hotel as Aaron and went to all the fancy parties with him in a chauffeured limousine. The premiere was a sensational success." Verna noted that Fine, unlike many of Copland's colleagues, "was never critical of his light music, because he felt that Aaron maintained the same integrity as in his serious pieces." Fine sensed that Copland "had discovered something special and often said he wished he could do something similar." Still, Fine, with his refined musical sensibility, was rather leery of Copland's vernacular style, especially when he felt it had invaded an ambitious and serious work.[5] A few years later, he wrote to Copland about his recent *Third Symphony*: "I am not entirely in sympathy with the symphony's populist tendencies, but you would not expect otherwise from me." One can imagine Fine being disturbed by the appearance of Copland's

5. Shapero noted: "Irving wasn't a great commoner like Aaron. He was elegant."

48

stirringly patriotic *Fanfare for the Common Man* in the finale, perhaps agreeing with Virgil Thomson that it sounded "stuck in." (Subsequently Fine relented somewhat, telling Copland that his symphony "does get better on hearing it a third time, and I think it will make its way surely. It has some of the noblest music you have ever written.")

From his late student years at Harvard and through the war as a faculty member, Fine had been associated with a loose-knit group of composers who esteemed and emulated the neoclassicism of Stravinsky and, to lesser degree, that of Paul Hindemith. Fine termed them a "later group of neoclassicists," while Copland called them a "Stravinsky school." According to Fine, lecturing in 1957, the members consisted of himself, Harold Shapero, Arthur Berger, Lukas Foss, Louise Talma and Leo Smit. According to Berger, in a 1955 article, they were himself, Fine, Shapero, Foss, Ingolf Dahl and Alexei Haieff. More recently, Berger cited himself, Fine, Shapero, John Lessard and Claudio Spies ("somewhat"), all of whom had studied with Nadia Boulanger. "Stravinsky came to Harvard to give the Norton Lectures in 1939," he said, "but I think that even if he hadn't we would have been Stravinskyites through Boulanger. We didn't need him in America to be Stravinskian." In Shapero's opinion, he and his colleagues were all "second-rate Stravinskys—just little off-shoots of the big man." He, Fine and Foss had been Stravinsky's "early American friends." Berger noted that Fine, while deeply involved for a long period in the neoclassic aesthetic, also had an attachment to romantic music. "I was an out-and-out neoclassic composer quite early, and Irving would be a little annoyed with me because I was so antiromantic." All of the various composers mentioned—some of whom were occasionally referred to, inaccurately, as the "Harvard Stravinskians" or the "Boston Neoclassicists"—matured and, to greater or lesser degree, broke out of the neoclassic mold. But Fine, as Shapero put it, "had some of the most unadulterated Stravinsky influence."

Foss remembered Fine as "a wonderful colleague, a very serious person devoted to music, incredibly talented and musical but not overly ambitious. He and Harold Shapero and I were always together, like a club. We were very neoclassic at that time, very involved with Stravinsky." In 1946

49

Stravinsky came to Boston and agreed to visit Foss in his studio and listen to his music. "I decided I couldn't do without Irving and Harold, so I invited them to join me and we all played our music for Stravinsky." Foss recalled Stravinsky's examining Fine's unfinished *Toccata Concertante* and asking why he had given a certain melody to the trumpet. "Irving said, 'because it sounds like a trumpet tune.' Stravinsky replied, 'then give it to the violins.' I don't know if he meant to startle Irving."

In a 1957 essay, Fine observed admiringly that the French-cum-Stravinsky neoclassicism in which he had been so immersed, "concentrates on elegance and taste as well as craftsmanship. It aims for an art thoroughly poised, detached, disciplined and serene." Even though it can be, at times, "a little precious," there is "an ideal balance between form and emotion [in this] aristocratic art." Neoclassicism in music "grows out of a search for order, which it attempts to establish by means of a restoration of contacts with pre-romantic musical traditions." Richard Wernick wrote that Fine himself "was a neoclassicist by temperament as well as training and had a deep personal commitment to the esthetic values of the eighteenth century."

Virgil Thomson once stated that "the formal preoccupations of Western neoclassicism do not lend themselves to emotional effusion," and Fine aptly cited the "cleansing satire" of Erik Satie and *Les Six* and the rejection of "the personal subjectivity of romantic music in favor of a cool objectivity or a bustling impersonality." Rhythm, in neoclassical music, "retains its regained vigor and much of its newly won complexity." Harmony "tends to become more normally functional or tonal, if not necessarily less dissonant."

Fine wrote that the music of Stravinsky "and his followers" is inclined to be "diatonic and tonal or quasi modal," their harmony pan-diatonic, "the result of the free and usually dissonant combination of any of the tones in the diatonic scale." In Stravinsky's music, diatonic harmony "is often peppered with unresolved neighbor dissonant tones, all of it tastefully set forth through his genius for spacing and texture." He accurately noted that much music labeled neoclassical is in reality neobaroque, though "undoubtedly 'Back to Bach' was the big slogan of neoclassicism"; and that the style had found perfection in Stravinsky's *Dumbarton Oaks Concerto*, "much as the neoclassical (neo-Mozart) style can be found at its best in Stravinsky's *Symphony in C* and [the opera] *The Rake's Progress*." Responding during a 1948 radio interview to a question about Stravinsky's influence on American composers, Fine mentioned "the [chord] spacing and the preoccupation with rhythm. We like to think that American composers are particularly interested in rhythmic problems, and Stravinsky's experiments with rhythms appeal [to us]." He expressed the opinion that "so-called neoclassic music has a very sharply jazzlike character."

# Chapter 6

■ IN SEPTEMBER 1944, COPLAND was in Mexico finishing his *Third Symphony*, and Fine wrote to him: "I am green with you know what. Your description of the Copland retreat in Tepoztlan made us drool at the mouth—to paraphrase blasphemously, 'as pants the hart for cooling stream, so pants our souls' for Aaron's Mexican mountains." He had been impressed by a Boston Symphony performance of Hindemith's *Four Temperaments*: "It was first-class Hindemith, which is very good indeed. I must confess that I couldn't really tell what was going on a good deal of the time, but the sounds were so pretty." In the same letter, Fine described the summer sessions at Harvard as "one of the bitchiest terms on record." Tillman Merritt, he reported, "is still acting as the department's Fuller Brush man," a reference to Merritt's fundraising activities, while Walter Piston "performs mysterious chemistry at his Belmont hideaway, appearing at the Music Building only when it is entirely necessary." As for his own activities, "little Itzick busies himself with choral conducting and Music 1 for the most part."

That fall Fine wrote his first music criticism, for the November-December 1944 issue of *Modern Music*, a magazine whose guiding light was Copland. This first of many reviews and essays for various publications is worth examining in some detail, for it reveals an acute and fastidious critical faculty, sometimes enthusiastic, sometimes severe. The article covered three Boston Symphony concerts and was entitled "Boston Opens an Exciting Season." Fine, unlike many careerist critics, does not seem overly fond of his own voice and makes his points concisely and readably, his opinions backed by technical expertise. William Schuman's *Prayer in Time of War* did not please, being "marred by the recurrence of clichés which a more self-conscious composer would have shunned or at least handled with more tact." For the most part, the music "was relatively restrained," but Schuman

53

"could do with a few more stylistic inhibitions." The piece "is a compilation of devices, effects and formulae rather than the product of a unified style." Conversely, David Diamond's *Second Symphony* "impressed by its freshness and individuality," especially in its first and third movements. Fine observed that "some members of the audience noted with obvious relief that the piece was not overly modern [but] this bespeaks a limited understanding of modernism, for the conservatism of the symphony was more apparent than real." In the orchestration of Arnold Schoenberg's *Theme and Variations*, Op. 43b, occasional "reminiscences of Bruckner, Mahler and Strauss cropped up to the annoyance of nearly everyone except myself." Noting that the work was "distinctly tonal," Fine, though respectful of Schoenberg's "technical mastery," astutely called attention to "the essentially academic quality of Schoenberg's music when divorced from the twelve-tone technic." He was amused to see that "most of the audience refused to believe that it was not listening to the most wicked twelve-tone music."

"A rousing good performance" of Bohuslav Martinu's *Concerto for Two Pianos and Orchestra* was saluted as "one of the memorable events of the season." Although the program note quoted the composer connecting his piece to the *concerto grosso* style, Fine demurred: "Except for the sequential character of the music and the presence of a driving, rhythmic motive typical of the eighteenth-century concerto style, I found little to support this contention." He liked the middle section of the second movement, which was "more diatonic and less 'fruity'" than the outer parts, whose "post-impressionistic chords and figuration" reminded him of Karol Szymanowski's music. He noticed unnecessarily complex textures in the opening movement and the finale, but praised the latter's "drive and go." Fine pronounced Hindemith's *Four Temperaments*, on an upcoming program, "among his most charming [works]," one that represented "a new departure for the composer in the care which he lavishes upon sonority." The thematic material "possesses a grace and lyrical quality which one associates with his more recent compositions."

The following spring, the Brazilian composer Heitor Villa-Lobos conducted a concert of his own works with the Boston Symphony, and Fine, writing again in *Modern Music*, thought that "all of the music comes perilously close to being swamped in a sea of banality. Certainly no clear-cut personality emerges." Also not to his taste were William Grant Still's *In Memoriam: The Colored Soldiers Who Died for Democracy* and Hindemith's popular and populist *Symphonic Metamorphoses on Themes by Carl Maria von Weber.* The former "is over-ripe harmonically and not very original," the latter "is a *tour de force* of often questionable taste, especially in its orchestration." *Music for English Horn and Orchestra,* Op. 50, by Fine's orchestration teacher Edward Burlingame Hill, fared better. "One of the most ingratiating of Mr. Hill's compositions, it is sensitive music of quiet dignity, impeccably written in a conservatively impressionistic style." (In response to this article, Copland wrote Fine: "Someday I expect to disagree with you but I can't imagine what about.")

Reviewing the 1945-1946 Boston season, Fine thought Stravinsky's *Symphony in Three Movements* "the most impressive and exhilarating new work of the season," although he questioned the word symphony in the title and criticized elements of the music. The "toccata-like" first movement was "the most completely satisfying formally," but the second movement's "rococo lyricism" seemed inconsistent "after the dynamic propulsiveness of the first movement." Even more problematic was the third movement, "the least convincing," with an underdeveloped fugue and an anticlimactic ending where "Stravinsky's fear of overstatement leads to a miscalculation of proportion." He concluded on a positive note: "While in many ways this score can be characterized as an uncommonly successful regression, [in it] Stravinsky achieves in the synthesis of old and more recent idioms something that is new. In his search for new sonorities and new forms of expression, he is still a young composer, the most youthful and forward-looking of them all."

Samuel Barber's *Cello Concerto,* Op. 22 was "an effective and attractive piece, the difficult medium handled with skill." But a Russian composer and three English composers were raked across the proverbial coals by an obviously irritated Fine. He thought Alexander Gretchaninov's *Elegy,* Op. 175 "an agglomeration of the eclecticism of Glazunov and Rachmaninov, which, although completed in 1945, could have been written in 1880." John Ireland's *The Forgotten Rite* was "as pale and ineffective a piece of musical landscape as has been heard here in many a decade," while "Koussevitzky's good taste has spared us up till now" Sir Arnold Bax's "turgid, hybrid" symphonic poem *Tintagel.* The *Threnody for a Soldier Killed in Action* by Anthony Collins, better known as a conductor, received the most devastating appraisal: "a hoax upon the public sympathies and a work whose musical substance is zero."[1]

Continuing his survey of the season, Fine wrote that Béla Bartók's *Concerto for Orchestra*, destined for classic status, promised only "to become one of Koussevitzky's better warhorses." It was "relatively long, though by no means diffuse [and is] in the composer's least aggressive manner." He especially responded to the second-movement scherzo, "where the trick of pairing wind instruments in succession comes off very well indeed." He described the elegy movement as "an intense Magyar lament, very queerly but effectively orchestrated," and noted that the intermezzo movement "could easily become my favorite night music with its charming folksong beginning and its broad slapstick parody of Shostakovich." Fine defended Russian composer Arthur Lourié's suite from his opera-ballet *The Feast During the Plague*—"this sometime Stravinskian music [of which] it is supposed to be smart to speak condescendingly." That music, he said, "reveals a seriousness, an integrity, that is altogether admirable. Why it should possess such individuality is a mystery, for the best passages seemed to

---

1. Here, Fine failed in his duty as a critic by ignoring relevant information about a most unusual work. The program book for the January 18/19, 1946 concerts of the Boston Symphony Orchestra did indeed credit Collins as the composer, but gave the following cumbersome title: *A Threnody for a Soldier Killed in Action; based on fragments left by Michael Heming (1920-1942), killed in action at El Alamein.* A note explained that Heming was a lieutenant in the King's Royal Rifles at the time of his death at age twenty-two. Further: "His father (a professional singer) showed these sketches to John Barbirolli, who sent them to Anthony Collins, then in America, to complete in full score." Barbirolli had conducted the first performance of the Collins/Heming *Threnody* in Sheffield, England in January 1943, and the work had been previously heard in the United States broadcast on a *March of Time* program, on the ABC radio network in January 1944.

be those in which the influence of Stravinsky was most apparent." (This puzzlement, coming from a Stravinsky disciple who would eventually fret under the dominance of the master's style, partakes of a certain irony.) Reviewing the premiere of Martinu's *Fantasy and Rondo* for piano, Fine observed (impossible to tell whether sarcastically): "This piece should be gotten out as a text book on how to string together a series of introductions to introductions. It must be quite a feat to write several minutes of music without a consequent phrase."

In the spring of 1945, Fine published a substantial article on two of his composer friends entitled "Young America: Bernstein and Foss," in which he characterized them as "the twin prodigies, the fair-haired boys of the contemporary musical scene." Leonard Bernstein was then twenty-six, and Fine recalled his amazing musical facility as a Harvard student in the late 1930s: "His extraordinary memory and his flair for improvisation were almost legendary at college. I remember with great nostalgia his appearance as piano accompanist at a series of historical films presented by the Harvard Film Society. *The Battleship Potemkin* rode at anchor to the accompaniment of Copland's *Piano Variations*, excerpts from *Petrouschka* and [his] own paraphrases of Russian folksongs." Fine then took Bernstein's unabashed eclecticism into account in a perceptive capsule critique that could have served as Bernstein's escutcheon throughout his composing career: "Numerous influences are at work on his music, and one doubts that they are completely fused. With Bernstein the dramatic and emotional elements get first consideration and stylistic derivations are of minor importance." Further: "Bernstein's mind is agile and intuitive, if not overly introspective. The blending of sophistication and naiveté in his music has great popular appeal." Fine pointed out "a partiality for jazz and Latin American meters" especially to be heard in the ballet *Fancy Free* and the musical *On the Town*. Always high-minded, he noted that although Bernstein might eventually develop "a truly modern popular style," such a course "has attendant dangers for the composition of serious music." While citing "occasional lapses of taste," he praised "the loftiness of the conception" of the *Jeremiah Symphony*, and registered the opinion that Bernstein's talents were essentially those of a theater composer. But, he warned, "it is dangerous to make any prediction about this young man [for] he can be anything he wants to be." (Verna Fine remembered meeting Bernstein for the first time in the fall of 1940, when she and Fine had just begun dating. "Irving and I were at a Boston Symphony concert and there was a vacant seat next to us. Lenny Bernstein sat down in it and Irving turned to me and said, 'Verna, I want you to notice this guy because he's going to be famous. He's the most talented musician I know.' As far as having a favorite conductor later on, Irving thought Lenny was the best thing since sliced bread. He could do no wrong, even with his flamboyance and vulgarity. Irving loved it when Lenny took over the New York Philharmonic in 1957.")

A few months before the appearance of the *Modern Music* article, Fine had written to Copland that he thought Bernstein's new musical *On the Town* "was terrific in many ways, but not entirely successful." He said he had had a long talk with him and was "terribly impressed with the growing seriousness which seems to be coming over him these days. His conducting performance at symphony some weeks ago was positively hair-raising." Copland responded: "I liked 'On the Town'—thought it lively, fast and lots of fun. It's making everybody lots of money too—so the question as to whether it's art will never be raised. With so successful a precedent we can all write musicals now—or can we?" On January 9, 1945, Fine had written to Bernstein: "I was awfully pleased to read about the great success that 'On the Town' is having in New York. Verna and I talked about nothing else for a few days after we had seen the show. I still have my reservations about the production as a whole, but not about the music, which is first-rate and far too good to be wasted on a musical comedy." He urged Bernstein to compose a serious musical play or an opera on a serious subject. "The peculiarly individual pathos and sentiment of your music suggest a more sustained type of lyrical drama."

As for Lukas Foss, then twenty-one, Fine clearly took him more seriously as a composer, and thus treated Foss's music and development to more detailed scrutiny in his article. A virtuoso pianist born in Germany, Foss was "one of the most gifted composers who has appeared on the American scene." So far, he had enjoyed "a less spectacular popular success" than composer-conductor Bernstein, because "his achievements are those chiefly of a composer." The precocious Foss had already "turned out an enormous amount of music" and was strongly influenced, initially, by Hindemith. Fine thought his early music "often lacks harmonic refinement" but found freshness in its "charming, almost Haydnesque tunefulness." Foss's *First Piano Concerto* of 1944 was based on an earlier clarinet trio rewritten as a clarinet concerto, and in its final form "it had accumulated new themes, a few additional purple harmonies and one or two mannerisms." The first movement had "some delicious themes," but, stylistically, it was "one of Foss's most heterogeneous concoctions." At odds with Foss's later contention that he had been "very involved with Stravinsky," Fine noted that the concerto's "shortwinded Finale shows Foss aware of Stravinskian neoclassicism for the first and last time." He singled out the ambitious 1944 Carl Sandburg cantata *The Prairie* as the young composer's "magnum opus," citing it as "one of the most impressive contributions to American choral literature during the past two decades." Although he disliked certain details of the score—"propulsive ostinati, repetitions and frequent squareness of phrasing"—he acknowledged that they seemed unimportant "beside the work's generous emotion and its extraordinary wealth of invention." At times, there was a pronounced Copland influence (Foss had conducted *Billy the Kid* and was "ready for a new influence"), but the writing was more polyphonic "and has not achieved Copland's transparency." Fine disapproved of Foss's recent *Ode*, finding it badly orchestrated and full of "overblown romanticism," and criticizing its overly sentimental harmony and "increasing tendency to build climax upon climax." The *Symphony in G* was more to his liking, and gave "the impression that Foss is developing an individual style that is more tonal, less dissonant, and perhaps more conservative than his earlier manner." He praised the "fine exuberance" of its scherzo.

The "Young America" article appeared in the May-June, 1945 issue of *Modern Music*. In a letter to Copland, Fine, who had not yet seen the magazine, complained about Minna Lederman, the editor: "I have just received my check for $23 for the Foss-Bernstein article and a note from Lederman telling me that she had made a few cuts. Judging by the size of the check she has lopped off a third of the article. If she has been as injudicious as in the past I shall need several bodyguards to protect me from the wrath of Lenny and Lukas." He added, "Actually, I was quite nice to them." Copland agreed with Fine's last remark, responding on June 5: "I liked your article in M.M. very much. I know from experience that articles on the young are not easy to do. Yours was definitely on the kind side—but why not?"

In an unpublished lecture later in life, Fine mused over the role of music criticism, feeling that it "is not living up to its proper function." He noted that criticism was practiced not only by newspaper and magazine critics, but also by performers, who decide programs; historians, who make use of the critical faculty; composers, who "select, refine, choose"; and even audiences, which applaud or withhold applause. He lamented the power reviewers have over careers, terming it "unfortunate, even intolerable," but blamed "the star system that operates here and abroad." The biggest problem with criticism, he felt, was the judging of new music, and "the only professional musicians who can usually be expected to have something interesting to say about new music are the composers. They may be wrong, but even in their wrongheadedness they can be illuminating." Although he had heard a musicologist at a Harvard symposium on criticism stress knowledge and scholarship, Fine insisted that, overall, "sensitivity, receptivity to music [and] general culture are more necessary to the music reviewer than specific musical knowledge. Add to this a certain humility—a recognition of the power of the pen—of the fact that adverse criticism commands more attention than favorable criticism." He concluded: "What is the old saying? 'One rotten apple can spoil a barrel'."

# Chapter 7

■ THE YEAR 1944 SAW NOT ONLY FINE'S INITIAL EFFORTS at criticism and the beginning of his friendship with Copland, but also the composition of two new works, one negligible, the other not. In November, he wrote Copland that he hoped to be able to come to New York in the near future, because "I shall soon be in the chips, since the advertising stuff came through. They now want a serenade and an intermezzo." The reference was to piano music commissioned by the Verney Fabrics Corporation of New York City, for an ad announcing their "Newsong" line of fabrics. According to Verna, under the terms of this odd but obviously lucrative assignment, Fine's music would be used exclusively for advertising. In an ad in *Harper's Bazaar* magazine in early 1945, a partial view of the first page of a *Serenade* for piano is juxtaposed with a female model wearing a dress and gloves in a pattern of loops, squiggles and squares, the latter possibly meant to invoke music manuscript. The hideous concoction, called "Album Print," is described as "textured harmonies created from today's challenging variety of synthetic fibres." What can be seen of the *Serenade* (the score seems to have disappeared, perhaps into the Verney Fabrics file cabinets) shows a graceful and melancholy waltzlike piece, harmonically conventional. Considering the circumstances of its appearance, Fine may have felt relief that his music went uncredited.

Fine's principal achievement in 1944 was the completion on October 23 of *The Choral New Yorker*, subtitled *Four Choral Patterns with Piano Obbligato*. He found his texts in *The New Yorker Book of Verse*, an anthology of poems that had been published in that magazine between 1925 and 1935, and the poets he chose were relatively unknown. His musical idiom is eclectic and has a good deal of variety: tonal, lyrical, but often relatively dissonant. The latter element, as always with choral writing, presents a higher level of performance difficulty than in more consonant music, certainly as compared to the previous *Alice in Wonderland* settings. In addition, the substantial accompaniment requires a rhythmically alert pianist.

The character of the music in each of the four pieces is quite different, keeping with the nature of the poems, while the part-writing is continually inventive, at times conceptually virtuosic. For elegance and sophistication, especially as regards color contrasts, *The Choral New Yorker* exceeds even the brilliant *Alice,* every bar showing Fine to be a master of the choral medium. As one critic put it a few years later, in this work "his remarkable technical equipment came forth to the use of the will to write."

The first piece, *Prologue: "Hen Party"* (*Moderato ma ben rimato*), dedicated to Fine's father, features a perky and declamatory vocal part that corresponds nicely to Peggy Bacon's wickedly satiric description of gossiping women. ("The pack gathers on the black Sunday/Mrs. Lathers and Mrs. Grundy give a party for all the witches; In aged ermine, the Queen viper, the Ace of vermin/The Pied Piper overlooked her and Cotton Mather should have cooked her.") Occasional echoes of Stravinsky and perhaps Poulenc can be heard in this vivacious yet droll music. The choral part is for mixed voices (SATB) with soprano solo.

*Scherzando: "Caroline Million"* follows without pause, connected by a semitonally dissonant D-natural from the last chord of the prologue. It is set for four-part treble chorus (SSAA) with soprano and alto solos. The text, by Kentuckian Isabel McLennan McMeekin, concerns a bloodthirsty, century-old hillbilly woman who sits by her fireplace smoking a corncob pipe and fingering a Bible: "Hot with desire to kill her lumpy daughter and feed her to the crows." This lively and witty music is jazzily syncopated, subdivision occurring within regular meter (thus, 4/4 divided into 3+3+2). The style sometimes approaches that of a Broadway musical, but never lapses into vulgarity.

Dedicated "to my Parents," the third number, *Concertante: "Pianola d'Amore"* (*Allegro risoluto*), is scored for three-part men's chorus (TBB). The determinedly silly text, by David McCord, evokes English comic-madrigal style as filtered through Gilbert and Sullivan. ("Sing hey, sing ho, sing heigh-o/For the blue that's in the sky-o.") Appropriately,

Fine's music—beginning with a spirited, almost jazzy piano introduction—is tonal, jolly and rhythmic. The syncopated *staccato* accompaniment chatters along with the chorus, at one point indulging in an assertive little bitonal cadenza. The ending is humorously abrupt.

The finale, *Epilogue: "Design for October"* (*Lento*), scored for mixed voices (SATB) with baritone solo, sounds an impressively elegiac note. A simple progression of mildly dissonant chords, used to great expressive purpose, is its foundation. Simplicity is also the hallmark of the poem, by "Jake Falstaff" (pseudonym of Herman Fetzer), a lament for the passing of summer: "Then I heard a voice saying summer is gone!/Gravely I watched the summer die, and the last of the crying geese go by/Summer is ended!" In their American-vernacular, open-air sound, the quiet piano introduction and the initial baritone solo suggest the Copland of *Billy the Kid* and *Our Town*; and indeed the influence of Copland prevails throughout, both in harmony and rhetoric. The choral writing is extremely mellifluous, albeit traditional, seeming so even during the dramatic dissonance that occurs in the piano part when set against unison chorus at the words "No more at morning will you hear the crying geese of the dawn." With its uncomplicated means and direct sentiment, *Design for October* impresses as the emotional crown of this splendid cycle.

*The Choral New Yorker* was given its first performance (under the title *Four Choral Patterns from The New Yorker*) in Cambridge at Sanders Theater on January 25, 1945. The combined forces of the Harvard Glee Club and the Radcliffe Choral Society were conducted by G. Wallace Woodworth, with Fine at the piano. The only newspaper review noted disapprovingly that this was "music of a brittle, cynical quality, consisting of one part jazz and one part ragtime." Witmark published the score the following year, and, upon receiving a copy, the Argentinian composer Alberto Ginastera wrote to Fine, praising the music as "very attractive and interesting" and citing his "magnificent technique." Nevertheless, *The Choral New Yorker* would never rival the popularity of the *Alice* sets.

Fine continued to be active as a performer in 1945, assuming the conductorship of the chorus and chamber orchestra of the

Harvard-Radcliffe Music Clubs and accompanying a soprano at Cambridge's Fogg Museum that April in a program of songs by Brahms, Bach, Mozart, Fauré, Debussy, Ravel, Tchaikovsky and Gershwin. His teaching schedule at Harvard remained constant, and on March 25 the *Boston Herald* announced his promotion to faculty instructor in music, beginning July 1. Verna remembered that after the war the incoming students were older, more mature and serious: "nice, bright kids who had been in the military. They were almost our generation and we enjoyed going out and having drinks with them. They weren't looking for fraternities and binges, but were interested in studying. Those were Irving's best music students at Harvard."

Fine had long been critical of the music department's indifference, even hostility, to the performance element in education, and in Tillman Merritt, who became chairman in 1942, he found an ally. Verna noted that "Irving had a lot of trouble at Harvard because it was run by musicologists and they weren't interested in live music. He fought to introduce the Basic Piano course." According to Daniel Pinkham, it wasn't until the late 1950s, when pianist Luise Vosgerchian joined the faculty, that "they began to take into consideration that a good performer might somehow nourish and bring insights into musicology." He remembered "old President Eliot" who, when confronted with a proposal to give academic credit for piano lessons, declared, "But that's manual labor!" And a faculty meeting during which Merritt praised a student as "a very good scholar and, moreover, a wonderful pianist," whereupon composer Randall Thompson responded loftily: "Oh, he plays the piano. Why, that's one of the social graces." Pinkham described Merritt, who was chairman of the music department from 1942 to 1952, and again from 1968 to 1972, as "a very curious character. Back in the 1940s, he was one of the most popular teachers on the campus from the point of view of the students. Then something happened to him and all the charm and jolliness disappeared. He became bitter and distant." Thompson, he said, "was probably enslaved by his wife, who owned Union Carbide. They had a beautiful, Federal-style house in Cambridge, but Mrs. Thompson would never let any of Randall's colleagues come to dinner because she considered them *declassé*."

According to Elliot Forbes, in his book *A History of Music at Harvard to 1972*, "by 1945 a wide-ranging change was in the making . . . stemming from Merritt's determination that students should *make* music as well as read about it." All candidates for admission as music majors were now expected "to show proficiency on a musical instrument," and before graduating each student must "demonstrate a minimal ability to play the piano." Merritt instituted the new Basic Piano program, and he wanted, in his words, "a highly competent pianist and teacher" imbued with "the scholarly ideals of the Harvard Music Department" to direct it. He chose Fine. Basic Piano, said Merritt, "is a real innovation at Harvard." It was "not for the sake of training piano virtuosi," but simply to make certain "that every student can use piano as a tool in his work."

Retrospectively appraising the situation at Harvard in a 1948 article, Fine noted that "in a place with the traditions of Harvard there is the problem of overcoming inertia and prejudice." Given without fee, the Basic Piano program had grown out of the discovery that some students "were articulate *about* music, but were *musically inarticulate* [because] the kind of music education some of our graduates were leaving with was at best two-dimensional, and at its worst superficial." Merritt's and Fine's post-war ideal for Harvard was to produce a "university musician," meaning "a man of broad interests and sympathies—no narrow specialist [but] a completely equipped musician able to perform on an instrument with competence [and] well grounded in theory [and] familiar with the styles and periods of music history." Even more important than musicological expertise, however, a student should be "intimately acquainted with a small portion of musical literature." The two men had decided that "the ability to perform on the piano was a necessary adjunct to most of these activities, and therefore concluded that the piano was an indispensable tool in any serious study of music."

In his report, Fine deplored the Harvard music department's continuing conservatism and the tenacious emphasis on theory and history. "Although it moves in the right direction, the [1945] Harvard [applied music] program, in my opinion, does not go far enough. It is inadequate in that it considers performance merely as an adjunct to other things—

as a tool for theoretical studies, and as a means of getting at music for the sake of analysis and historical investigation. It makes no direct provision, however, for the enjoyment of music as an art (unless it be through listening)." Stressing performing skills, Fine observed that, though improved, the 1945 program "makes no provision for instruction in other instruments" than the piano. This failure, he felt, "impoverishes the musical life of the university community." He recommended not only more piano instruction but lessons in orchestral instruments, and concluded his essay on a sour note: "It is apparent today that technological advances are progressively restricting the demand for professional musicians. There is a growing danger that Americans will become a nation of musical spectators."

The Basic Piano program began in the fall of 1945, and Fine received a five-year appointment to the faculty. Ever doubting, he had written to Copland the previous winter that although the music department had suggested the appointment, he was not sure the administration would approve it, "since I am not distinguished enough to reward in such a way."

On September 12, just before the start of the term, Fine wrote to Copland that the still-deserted Harvard music building "is a rather noisy place these days. They are putting air-conditioning and sound proofing in the basement for the new practice-rooms that we are installing for our applied-music program." A few weeks later, he noted that although his schedule involved teaching twenty-five hours a week, he did not find it oppressive. "My only regret is that there is no time for the things I like best. I have had to drop out of the Glee Club and to shelve composition for a while." The latter allusion was to a work for violin and piano on which Fine had labored during the summer months. With the austerities of the war years a thing of the past, he and Verna spent much of that period in a rented cottage in Centerville, Massachusetts, on Cape Cod: "a little six-room job with three bedrooms, completely furnished with every convenience [including] an oil stove and a fireplace." Despite such comforts, creative work did not go well, the weather was often bad and he missed seeing other musicians, so that by August he was depressed and frustrated. "This vacation is too long," he grumbled to Copland, "and I am becoming lazy and jumpy. I suppose that I should be happiest punching a clock at eight every morning and leaving for home, the wife and the kiddies at five in the afternoon. It will be good to get back into some kind of routine." One of the summer's rare pleasures was a visit from Harold Shapero: "Harold was down for a few days last month, played his serenade [in D major for string orchestra] for me (his technical grasp is more extraordinary than ever), improvised constantly, went fishing for one afternoon and departed the next day."

Fine had borrowed a violin and was trying to learn its secrets. "Thus far I can play the first page in Sevcik's 'Preparatory Trill Exercises' [and] the G major scale and arpeggio. Most of the time is spent in figuring out various triple-stop combinations, harmonics, etc. It is probably a great waste of time, and agony for Verna, but seems a good way to pass the rainy days." He engaged a violin teacher, "a kindly middle-aged lady who is constantly reliving her student days in Berlin." But on August 13 he wrote that "I am already past shame in admitting that I have done little or nothing." Nonetheless, on returning to Cambridge in September, he informed Copland that "actually, I have written one movement of a sonata for violin and piano and that needs plenty of retouching. This is my sole achievement during the summer. I don't think it's bad." He remarked that Verna liked the music and then described it as "depressingly piddling." "In my present scheme of things," he said, "a minute's music is a tremendous accomplishment." Mentioning the "highly neurotic state" of David Diamond, recently described to him by Leonard Bernstein, Fine observed that "my present experience is that nerves and writing don't mix, but then there are numerous instances to disapprove that theory."

The only work that Fine completed in 1945 was a three-minute piece in E-flat major and simple A-B-A form for *a cappella* women's chorus (SSA) entitled *A Short Alleluia*. Although gesturally clichéd (similar to most alleluias through the ages), this music is rendered effective and attractive by its frequent meter changes, carefully calculated dynamics and an unexpected modulation at the climax, leading to a stern dissonance that resolves to a pure B-flat-minor chord. It was written for the Bryn Mawr College Chorus, but whether that group ever performed it is not known. *A Short Alleluia* was published posthumously in 1973. Meanwhile, in late 1945, Fine privately plied his critical skills in a letter to Copland, with capsule evaluations of new works played by the Boston Symphony. "We have had three premieres within the past month," he reported. "Martinu's Third [Symphony] (worth about a B+), Menotti's [piano] concerto (grade C trivia) and Prokofiev's new symphony [No. 5] (exhilarating but not worth all the fanfare it got)." In the same letter, Fine expressed disappointment with a recent Foss piece. "Lukas has played his 'Song of Anguish' for us (also for Boulanger, Harold and anybody else he can snare into listening). It is relatively free of the usual influences, and yet seems less fresh than his 'Prairie' or symphony. In spite of some beautiful passages I feel that he falls considerably short of the emotional level of the text (excerpts from Isaiah)." Soon after, at the same time he was writing the harsh appraisal of the Boston Symphony's mini-festival of British music that would appear in Modern Music, an incensed Fine told Copland: "We have entered upon a desert-like stretch in so far as the symphony concerts are concerned. Sir Adrian Boult is conducting and a more apathetic—rather, dull, individual I have never seen upon a conductor's podium. And who was it that talked about a Renaissance of English music? Talk about the provincialism of Sibelius. The affected rusticity and antiquarianism of guys like Vaughan Williams is far more obnoxious." He found "particularly irritating" the "wave of anglophilia gripping Boston Symphony audiences" and denounced the orchestra's management as "a notorious gang of tories who seem to believe that the British are great artists since they are all great people—brothers of Churchill, so to speak."

In a January 20, 1946 letter to Copland, Fine noted that he was "copying the fiddle sonata—which means further revisions and delay. It has a cloying prettiness which I delude myself into thinking is depth and passion. There are shades of Beethoven, Tchaikovsky, Brahms and a few live snatches of Stravinsky, Copland and Shapero." In later years he would tend to deprecate his *Sonata for Violin and Piano* as a kind of sin-of-my-youth effort—an overly severe view that has, nonetheless, some validity. After reading through the sonata in 1955 with Joseph Fuchs, Fine wrote to Verna: "What a funny uneven young piece that is. Full of awfully nice things but so often inept in the way it progresses from idea to idea." In a 1960 program note, he characterized it as "an early work belonging to a manner somewhat remote to its composer [today]." And in a 1958 letter, he stated that he had been "strongly under the influence of composers whom I admired (and still do!). Stylistically it can be related to Stravinsky and Copland; however, there are indefinable personal qualities in the sonata which characterize both it and all my subsequent works."

In a work so saturated with derivations, it is difficult to know exactly what Fine meant by "indefinable personal qualities." The sonata is basically a neoclassic score, especially in its lively rhythms and transparent textures. Stravinsky is certainly a strong influence (Arthur Cohn would write that Fine was "as true a disciple as one could find"), and possibly Piston and Prokofiev, along with Copland and, oddly enough, Brahms, in relation to some of the harmonies and melodic outlines. (Noël Lee, who often performed the sonata, thought of it as "sort of Brahmsian-American neoclassic.") The piece is well made, with considerable attention to detail, a concern for formal balance and symmetry everywhere evident. It is, at twenty minutes' duration, a substantial concert work. Musical ideas are mostly diatonic and lyrical (requiring a violinist with good intonation in the high register), except when rhythmic energy, particularly in the piano part, predominates. Recognizing, as did Bartók, that the two instruments are sonically incompatible, Fine seldom allows them to share material but is careful to give them equal roles. The work is cast in three movements, the only time he would employ the standard fast-slow-fast format in any score.

An impartial appraisal of Fine's violin sonata would have to note that it illustrates the tenet that his problem as a composer was never one of technique but rather of personality. Although some of the romantically soaring violin lines are unlike anything found in any of its avatars, as are occasional harmonic complications, at no point does a clear voice emerge. Yet the sonata's eclectic virtues go far to make it an attractive and effective addition to the chamber repertory. Soon after it was finished, Fine showed it to Stravinsky, who thought the music "very sympathetic" and complimented "the clean quality of the writing." Fine himself described the sonata's idiom as being "essentially tonal, diatonic and moderately dissonant, neoclassic in its formal approach, and (according to some critics) neoromantic in its expressive attitudes."

The first movement (*Moderato; Allegro moderato, giusto*) is in sonata form, as is the third movement, both, said the composer, "with one minor modification: the contraction of the recapitulation by omission or elision of the first theme group." The lyrically poetic opening (marked *dolce* in the violin part) sets forth the thematic material (ending in a rich minor-second chord), which undergoes extensive development in the subsequent allegro. That section is playfully syncopated, with a pleasing continuity of contrasts between short, restless phrases and more sustained melodic writing that is interrupted by a fugue (the only one in Fine's mature output). This last is dry and academic sounding and decidedly intrusive, but it should be noted that the first three notes will generate the following movement's theme and, by slight stretch of imagination, the fugue-subject can be heard as being related to the rhythmic opening of the finale. A sparkling little coda brings the movement to its end.

Fine stated that the structure of the lyrical second movement (*Lento con moto*) is "more difficult to describe" than the outer movements. "The first part of the exposition contains the initial double theme (or theme with countermelody in the piano), transition and closing theme; the second part omits the transition and adds a brief coda. In the recapitulation, the opening theme is entrusted to the piano, the countermelody to the violin. [Here,] the medium is treated in duo fashion, the two instruments often being treated in free and occasionally imitative polyphony." The movement begins in Copland's most seductive, "white-note" style (excepting two saccharine violin *glissandi*), and then, after some melodramatic rhetoric and a return of the opening lyricism, becomes rather diffuse harmonically. Partaking of variation technique, this curiously constructed movement is essentially romantic in expression.

Fine described the high-spirited finale (*Vivo*) as "more bravura in character." It contains mildly virtuosic violin writing and a piano part abounding in tricky rhythms. Bowing effects such as *martellato, saltando, détaché,* and *richochet* add color, as do occasional triple-stop *pizzicato* chords. The music is rhythmically intricate throughout, with striking contrasts between the instruments. Near the end, material from the first movement returns in the piano for a gripping *allargando* climax. The work ends with a short, brittle but witty coda.

Fine's *Sonata for Violin and Piano* had a tryout performance at Harvard on February 6, 1947, performed by its dedicatees, violinist Angel Reyes and composer-pianist Jacques de Menasce. The official premiere was given by the same forces in New York a few days later, on February 9, at Times Hall, along with sonatas by Prokofiev, Milhaud and de Menasce. Both program books listed the Fine sonata as a first performance. Writing in the *New York Sun,* Harold C. Schoenberg thought it displayed "a worthy modicum of individuality and a satisfactory feeling of events proceeding to a logical conclusion." Howard Taubman observed in the *New York Times*: "To one hearing music by Mr. Fine for the first time it signalized the arrival of a gifted composer. This sonata has logic and lucidity, tasteful workmanship and abundant vitality. If [it] reflects more of energy than depth, to judge it from a single hearing, that is not a bad balance for an up and coming composer." Two weeks later, on April 24, the sonata had its formal Boston premiere, at the Institute of Modern Art. This time, the performers were Alfred Krips and Fine himself. The program also had works by Shapero, Foss, Talma and Copland, and Fine and Foss served as a duo-piano team in Copland's *Danzon Cubano* and Talma's *Four Handed Fun.*

The performance of the violin sonata in New York marked Fine's debut as a composer outside the Boston area, and the score was published by Witmark a year later. His first instrumental composition for the concert hall had fared well.

# Chapter 8

IN JANUARY 1946, COPLAND asked Koussevitzky to engage Fine to teach harmonic analysis during that year's six-week summer season at Tanglewood, near Lenox, Massachusetts, where the conductor had established a music school. That winter, Verna had been periodically incapacitated with back pain and flu, and the Fines had moved temporarily into Florence Rudnick's comfortable suite in Boston's Lafayette Hotel, where, Fine wrote Copland, he was finally free "from the endless round of cooking, dishes and bed-pans. I am trying to write while mother and daughter are carrying on an animated conversation (of a gossiping nature) which I have been straining to hear." On January 20 he wrote that he had heard nothing about Tanglewood: "Am I to be notified officially of my appointment or disappointment?" He noted that, in any case, he would have to obtain permission from Harvard.

The invitation from Tanglewood arrived. Although in a postcard Fine said that "the outlook is bright," he was clearly worried about Harvard: "It is so easy to get tripped up in the incredible red tape in this institution." Verna remembered that "the music department at Harvard was opposed and wanted to block him going to Tanglewood. The summer, they said, is for research and recuperation. You're not supposed to take another job, much less get paid! There was tension between Irving and the music department, because Irving liked musical music. He finally went to Paul Buck, the Dean [of the Faculty of Arts and Sciences], and said, 'You know, music at Harvard is very sterile, so I look forward to going to Tanglewood and hearing and performing live music. This is what it's all about'." Fortunately, Dean Buck was sympathetic and granted permission. Fine gave Copland the good news on February 28: "I might add that the Dean stated that his sanction would not bind him for the future."[1] (A week later,

---

1. Indeed it would not. Although Fine had no further trouble with

Copland replied: "I was relieved and pleased to hear that the Dean had listened to reason. Your name was already in the catalogue and I was holding my breath in case anything went haywire.")

More routinely, Fine expressed irritation with Minna Lederman, writing to Copland upon receiving a proof for his *Modern Music* article entitled "Bartók's New Koussevitzky Number": "My impression is that the magazine has become one of the Luce publications. The style of the proof was hardly recognizable as my own." In February he was back at the Cambridge apartment and in a happy mood, thanks to a Boston visit by Stravinsky, who conducted the local premiere of his *Symphony in Three Movements*. "We had a wonderful time," he informed Copland. "I like the new symphony very much, especially the first two movements. Boston critics were rather rough on him, but somehow I have the impression he doesn't particularly care about critical comment anymore." Fine and other composer friends, including Shapero, Foss, Claudio Spies and Alexei Haieff, had met with Stravinsky at Foss's studio and played him their recent music, the occasion at which Fine had unveiled his violin sonata. "He wasn't too specific in his criticism although he pointed out the dangers of 6/8 time in Lukas' symphony. In Harold's music he noted a

---

Harvard about spending his summers at Tanglewood, it was quite another matter when, the following year, Koussevitzky recommended him to be the conductor of Boston's prestigious Cecilia Society, which held concerts during the academic year. As Fine wrote to Koussevitzky on May 24, 1947: "I first saw The Provost of the University, Dr. Paul Buck, who said he considered the request irregular and that it would be necessary for me to obtain the opinions of my colleagues in the music department. This I did [and] I reported to the Provost that my colleagues were not opposed to the matter. [Consequently,] I was astonished when [Tillman Merritt] informed me that Dr. Buck had spoken to him about the matter and had said that if I were to take on the Cecilia Society, I should have to give up half of my job and salary at Harvard." He concluded: "I could see that in order to maintain harmonious relations all around, it was best to forget about the matter. Furthermore, if I were to take a cut in salary at Harvard (no matter what the Cecilia Society should decide to pay), I should never be able to make ends meet next year."

few places which will probably be difficult in execution, but one could see that he was profoundly impressed. After the music-making, we had a gay dinner party lasting three hours at the Athens Olympia. When we said good-by to him [the next day], he asked Lukas to send him a copy of his *Song of Anguish*, Harold his *Serenade*, and me the fiddle sonata." Copland replied: "Your description of the Stravinsky seance sounded historic. When am *I* going to see that Violin Sonata of you'n?" (On July 9, after receiving Fine's sonata, Stravinsky wrote: "I liked this score so much when you played it for me the last February in Boston. Glad to hear it.")

On April 13, after a visit to Copland in Ridgefield, Connecticut, Fine invited him to stay with them in Cambridge at "our present little apartment," offering the information that "our studio couch is comfortable, there are a certain number of books and pieces of music at hand, and there is also a handy keyhole at the head of the bed, through which you can observe the activities our neighbors carry on in the supposed privacy of their bathroom." Verna and her mother had just returned from a Florida vacation, and "the cloistered calm of my studio is completely shattered by the noise of Verna's stomping, shrieking and baby chatter." But, he added contentedly, "it is all a very pleasant change." Fine noted that both Shapero and Haieff recently had been given Guggenheim grants, and that Copland seemed to have mysterious foreknowledge of the awards. "Bearing this in mind I have begun writing a symphony, an oratorio, a chamber-opera, six tone-poems, and a brace of chamber works for all sorts of instrumental combination. I shall then study every inflection of every chance remark that you might make throughout the summer and will have each of your letters examined by a competent analyst, so as to determine what my future *als Komponist* [as a composer] will be." He congratulated Copland on securing "a dream cottage" for the upcoming Tanglewood season and worried whether he could find and afford a suitable place for himself. "Verna and I are going up to Lenox again this week [to] spend a day or so looking around." He had even considered buying a trailer.

Tanglewood was to play an important role in Fine's musical life. He would spend portions of nine summers there, between 1946 and 1957, as a member of the Berkshire Music Center's composition faculty. He had known Koussevitzky slightly since the late 1930s, having often gone backstage after Boston Symphony concerts. "Irving was a familiar face, as a student," Verna recalled. In 1944 Copland introduced Fine to Koussevitzky as a potential teacher. Tanglewood had closed in 1942 because of the war, and Copland told Koussevitzky that when the school reopened the composition department would need additional academic courses. According to Verna, Koussevitzky, whose English could be picturesque, declared to her husband: "My friend, when the war is over I'm going to hire you to teach harmonical analysis." Interestingly, by 1945 Fine knew Koussevitzky well enough to be asked to re-bar sections of Copland's *Appalachian Spring* suite, to make them easier to conduct. It was known that Koussevitzky had trouble with meter changes, but, said Verna, "Irving refused at Aaron's request, and eventually 'Koussie' struggled through those difficult rhythms."

It was Koussevitzky's custom to rely on the assistance of younger musicians when confronted with a contemporary work he meant to conduct. "He couldn't read scores very well," said Harold Shapero, "so when a new one came along he always had a troubleshooter to play it on the piano. In the initial years, it was Nicholas Slonimsky. Then, at one point it got to be Irving." Verna recalled that "Irving could read a score the way Leonard Bernstein could: he would take a new orchestral piece and sit down at the piano and play it. He was a fabulous sight-reader." Both Verna and Shapero remembered an amusing incident from 1945 involving the recent *Fifth Symphony* of Prokofiev. "I got this from Irving," Shapero reminisced. "One night, Koussevitzky telephoned him and said, 'I have the Prokofiev symphony and I want you to come over and tell me how it is formed and everything about it.' So they start on the slow movement, and Koussevitzky nudges him on the shoulder and says, 'It's a *passacaglia*, no?' 'Well, not really,' says Irving, and goes on through the movement in his pedantic way for half an hour, showing him it was a five-part song form or something. And at the end of all of this, Koussevitzky says: 'But it's a *passacaglia*, no?'"

Tanglewood had a somewhat complicated history. At Stockbridge, Massachusetts in 1934, the American composer and conductor Henry Kimball Hadley (1871-1937) had established the Berkshire Symphonic Festivals, with the New York Philharmonic as resident orchestra. Two years later the Boston Symphony replaced the Philharmonic. Only three concerts were given that summer—under a large tent in an open field at Holmwood, a former estate of the Vanderbilt family—but almost 15,000 people attended them. In 1937 the Tanglewood Estate, owned by the Tappan family and comprising over 200 wooded acres in the scenic Berkshire Mountains, was donated to Koussevitzky and the trustees of the Boston Symphony. There, the orchestra gave three summer concerts. When torrential rain ruined the second concert, it was decided that a permanent structure should be constructed, and a fund drive began. Koussevitzky chose the distinguished architect Eliel Saarinen, but Saarinen's plans proved too elaborate for the $100,000 budget and had to be simplified. The Shed, a roofed open-air concert hall overlooking Lake Mahkeenac, was inaugurated on August 4, 1938, and Tanglewood became the official summer home of the Boston Symphony. (In 1988, on its fiftieth anniversary, it was renamed the Serge Koussevitzky Music Shed.)

Since his youth in Russia, Koussevitzky had dreamt of establishing an elaborate music center where, as he put it in 1939 to the Boston Symphony trustees, "the greatest living composers would teach the art of composition, the greatest virtuosi the art of performance, and the greatest conductors the mystery of conducting orchestras and choruses." He felt that in the United States such an elite institution "would result in a creation of new and great values in art [and] in the education and training of a new generation of American artists." So, in 1940, he founded the Berkshire Music Center.

Koussevitzky organized the Center into two divisions: the Institute for Advanced Study, which included composers and their pupils, his own conducting students and an opera program; and the Academy, or Department of Music and Culture, for student performances in chorus and orchestra. To teach thirteen young composers that first season, he selected two renowned but dissimilar figures: Aaron Copland and Paul Hindemith. There were also lectures by Olin Downes, Archibald T. Davison and Randall Thompson, among others.

At the opening ceremony, Thompson's commissioned *Alleluia* for chorus was premiered and Koussevitzky, referring to the war raging in Europe, declared: "If ever there was a time to speak of music, it is now in the New World."[2]

Harold Shapero was one of the composition students in the initial class, and he felt that Tanglewood "was not very organized that first year." However, for Leonard Bernstein Tanglewood "was wonderful. I came in as a [conducting] student, and Aaron came in as head of the composition department, but we both became so close to Koussevitzky. He adored Aaron, Aaron adored him. It was a marvelous summer." Bernstein wrote to his brother: "The inspiration of this center is terrific enough to keep you going with no sleep at all." Lukas Foss also remembered 1940 in the Berkshires: "At Tanglewood, Koussevitzky was very important to me. All of us profited from his interest in American music. Koussevitzky tried to help me—he even gave me his suits after having worn them four or five times."

Copland prevailed upon Koussevitzky to let him commandeer student instrumentalists to play pieces written by his students, certain it was the best way for young composers to learn to hear what they put down on paper. By the following year, the Chamber Music Hall, the Theatre-Concert Hall and several studios had been constructed.

For the first two years after 1940, the school and the Boston Symphony concerts (each event usually drew between eight and ten thousand people) were an immense success. There were also recitals, chamber-music programs, opera workshops and lectures: a veritable hive of activity overseen by the benign yet sometimes imperious Russian conductor. Sixty years later, Shapero reminisced: "Koussevitzky was a marvelous fellow with a lot of vision, and he had the vision of American music being important. He brought Aaron in to Tanglewood, which was the best thing he did. He was a very elegant man by deep instinct, but he was also a fearsome, illogical martinet who could drive you crazy."

In 1942 there were grave changes at Tanglewood

---

2. Koussevitzky always referred to the first event of the Tanglewood season as the "commencement," and Thompson's *Alleluia* was a staple at such occasions.

brought on by the war. Because of gasoline shortages, the music festival had to be canceled, and the Boston Symphony's board of trustees voted to stop funding the school.[3] But Koussevitzky refused to close it and used his own money, along with contributions, to keep it open that summer. He arranged composer forums at the Lenox Library and replaced the Boston Symphony with two student orchestras. He even conducted the "first" orchestra in the American concert premiere of Shostakovich's much-touted *Leningrad Symphony*, a coup that brought considerable publicity. Nonetheless, as Copland wrote, "the school and the festivals became war casualties in spite of the successes of 1942; neither would resume in full force until 1946."

Fine, who was one of Koussevitzky's final protégés, began a long and happy affiliation with Tanglewood in late June 1946, teaching harmonic analysis at the Berkshire Music Center's Institute for Advanced Study. Copland was head of the composition department and was thus Fine's nominal superior, a professional relationship both men found congenial. Copland remarked that "titles didn't mean too much. Everybody took care of his own classes and his own work." Fine in the classroom, Harold Shapero noted, was "a very skillful teacher, especially good at harmony." In Verna's opinion, "because Irving was in the academic world, Aaron often turned to him for teaching and organizational ideas. They did a lot of co-lecturing. Both were good administrators."

As a matter of policy, Koussevitzky had decided to invite a distinguished non-American composer each summer to share composition duties with Copland. (Each student had two private lessons a week, along with two group sessions.) That year's choice was Bohuslav Martinu, a Czech who spent the war in the United States as a refugee and, a few years earlier, had written the first of his six symphonies for Koussevitzky. Not long after the Tanglewood season began, Martinu seriously injured himself when he fell onto his head from a balcony in Great Barrington, where he was staying. For a short period, his eight composer students were taught by Fine,

---

3. The Berkshire Music Center's letterhead stationery contained the phrase: "Maintained by the Boston Symphony Orchestra in connection with the Berkshire Festival Concerts."

until Copland could arrange for Russian-born Nikolai Lopat-nikoff to replace Martinu.[4]

In 1946, in addition to Copland, the school's administrative staff included Tod Perry, Koussevitzky's executive secretary, and Leonard Burkat, whom Fine recommended to Copland as librarian. As noted, Fine taught harmonic analysis, and his lectures were often related to works being performed at the festival; according to Verna, he also taught composition to students who needed basic technical training. Robert Shaw and Hugh Ross were instructors in choral music, Gregor Piatigorsky in chamber music and Olin Downes in music criticism. Lessons in instruments were given by members of the Boston Symphony. Boris Goldovsky was in charge of the opera program, and that summer Leonard Bernstein conducted the American premiere of Benjamin Britten's *Peter Grimes*, a mostly student production that turned out to be the season's highlight. Four hundred students had enrolled at Tanglewood, many on the GI Bill of Rights recently passed by Congress.

Several of that year's composition students went on to major careers, among them Ned Rorem and the Argentinian Alberto Ginastera. "It was the happiest summer of my life," said Rorem. Ginastera remembered that "at Tanglewood, Koussevitzky was like the Czar. We were very much impressed each time we saw him, especially when he wore a cape with red silk inside." Leonard Burkat termed Koussevitzky "our lord and our master. This was his place. He had thought it up—invented it—and brought it into existence. He made it exactly what he wanted it to be—a kind of meeting place for people he considered to have the best musical minds and the greatest musical skills and the highest artistic aspirations." That extraordinary environment was tailormade for Fine, the complete musician, and three years later he would write to

---

4. Bad luck dogged Koussevitzky's choices. When the Swiss composer Arthur Honegger came to Tanglewood in 1947, he promptly suffered a heart attack. Copland replaced him with the American Samuel Barber. The following year, the Frenchman Darius Milhaud, though gout-ridden, made it through the season. In a letter to Copland, he referred to Koussevitzky as "the magician of this musical land."

Koussevitzky: "I have a powerful feeling of loyalty to the school and its ideals, and I have a sense of *belonging* to Tanglewood in a way that I have belonged to little else in my life." Verna reflected that "in those Tanglewood days we all lived together: Aaron Copland, Lukas Foss and sometimes even Leonard Bernstein (he'd come to snitch a free meal). They all played music for each other. It was a wonderful time, when the composers were relaxed and we had Koussevitzky as the godfather in the best sense of the word."

During the following summer, 1947, in addition to being a faculty member at Tanglewood,[5] Fine became a student in Koussevitzky's conducting class. Koussevitzky thought that composers should learn to conduct and he invited Fine to study with him. "Every week, as a student conductor, you had to learn a new piece," recalled Verna, "and Irving said it wasn't easy." One week Fine was assigned the Brahms *Haydn Variations*, and took the score home to study. "He decided he'd sneak into the Tanglewood library and get the record. In those days, records were 78s and it was a big album. He was just coming out of the library when who does he bump smack into but Koussevitzky. My husband was very fair in complection and he turned crimson. He said, Oh, Maestro! And tried to explain that he still was going to study the score but he needed a little assistance and was going to stay home and listen to the record and learn it faster. I know it's not correct, he admitted. Then Koussevitzky put his hand on Irving's shoulder and said, 'Mine son, dunt vurry, dunt vurry. What goes on in the kitchen you dunt haf to know in the dining room'."

---

5. Along with the usual theory classes, Fine gave four lectures on American music: the first on the earliest period (Indian and regional folk music, William Billings); the second on post-Civil War composers (John Knowles Paine, George Whitefield Chadwick, Edward MacDowell, Arthur Foote, Horatio Parker); the third on neoclassicism versus atonality (heritage of Stravinsky, Schoenberg, Hindemith and Ernest Bloch); the fourth on Piston, Roger Sessions and Howard Hanson. In early 1947, Fine had delivered comprehensive lectures at Amherst College on the history of American music. During the summer of 1948, he gave two lectures on the Bartók string quartets at Tanglewood.

Apropos that Brahms score came a classic Tanglewood anecdote, one often repeated by Fine's colleagues and one which he liked to tell on himself. Leonard Bernstein related it in a 1966 radio interview. "It was after a performance he conducted [on July 4, 1947]. I remember it. I was there. It was the Brahms *Haydn Variations,* on which he had worked very hard, and it didn't come off very well. Koussevitzky was standing in the wings waiting for him as he came off the stage, and patted him on the shoulder and said: 'Fine. Fine. It was awful'."[6]

Another story Fine enjoyed telling was about the time, in 1949, when a pianist became ill just before a Boston Symphony rehearsal at Tanglewood of Martinu's two-piano concerto. Koussevitzky unexpectedly enlisted Fine to play one of the solo parts, although Fine had never seen the score. Verna remembered: "Lukas Foss was the other pianist, and Irving said it was a total disaster. When Irving would make a mistake he would grimace, like he was getting an injection. Finally Koussevitzky stopped the rehearsal, glared at Irving, and said: 'Ven ve make mistake in this orchestra, ve don't laugh, ve *veep!*'"

6. According to Richard Wernick, when Fine related this story he always quoted the conductor as having used the word "terrible." In July 1947, along with the Brahms variations, Fine conducted the Department II Orchestra (advanced players) in Haieff's *Divertimento,* the first movement of Mozart's *Symphony No. 35,* Beethoven's *Consecration of the House* overture and Copland's *Quiet City.*

# Chapter 9

■ AFTER THE "STERILE" ENVIRONMENT AT HARVARD, the volatile atmosphere of Tanglewood, where Fine frequently met with performers and often attended orchestra rehearsals, was likely the stimulus behind his first symphonic work, the *Toccata Concertante*. He began it in Cambridge in late 1946. No commission was involved, although Koussevitzky may well have said: if you write an orchestral piece, I'll play it.

The score (working titles were *Symphonic allegro* and *Sinfonia*; then *Masque* with *Toccata Concertante* as the subtitle) was composed during 1946-1947, but Verna noted that its themes "were germinating for ages." She remembered that "when I met Irving in 1940, he sat down at the piano in my college dormitory and played the opening theme. It was in his head way back then."

In 1947, Fine received the first of several fellowships to the MacDowell Colony, a woodland retreat for artists in Peterborough, New Hampshire, founded in 1908 by the widow of the American composer Edward MacDowell. It was there, on June 5, that he finished composing the *Toccata*.[1]

Meanwhile, he had been involved in two Stravinsky projects. The first was something of a coup. With the composer's permission, he conducted two sections of the as-yet-unfinished *Mass*, the "Kyrie" and "Gloria," at Harvard on February 26, with the wind parts arranged for two pianos.[2]

---

1. A quarter of a century later, in 1972, one of the Colony's earliest cottages, the Youngstown Studio, would be rechristened the Irving Fine Studio.

2. Besides the Stravinsky, this adventurous, mostly-choral concert by the Harvard and Radcliffe music clubs included the Boston premiere of Copland's *The Lark*, the premiere of Lukas Foss's *Tell This Blood*, the first American performance of Francis Poulenc's *Secheresses* and the premiere of Robert Middleton's *Madrigal*, all conducted by Fine. Also heard were Hindemith's

(The previous October, Alexei Haieff had written Fine from Hollywood that Stravinsky had asked him to convey that "he is very happy" about the plan to air the excerpts, adding: "One thing though, before he sends you those scores he wants to have them copyrighted.") Then, on March 15, Fine served as pianist in the *Symphony of Psalms* at Carnegie Hall, at a Boston Symphony concert conducted by Koussevitzky.

Immersed as Fine was in Stravinsky's music during early 1947, it is not altogether surprising that the forthcoming *Toccata Concertante* turned out to be his most quintessentially Stravinskian score. As Leonard Slatkin would comment, with only slight exaggeration, many years later after conducting the work with the New York Philharmonic: "It is certainly a rare example of a composer turning to another composer for a huge influence which, if you didn't know Irving Fine wrote the piece, you would swear it's a piece written by Stravinsky that we never heard of."

Fine, then thirty-two years old, arrived at MacDowell on June 2, 1947, and the following day he described his situation in a letter to Verna. "My studio, 'Chapman', is the farthest removed from everything. It has no running water nor does it have a toilet. Nevertheless, it has had some pretty well known occupants in its time—Copland, [Roy] Harris, [Marc] Blitzstein, Douglas Moore. I began working at about 8:45 this morning and continued until shortly after 4:30 this afternoon. Wrote about a page and a half of music and am now actually writing the coda of the symphonic piece—as yet no orchestration attempted. There is no question but that one can get

---

four-hand piano sonata and works for two pianos by Milhaud and Theodore Chanler.

Chanler's piece was entitled *The Second Joyful Mystery, Fugue for Two Pianos*, and in December 1947 Fine enthusiastically reviewed the recently published score. He termed it "beautiful in a nostalgic, 'old-worldly' way" and "gentle and evocative." It exhibited "qualities of sensitivity, refinement, and decorum rarely encountered in American music these days." The idiom was "essentially diatonic and consonant" and made its point "without display of contrapuntal erudition, and with flowing melodic lines." Fine cited Chanler's "meticulous regard for detail," which suggested to him the influence of Fauré. Although he found the music "not particularly adventurous," it was "altogether admirable."

more work done here than at home. For one thing, one can pound the piano and shout without feeling self-conscious." The letter is signed "Yahving," approximating Verna's usual distortion of his name.

On June 6, in a letter that begins "Darling monkeyface," Fine writes: "As I told you yesterday, I have actually finished the composition. Now the dirty work begins. The next step is tabbing the piano score with all the instrumentation I can think of. It looks as though I am going to have to use a large orchestra, for the coda is quite big though by no means long." He then complains that there is little to do in the evenings except play pool, at which he is far from proficient. This letter ends with an inquiry to his pregnant wife: "Are there any signs of the little guest as yet?" and is signed "Swaitsie-pie."

The next letter, dated June 10, reports on the routine at the Colony, which is "much the same every day. We breakfast together; depart to our studios for the day; return for dinner; play croquet or billiards, read or go to the beer joint in the evening." Fortunately, he has the companionship of his friend Harold Shapero. "Harold is knocking off his five or six measures a day. He is working on some piano music [*Variations in C Minor*]. As you might expect he is also playing a lot of Beethoven's sonatas." At the end of the letter comes the first reference to a new piece. "I have decided to try to gather some themes while I'm up here, since I find that working on the orchestration is a real bore as well as a chore. Needless to say it is going very slowly. I made and gave up at least four beginnings and have now decided to go on as well as I can and return to the difficult parts later. It has taken as long as four hours to do one page of scoring and there are approximately seventy pages in all to be done." On June 19, the *Peterborough Transcript* announced that Fine was in residence at the Mac-Dowell Colony "working on an orchestra overture called 'Symphony Allegro'."

At the end of the month, Irving and Verna were off to Tanglewood for six weeks of teaching and concerts. A highlight of the summer was a course in American music, perhaps the first of its kind, taught alternately by Fine, Copland and Bernstein. With the exception of the first few pages, the *Toccata Concertante* remained unorchestrated, and in the middle of August Fine returned to MacDowell with Verna to continue work both on it and on a suite of piano pieces begun earlier in the summer. Additionally, he spent "one week of agony" writing a 6,000-word article, "The Story of Twentieth-Century Music"; this would be published by the Grolier Society in 1948 as a chapter in the *Book of Knowledge*, and he was paid $200, a good fee in those days.

On August 27, Verna wrote to Copland, who was in Rio de Janeiro on a State Department tour: "Irving had a mild 'blackie' [Fine's term for a depression] after leaving Tanglewood. He said it was because he missed you and the wonderful influence you have over him. He is now finishing up his little piano pieces and the scoring business." Shapero, Foss and Louise Talma were all in residence, so there was agreeable company during the long evenings at Colony Hall. Back in Cambridge at the beginning of October, Fine reported to Copland that "I still have forty measures of coda to orchestrate in my as yet unnamed piece for orchestra, but then [at Mac-Dowell] I did manage to do forty-five pages of scoring (which seemed pretty good to me). Moreover, I wrote a set of four variations and a waltz and trio to go in the piano suite [*Music for Piano*, Fine's major keyboard work]. This latter is now finished." He also mentioned starting a choral piece, apparently never completed, for G. Wallace Woodworth.

Verna was then in the late stages of pregnancy. During her stay in Peterborough, her vitality had not lessened. She had been "reading mystery stories; balancing the check-account; typing and editing the Book of Knowledge article; and sunning herself outside the studio. Her belly is, as you might expect, very large and firm and slightly bruised by the gymnastics going on inside. It received the major part of the sun-tan. For some peculiar reason or other, she is now possessed of such vigor and energy that she can become quite exhausting to a person like myself who, as you know, [has] a very small battery."

The first of the Fines' three daughters, Claudia Carol, was born on December 12, 1947. For some time, they had wanted a child, but Verna had serious infertility problems. In later years, she liked to tell the story of Claudia's conception, which had occurred in New York in early 1947. As Claudia herself related it, "My mother had been in fertility workups and was constantly checking to see if her basal body temperature had risen. They were staying with Louise Talma, sleeping on a pullout couch in the dining room. One morning my mother realized she was ovulating, and she yelled: 'Yahving, this is the right day! We have to do it!' My father said, 'But there are people around,' and my mother replied, 'It's okay. Let's do it!' So they closed the sliding doors to the dining room after putting Lukas Foss on guard outside."

In October 1947, Fine informed Copland that he had finished the first draft of the *Toccata Concertante* "and am now trying to clean up the mess." He subsequently played the work for Koussevitzky, who liked it and promptly scheduled the premiere for the following season of the Boston Symphony. October 18, 1948 was the date of the first rehearsal. The day before, Fine wrote Copland that Koussevitzky "is beginning to complain strenuously about the difficulties of the score and, above all, about the minuscule note heads Karl Kohn [the copyist] has made. If he should ask me to conduct the piece, I'm sure I'd pass out on the spot."

On Friday, October 22, Fine's ebulliently rhythmic *Toccata Concertante*, dedicated "To my Wife," had its first performance, at Symphony Hall by Koussevitzky and the Boston Symphony, on a program entirely devoted to twentieth-century music.[3] The work was well received by the Friday audience and, according to *Musical America* magazine, its composer was "roundly applauded." On Saturday evening, there was a repeat performance. Fine himself conducted the Boston Symphony in a performance at Harvard, in Sanders Theater, on December 14. Then, on January 2, 1949, at a Sunday afternoon concert at Symphony Hall, Koussevitzky played it again. "In his early life," said Verna, "Irving always wrote choral or chamber music, and he always said, 'I can't orchestrate. I don't think I can do a big piece.' But when he heard the *Toccata Concertante* he was very pleased that he'd done it right." Koussevitzky later described the brilliantly executed and vibrantly scored ten-minute work as "a contemporary minor masterpiece." The instrumentation is for piccolo, two flutes, two oboes, English horn, two clarinets, bass clarinet,

3. The other pieces were Vaughan Williams' *Sixth Symphony*, Ravel's *Piano Concerto in G* (Jesús Maria Sanroma, soloist) and Richard Strauss's *Till Eulenspiegel*.

two bassoons, contrabassoon, four horns, two trumpets in C, three trombones, tuba, timpani, percussion (snare drum, suspended and crash cymbals, bass drum), piano and strings.

For the premiere, Fine provided a concise program note that is worth quoting in full.

"The word *toccata* is commonly used to describe improvisatory display pieces for keyboard instruments. It has also been used in connection with concerted music of a fanfare-like character. It is in this latter sense that I have used the term. In writing this piece, I was aware of a certain affinity with the energetic music of the Baroque concertos. Hence the qualifying adjective, *concertante*. Moreover, this adjective seemed particularly appropriate because of the soloistic nature of much of the orchestration, especially in the second theme-group and the closing sections of the exposition and recapitulation.

"The piece is roughly in sonata form. There is a short fanfare-like introduction [*Allegro energico*] containing two motives that generate most of the subsequent thematic material. The following exposition contains a first section that makes prominent use of an *ostinato* and is rather indeterminate in tonality. A transitional theme, announced by the trumpet and continued by the flute and the bassoon, is abruptly terminated and followed by a second theme-group more lyrical in character. In this section the thematic material is chiefly entrusted to solo wind instruments supported by string accompaniment. The whole of the exposition is concluded by additional woodwind dialogue and scattered references to some of the preceding material.

"There are several episodes in the development, one of the most prominent being a *fugato* announced by the clarinets and based on the opening *ostinato*. There is no break between the development and recapitulation, the return of the first material commencing at the climax of the development. The second and closing sections of the exposition are recapitulated in the main tonality without significant changes except for a few in instrumentation and texture. The whole piece is rounded off by an extended coda."

In Fine's description of his *Toccata Concertante* there is no mention of a fairly prominent feature: the octatonic scale. Certainly its use here is Stravinskian and also eminently Russian, as it was a favorite of Stravinsky's teacher Rimsky-Korsakov. Other direct Stravinsky influences are heard in the *scherzando* music and in the numerous virtuosic woodwind passages. There are, however, parts of this work that are not at all Stravinsky-inflected, most notably the thematically complex, heavily scored, joyously bombastic music about half way through (at rehearsal numbers 25 and 27), which has nothing to do with Stravinsky's pellucid neoclassicism but is more akin to similar moments in symphonies by Prokofiev and Miaskovsky. Some of the melodic writing seems personal, especially the lyric theme one bar after rehearsal number 9 in the solo oboe.

Three days after the October 22 premiere of the *Toccata Concertante*, Verna wrote to Copland: "At last peace and calm. Am glad Irving does not have a big performance every weekend. I couldn't stand the strain." She reported that the two initial performances went well, but that the piece "went better in the Thursday rehearsal. The time changes make Koussie nervous in concert only. It seems he doesn't mind such things at all in rehearsal." She continued on a slightly disloyal note: "The reviews were good, even one out and out rave! (That good *I* don't think it is.)" On December 11, Fine himself wrote to Copland, sounding puzzled. 'What's happening to the critics anyway? They were almost ecstatic over Sonny's [Shapero] old fiddle sonata when it was done in New York recently; and they even had nice though slightly condescending things to say about my orchestral piece when it was done in Boston."

On the day after the premiere, four newspaper reviews appeared. In the "rave" mentioned by Verna, Cyrus Durgin noted in the *Boston Daily Globe* that "all over the lobby at intermission, they were punning on Fine's name and his piece. The Fine music is fine music, indeed; no piddling little curtain-raiser, but a well-proportioned toccata in a concertante style, fully but deftly orchestrated, logically constructed and sparkling." Durgin seems to have been ignorant of Stravinsky's neoclassic style: "Knowing Fine's great admiration for Stravinsky, I had half-expected the Toccata to be deeply influenced by that composer. But the work actually is distinctive and original, with only a few Stravinskyan touches." He continued, more accurately: "The ideas are salient, the texture alive but by no means a mass of dissonance. You might call the style impersonal, in its bustling way, yet at the same time it is music of both color and feeling. This Toccata looks like a worthy addition to the repertory." The *Boston Post* thought it the work "of a young composer who has not yet found himself [although] Mr. Fine here displays technical skill and agreeable powers of invention." The *Boston Herald* pronounced the *Toccata Concertante* "a brief but highly competent orchestral essay [that] displayed a fine economy of style, a sure orchestral sense and an attractive though slightly dry melodic invention." Clearly befuddled, the critic of the *Christian Science Monitor* professed to hear the influence of Walter Piston, "to whose compositions this work bears a strong family resemblance," citing "hints of a gift for melody, a strange quality indeed in a young modernist."

Koussevitzky brought the *Toccata Concertante* to New York on January 15, 1949, as part of the second concert of his second "American Music Festival" at Carnegie Hall. The ambitious program also included David Diamond's *Rounds for String Orchestra*, Howard Hanson's *Piano Concerto* (Rudolf Firkusny, soloist), Roy Harris' *Symphony No. 3*, Edward Burlingame Hill's *Music for English Horn and Orchestra* and Copland's *Lincoln Portrait*. Verna remembered that "Koussevitzky was very excited about the *Toccata*, so he took it to New York as part of his big concert series of contemporary American music. He lost his place in the beginning. It was a little touch and go." A reference recording of that performance does not bear out Verna's memory; if Koussevitzky did indeed lose his place, his orchestra seemed not to have been unduly troubled. It was in fact a dynamic and for the most part accurate presentation of this beautifully crafted but rhythmically and contrapuntally intricate score.

The reviews, however, were disappointing. Virgil Thomson wrote in the *New York Herald Tribune* that "Irving Fine's *Toccata Concertante*, though largely derivative, has a grace about it that lifts it above that sectarian devotion to Stravinsky's later works that marks the Boston school of today." Oddly enough, he found its form "casual," although he liked "a certain prettiness of material." Rather bizarrely, he accused Fine's piece of "having introduced for the first time in American composition the direct influence of [the contemporary

French composer] Henri Sauguet." The critic of the *New York Journal American* cited an "academic style," noting that the *Toccata* "created no stir musically. The audience applauded politely." In the *New York Times*, Olin Downes was somewhat more positive, terming it "a good job by a gifted pupil of Piston, Hill and Merritt [and] Nadia Boulanger" and "a good piece of student's work," citing the music as "lively and considerably more sophisticated" than Hanson's concerto. The *New York Telegram*'s correspondent thought Fine's piece "briskly worked out [and] featuring a clever alignment of orchestral choirs."

A half century later, and with the advantage of hindsight, the *Toccata Concertante*'s worth, along with its derivations, had become more apparent. David Diamond pronounced it "a brilliant piece, a kind of take-off from Stravinsky. Irving had a thing about Stravinsky; we all did. He was particularly taken with *Persephone* and *Oedipus Rex*, and he talked a lot about *Apollo*, which he loved." Lukas Foss said, "The *Toccata Concertante* is wonderful. Most of his music is Stravinskian. His early work was certainly neoclassic." Harold Shapero acknowledged that "the *Toccata* does have Stravinsky," but stressed that "it also has a lot of tunes that don't belong to Stravinsky." Arthur Berger stated that "it's a good piece, but it's too close to Stravinsky. That's interesting, because the general feel of Irving's music is not Stravinskian: it has a romantic flow and doesn't have the bite and sharp edges of Stravinsky—the way he cuts up his music to make you uncomfortable. But thematically, here and there, it's surprising how close the *Toccata* is."

Leon Kirchner felt that Fine was "the most rounded and fluent of the Boston Stravinskians. Some of his works, like the *Toccata Concertante*, mime Stravinsky to a great extent, but they were done with a real authority, as if he were a giant student." Jack Gottlieb, who studied composition with Fine at Brandeis University, called the work "an Americanized kind of Stravinsky. That's in the rhythms, mostly." Joel Spiegelman, who conducted a 1993 recording of the *Toccata*, stated: "It's a tremendous piece. And without question there are places in it that are close to Stravinsky: the melodic fragmentation and some of the harmonies." Ned Rorem praised the *Toccata Concertante* as "terribly skillful, diatonic music of its time. The thing is, what of Irving Fine is coming through? Because he *isn't* Stravinsky. I admire his ability to put fast music together in that piece. It doesn't slow down and reflect upon itself; it's fast for about ten minutes at the very same tempo. I can't do that."

A photograph was published in the July 28, 1949 issue of the *Harvard Crimson* with the caption: "Serge Koussevitzky stops a rehearsal to give conductor Irving Fine '37 of the Harvard faculty a few pointers. Fine is leading an all student orchestra." The occasion was undoubtedly a rehearsal at Tanglewood of the *Toccata Concertante*. Fine conducted it on August 13 at an afternoon concert in the Shed, and it seems never again to have been performed during his lifetime.

The *Toccata Concertante* is one of only two works originally conceived for full orchestra that Fine completed, and his other endeavor of the year 1947, *Music for Piano*, is his only major score for his own instrument. It was composed during the summer at the MacDowell Colony, and by October all finishing touches were in place. Fine dedicated this four-part suite, lasting about fifteen minutes, to Nadia Boulanger, in celebration of her sixtieth birthday. As might be expected from a pianist of his caliber, the keyboard writing, often two-part, is extremely felicitous—crisp and brilliant though not virtuosic in the traditional sense. Here, Fine was concerned primarily with lyricism, but also with clarity of texture and form. Although aesthetically lightweight, *Music for Piano* is another of his successful and attractive neo-Stravinsky concoctions, this time with distinct echoes of open-air Copland. No strongly defined personal voice emerges. ("The presence of self in music is a flaw," Fine once wrote), but the suite charms, amuses and impresses with its spontaneity and sheer musicality: a lively, elegant, modest and thoroughly lucid score on Classical lines, tonal and only mildly dissonant. Stravinsky himself wrote Fine in early 1948: "I was very much pleased to play over your graceful piano album, so elegant in its writing."

With its catchy march tune, the brief *Prelude* (*Allegro moderato*) is cheerfully melodic and cleverly syncopated, cast in A-B-A form. The opening harmony of the ensuing tripartite *Waltz-Gavotte* (*Grazioso*) is slightly jarring, as if clearing the air, but then the tunefulness returns, along with a recurring *staccato* passage strikingly imbued with a whiff of sardonic Prokofiev. A harmonically deceptive cadence prefaces the *gavotte* middle section (*Vivace*), which is contrastingly rhythmic. The waltz-music ends the movement gracefully. The following movement, titled *Variations*, consists of a decidedly Coplandesque theme (*Andante*), marked *dolce* and *expressivo*, and three short variations, the first two filled out by expeditious sectional repetitions. Variation one (*Allegro*) is fleet and sportive; variation two (*Andante*) is reflectively lyric; variation three (*Lento assai*) is initially quite à la Copland but then becomes more personal and dramatic in rhetoric. The *Interlude-Finale* follows without pause, wherein more harmonic slight-of-hand leads to high-spirited, syncopated, "fingery" music with passing references to previous materials.

In a December 11, 1948 letter to Copland, Fine noted: "My piano pieces have had their fifth first performance. (Luise Vosgerchian is doing them in New York on December 19th.) Leo [Smit] does the best job of them, although he schmaltzed up the Waltz and first variation when he played them at the Harvard Musical Association last month." That occasion, on November 19 in Boston, had been, he decided, the official premiere of *Music for Piano*, although Smit had previously given a try-out performance at Harvard. Earlier that year, the *Boston Herald* announced that Karl Kohn would play the work "for the first time in public" at Kirkland House, Harvard, on February 15. Then Vosgerchian played it in Boston on December 10 at Jordan Hall, where the program listed it as the premiere (this last would seem to have been the fourth first performance; perhaps Fine miscounted). One Boston critic was pleased by "some pretty melodies," thought the casual listener "might wonder what of the second movement was waltz and what was gavotte" and was intrigued by the variations, which "showed proof of a fertile imagination." When Vosgerchian introduced *Music for Piano* to New York later that month, the reviews were tepid. The *Herald Tribune* acknowledged that "some of its themes had a certain engaging Old-World atmosphere," while the *New York Times* cited it as "clean and unpretentious [while making] effective use of light sonorities." When the score was published in 1949 by G. Schirmer, one reviewer termed it "the sort of thing on which one can shower non-committal praise," registering the opinion that it "has no more weight than a grain of salt."

Pianists, however, liked *Music for Piano*, and several added it to their repertories early on, including Seymour Lipkin and Noël Lee.[4] Fine himself occasionally played it, for instance in March 1952 at Boston's Museum of Fine Arts, when he and Harold Shapero also performed the latter's early four-hand piano sonata. In 1954, Fine recorded two excerpts—the third and second movements, in that order—an exemplary performance exhibiting the "maximum of clarity" that he had requested in a note in the score.

A particularly astute contemporary critic, Klaus George Roy, praised *Music for Piano* in 1954 as "one of the most idiomatic and ingratiating American keyboard works of our period," concluding: "It is an utterly delightful set of neoclassic pieces." More recently, Arthur Berger said: "The variations are wonderful, such inspired music. For me, that is the great Irving. That belongs to the great music of all time." Richard Wernick noted that "*Music for Piano* is a Fine-cum-Stravinsky piece, but it's also similar to a lot of the things Harold Shapero was doing at the time," and Shapero himself remembered: "When Irving was younger, I had a problem with him, a strange problem. Too many of my qualities were appearing in his music. I don't claim to have much originality, but the little I have was being incorporated. Not the literal notes, but a certain kind of lyric melody I was doing then. I'm sure it was unconscious, but my three little piano sonatas are sort of incorporated in his *Music for Piano*. And there's a variation there that is completely generated from the variations of my big sonata in F minor, which is a failure but has a very beautiful theme in the second movement (his theme is also very pretty). That derivation stopped completely when he went twelve-tone." Shapero added: "Irving was more practical than I was and his pieces were much more performable, much more neatly written for piano."

Composed in 1944, Shapero's three short sonatas were based on Classical models and principles. Fine's interest in them may have been provoked by a 1946 letter from Copland:

---

4. In April 1962, a few months before his death, Fine received a postcard informing him that *Music for Piano* had been played in Rome, on the harpsichord.

"I've been looking closely at those amateur sonatas. The boy has everything. He seems to be sitting tight atop his own musical powers. If they ever get loose—the whole world will stop and listen." In 1950 Copland told Fine that he had walked into the Schirmer music store in New York and noticed, appropriately enough, the published score of "your piano pieces on display, big as life, right next to Sonny's sonatas."

The year before, referring to a recent Shapero score, the *Variations in C Minor* for piano, dedicated to Copland, the latter wrote to Fine complaining of Shapero's "Beethoven psychosis," saying that Shapero had promised him that those variations marked its end. In a 1964 book admired by Copland, *Music in a New Found Land*, by the British music historian Wilfrid Mellers, Mellers termed Shapero "the most talented of the group [that stemmed] from Stravinsky and Copland," but noted that Shapero "could not or would not tear himself from the past." His model for the 1944 sonatas had been Haydn, wrote Mellers; and the subsequent *Symphony for Classical Orchestra* and piano variations "are impressive pieces, remarkable for their very attempt to use Beethoven as (in Stravinsky's sense) a mask. One may still think, however, that the attempt was misguided."

In a 1952 record review of Shapero's *Piano Sonata No. 1*, Fine's strong enthusiasm for this music was no longer apparent, perhaps because by then he himself had moved on to serialism in an effort to escape the limitations of neoclassicism. His appraisal was accurate if cool, noting with regret "the academicism latent in Shapero's music." He described the sonata as "a sparkling little work comprising four short movements." Further: "The formal continuity is essentially Classical, more specifically Haydnesque. The harmonic material also derives from the Classical period, but with modernizations. The texture is homophonic and extremely sparse. The writing is notable at all times for its finesse—its air of fresh contemporaneity. Apart from an occasional dryness, the instrumental treatment is felicitous and idiomatic without ever falling into stereotyped figuration." In summation: "The charm and accessibility of Shapero's Sonata are deceptive. In spite of its modest proportions, it is not without pretensions, for it is the work of a highly sophisticated composer possessing a subtle mind, a strong personality, and working under self-imposed restraints."

Fine's own *Music for Piano*, seemingly indebted to Shapero's little sonatas, was orchestrated in 1972 by Joel Spiegelman, who had been a friend and colleague of the composer at Brandeis. This was done at the request of Verna Fine. Although the symphonic version (published in 1999 with the title *Music for Orchestra*) is expertly and coloristically scored, Spiegelman clearly aimed more at neo-romantic elegance than neo-classic dryness. In the fast sections, especially, more of the percussive ambiance of piano sound would have been welcome. Spiegelman observed that the original version "is very pianistic, and to orchestrate it was challenging. On one hand, I tried to be true to it, but I was also looking for creative solutions. I felt that my principal aspiration was to re-imagine in orchestral terms the colors that a pianist might bring to the work." Upon hearing this orchestration, Ned Rorem remarked that the third variation especially was "personal and touching, very beautiful." Fine, he said, "had an innate sense of tune."

# Chapter 10

■ DURING THE LATE 1940S and into the following decade, the Harvard music department remained—despite the innovative Basic Piano program—primarily the domain of musicologists and theorists, a place where music's *raison d'être* seemed to be as an object of study. In that environment, Fine, with his activities as a pianist, conductor, organizer of student concerts and summer defector to Tanglewood, may well have been regarded as a troublemaker by the old guard of the faculty—a square peg, so to speak. And it didn't help that Fine's relationship with the department's chairman, A. Tillman Merritt, had deteriorated. Leon Kirchner remembered that "Irving disliked his character. They were opposed. Merritt was an intensely jealous man, a man who could not contain himself." Esther Shapero recalled that "Irving didn't really like him at all, and resented him terribly."

Along with other colleges and universities, Harvard had a system called "tenure track," which in its case meant that after five years as an assistant professor one either must be promoted or leave. So it was that early in 1948, his fourth year as assistant professor, Fine started to worry about his future. On March 3 he wrote to Copland: "I have begun to think about another job. Apparently there is little chance of my receiving a promotion here since the department has to choose between Dick French [a musicologist and a favorite of Merritt] and myself. You can make your own conclusions about the result of such a choice. Doc [Archibald T.] Davison has already advised me to start looking, although his own feeling is that I deserve the promotion."

There was also the Jewish issue. "The music department was notoriously anti-Semitic," stated Verna. "Aaron Copland used to joke, in the 1940s and 50s, 'Gee, Harvard has to scrape to get teachers, so how could they avoid appointing, in the music world, someone of Jewish origin?" Kirchner finally got tenure in 1960. He was possibly the first Jew so honored

97

by the department since its founding. "As Aaron put it: 'That took some doing'," said Verna. Kirchner himself reflected: "I think I 'passed.' Frankly, I don't think that Randall Thompson knew that I was Jewish. I've heard that the Harvard music department had a reputation for being anti-Semitic. But the most unfortunate thing for the anti-Semites there, if there were any, is that the most gifted people were usually Jewish." He noted "a rather negative quality" to Fine's relationship to a department that had oriented itself "more and more toward musicology."

Daniel Pinkham called attention to "the latent anti-Semitic feeling" at Harvard. "There was a certain apprehension about what the Jews might do. It was the *Zeitgeist*, the spirit of the times." Such fears were no doubt enhanced by the founding of the State of Israel in May 1948. Besides, the music department was run along the lines of a Boston gentlemen's club, and who had ever heard of a Jewish gentleman?

Also to be considered was the well-known "Jewish Quota" (which disappeared a few years after the war) for students, a discriminatory policy practiced not only at Harvard but also at Yale, Princeton and Dartmouth. "They were very small quotas," said Martin Bookspan, "and at that time Harvard's attitude toward Jews was not terribly enlightened. There were very few Jewish professors at the University. I had a feeling of anti-Semitism with Tillman Merritt." Harold Shapero detested Merritt. "You couldn't trust him. He was a monster who did monstrous things: the resident department s.o.b. You couldn't like him. I'm sure Tillman was unconsciously anti-Semitic. Harvard, the whole university, was full of that. When I was an undergraduate, I could feel it." Shapero's hatred of Merritt, however, may have been provoked by rejection. "When I was graduating in 1941 and Irving was an instructor, he suggested to Merritt that they hire me as a teaching fellow in theory. I was flattered when Merritt said, we don't want any 'geniuses', we want someone who fits in with the department."[1]

---

1. It should be noted that Shapero was, from his student days, what is known as a "character," renowned for idiosyncratic and egocentric behavior. Daniel Pinkham remembered hearing a story of a Shapero/Walter Piston confrontation. "One day when Sonny was

In Merritt's defense, Noël Lee termed him "an enterprising, visionary man of great charm and organizational talents. What he did at Harvard during the war was fantastic. One of his first projects was an attempt to convince Béla Bartók, living precariously at the time in New York, to become associated with the Harvard Music Department in any capacity he wished but without any specific duties." Bartók had come to Harvard in 1940 for a lecture-recital and, urged by Merritt, he agreed to return in February 1943 to give conferences on Central European folk music along with seminars with graduate students of the music department. Ill with leukemia, he managed to give only three conferences before being hospitalized in New York. According to Lee, Merritt "continued communicating with Bartók" and once "personally paid a hospital operation fee."

One of Merritt's most important projects was a 1947 Harvard symposium for which several prominent American and European composers were commissioned. Copland wrote his choral work *In the Beginning*, Hindemith his *Apparebit Repentina Dies* for chorus and brass instruments, Schoenberg his *String Trio*, Piston his *String Quartet No. 3*; the other composers were Martinu and Malipiero.

Off campus, anti-Semitism came openly into Fine's life during 1948, but it had nothing to do with tenure at Harvard. A couple of years before, two senior faculty members, Woodworth and the composer Edward Ballantine, had proposed Fine for membership in the Harvard Musical Association, an exclusive, all-male Boston club on Beacon Hill. Since then nothing had been heard. Verna said that "both of us had a feeling about it—you have a sixth sense when you're Jewish. One day Irving came home after lunch with Ballantine and said that Ballantine and Woody had had a letter from the club

_____

in Piston's composition class, Piston looked through one of his scores. He said, 'Ah yes, Mr. Shapero, I see the problem here. Now, Bach would have taken care of it by doing thus and so.' A few pages later, Piston said, 'Ah, a different problem. Bach would have solved it in such and such a way.' At that point Sonny had had quite enough, and he exclaimed: 'I *hate* Bach!' Very quietly, Piston got up from the piano, went over to the window and looked out over Harvard Yard. Finally, he said: 'You know, I'm so glad that Mr. Bach wasn't here today. He'd feel awful'."

saying they're sorry but they cannot accept the nomination because somebody on the admissions committee had black-balled Irving because he was Jewish. Ballantine was incensed. Irving said Ballantine hadn't realized that such a thing as anti-Semitism existed, he was such a sheltered gentleman. So Ballantine looked up the charter and it said that the Harvard Musical Association was formed to help the Harvard music department—and here they are turning down a person on the staff. It was a terrible scandal in academia, and the whole music-department faculty resigned in protest, except for Tillman Merritt. [Merritt said he couldn't resign, for that would damage his fundraising capability with the club's wealthy Brahmins.] The next thing we heard was that the entire admissions committee of the Association had resigned to avoid a public scandal, because it was going to be a *cause célèbre* and would have been wonderful front-page news. So, in 1948 Irving was finally elected to membership. Then he had to decide what to do: should he turn it down? I said, you've got to save face. Join and never attend. He didn't want to go there anyway, with a bunch of anti-Semites. He did join, and the case was closed." There was an ironic footnote to this affair. Fine resigned in 1951, explaining that he was going to spend a year abroad where the club had no facilities. The following year, Leo Smit gave a concert at the Association and programmed Fine's *Music for Piano*. "Irving went as a guest," said Verna, "and he said it was funny because someone got up and made a speech proudly noting that the composer was a former member."

Fine fretted about his academic situation during all of 1948, with good reason as it turned out. On December 11, he wrote to Copland: "The AXE has fallen at Harvard." The Dean of the Faculty of Arts and Sciences had asked the music department to make a recommendation about Fine's future status because his five-year appointment as assistant professor would be finished the following spring. "The senior members were instructed to bear in mind the fact that Dick French and I were in competition with each other for promotion and that only one of us could be promoted. As you know, I had anticipated all of this for some time, so the result was not unexpected." Piston informed Fine that the department had decided to vote unanimously not to recommend his promotion, even though there might have been some disagreement over that decision. "This was done, Walter said, to avoid hard feelings. I don't understand what he meant by that; for to me the unanimous vote was the worst kind of slap in the face. I should have been comforted to know that not everybody thought that Dick was a better man than I. In any event, Tillman and Walter shed copious tears about the difficult decision they had been forced into making!! And they practically *sobbed* that it had been made especially difficult because I had been such an asset to the Department. The only thing that cheered them was the fact that they knew I would get a good job. After all, I had such good contacts!"

Richard French recalled that "it was generally known that Irving didn't get along with Merritt. Merritt had strong likes, but I don't know about his dislikes. We were good friends, and I never had any trouble with him myself. He and I did a lot of things together, including putting on a symposium of music criticism. But I can understand people not liking him." Interestingly, the promotion French received did not include tenure, and he left Harvard a year after Fine to join a music publisher in New York.

Many of Fine's friends and colleagues attributed his being denied tenure to anti-Semitism, and according to Verna he himself believed it was a contributing factor. Caldwell Titcomb remembered that Randall Thompson, who had a good deal of influence in the music department, "was known to be anti-Semitic. I'm sure he would not have wanted to give Irving tenure. But Piston was a big supporter of Irving." Verna said that "Thompson was hostile to Irving, but I don't know if it was because of Irving's music or Thompson's anti-Semitism. I don't think Piston was like that—although maybe he protested too much, because he always used to announce that he had a Jewish grandmother when nobody had asked him. I think Walter just didn't want to get involved in the politics of the music department, all the in-fighting. He was a reserved man who didn't go out on a limb for anybody." But Harold Shapero recalled that Piston "was capable of strange remarks. One day when I was having a composition lesson with him, he hurt my feelings. He forgot I was Jewish and said: 'There are so many Jews in New York'." As for Thompson, Shapero classified him as "a real Christian-type WASP, so his anti-

Semitism would have been pure and unadulterated." Verna noted that after Fine died, Leon Kirchner had looked into the early records of meetings in the department and private notes from the period when Fine was being considered for tenure. "They didn't want to give Irving tenure because he was too power-hungry," she said. "It was such nonsense." Arthur Berger agreed. "I don't think Irving knew how to do anything for himself. He wasn't vain enough to push himself." Lukas Foss thought Fine "not overly ambitious, certainly not like Harold Shapero. I once asked Harold how he was going to get over his Beethoven complex. He said, 'I've found the answer: greater than Beethoven.' It would be inconceivable for Irving to say that kind of thing." Verna felt that Fine's popularity with the students "was held against him by the upper crust at Harvard. The tenured professors there, including Randall Thompson, resented him."

They may also have resented her. Fine's friend, the composer Milton Babbitt, remembered that the scuttlebutt at Harvard was that "many members of the music faculty didn't like Verna. She was *very* 'Jewish': aggressive and strident, and she could be vulgar. At faculty get-togethers, she was noisy, brash and sharp-tongued, and people suspected that she had caused problems as far as Irving getting tenure." Babbitt also noted: "Never forget the Jewish aspect of Irving. He thought of himself as a Jew." As for Randall Thompson: "He was an official anti-Semite—that I can vouch for—and a curmudgeon. Randall's anti-Semitism took a form so that he could easily have been a member of the Hitler Union."

On the tenure issue, Kirchner observed: "I think there was a tiny bit of anti-Semitism involved, but it's too simplistic to say it was the cause. I was told that Irving was an empire-builder—that was Randall Thompson's idea. He had left Harvard under a cloud because he had done incredible things: he was one of the first to organize concerts of wonderful contemporary music, very well presented apparently. He also put together concerts of music by student composers. Luise Vosgerchian always said it was a golden time at Harvard when Irving was there. But the music department wasn't interested in concerts, and he was thought to be an operator. If you don't get tenure at Harvard, you're finished."[2]

Kirchner's analysis is probably closer to reality than the

idea that behind-the-scenes anti-Semitism, rather than a factor, was the root cause. If that had been so, it would seem exceedingly odd that during the same year the entire faculty of the music department should resign from the Harvard Musical Association in support of Fine when he was blackballed. Harvard in the late 1940s was simply no place for a performer-oriented composer. Richard Wernick remembered that "Irving felt Harvard was getting a little stultified, turning into an old-fashioned place." The empire-builder theory, however absurd, rings true. As Richard French put it, "That could have been the impression he gave. They were very rigid at Harvard. Ironically, I think he was better able to prosper at Brandeis University than he would have at Harvard. He found a community there that was more congenial intellectually." To misquote a famous line from Charles Dickens, Fine would go to "a far, far better place."

Whatever the reason for the rejection, Fine was bitter over it the rest of his life. Noël Lee said, "I gathered that the big trauma of his career was being denied tenure at Harvard." Wernick recalled him "talking about it gently, and using the expression anti-Semitism. But he was on friendly terms with Piston, and he never condemned Randall Thompson or anyone else." A friend of later years, Arnold Modell, recollected Fine's mentioning "that he thought he had been denied tenure because he was Jewish. That was taken for granted back then. I think he felt humiliated by that rejection." Harold Shapero said that the rejection "left a lifelong scar. It was the abstract idea that if I don't make it at Harvard then I'm not first-rate. It's a neurotic view, because that's not what happened." He added: "But Irving was not as mild-mannered as everybody thought. If you knew him well, you knew that the ambition was considerable."

Along with the premiere of the *Toccata Concertante* by the Boston Symphony, Fine's musical accomplishments of 1948

---

2. Even after the passage of half a century, the author's attempts to examine the notes of the Harvard University Music Department's 1948 tenure committee were blocked by the Draconian privacy policies of both the Music Department and the University Archives.

were two: presenting the Boston premiere of Stravinsky's opera-ballet *Les Noces*; and composing his *Partita for Wind Quintet*.

Written in 1917 and first heard in 1923 in Paris, the Russian-folkloristic *Les Noces* (or *The Wedding*) had not been performed in the United States since 1934. In 1947 Fine proposed to Stravinsky the idea of producing it in Boston, and the composer replied: "Who will conduct it? Try to get my records made by myself in London in 1934 (in English), this for the right information concerning tempo, dynamics, etc." Fine decided to conduct the work himself.

The scoring of *Les Noces* is for mixed chorus (sixty voices at Fine's performance, with soloists brought in), four pianos and a percussion battery. In a February interview with the *Harvard Crimson*, Fine termed the music "sensational" and noted that the prominent percussion parts result in a "clamorous, gong-like music." He continued: "There is nothing like it. Some people think it is the most important work Stravinsky ever wrote." The performance was on May 3, 1948, at Paine Hall, Harvard, by the forces of the Music Club, an organization sponsored by Boston's Institute of Modern Music.

Meanwhile, in March Harold Shapero's ambitious and controversial, militantly neoclassical *Symphony for Classical Orchestra* had been premiered by the Boston Symphony under Leonard Bernstein. On the sixteenth, Fine wrote to Copland that "Sonny's Symphony had considerable public success but very mixed critical reaction. Only Williams of the Herald was favorable and Durgin panned him (Sonny I mean) as the Mahler of Newton Center. Everybody seemed to agree that the symphony was long." Fine then himself became critical.[3] "I felt that the last movement had the greatest miscalculations

---

3. Whether or not there was any correlation, it should be remembered that this was a time of some tension between the two friends, provoked by what Shapero considered Fine's borrowings from his works. On a postcard that year, Shapero used his pet nickname for Fine, "Iggy," inspired by Fine's first two initials, perfectly aware that Fine disliked it. Richard Wernick recalled that, years later at Brandeis, "Irving hated Shapero every time he did it in front of students." In a 1944 letter to Copland, referring to his newly printed Irving Gifford Fine letterhead, he had declared: "I'm getting

in proportion. Strangely enough the slow movement seemed fine—in fact, was completely successful in every way. The same could be said about the scherzo. The first movement (which we both thought was the most perfect) was actually the most disappointing. Too much busy work going on and the main line often completely obscured." (In a 1966 radio interview, Bernstein would call the Shapero symphony "a perfect piece, an absolute masterpiece," but note that "its time limit is over-extended. This is a symphony for Classical orchestra in very Classical forms, and it *should* occupy a place on a program equivalent to that of a Haydn or a Mozart symphony, instead of which it is much longer than that.")

In the same letter, Fine went on to praise Piston's new *Symphony No. 3*, also introduced by the Boston Symphony. "It is the most perfectly proportioned large scale work that he has written, although again you don't remember any tunes."

That spring Fine and Copland were planning a lecture course dealing with very old and very new music for the summer session at Tanglewood, and it was there that Fine composed his *Partita for Wind Quintet* in the summer of 1948. Although the scoring is for the standard combination of flute, oboe, clarinet, horn and bassoon, he may initially have planned a work for only three instruments. In February, Stravinsky had written him: "All best to your TRIO" (the capital letters are his). In any event, it is appropriate that the new piece should have the Master's benediction, for it turned out to be, for the most part, business-as-usual: robust Stravinskian neoclassicism, masterfully done.

Similar to the violin sonata and the *Toccata Concertante*, the *Partita* was uncommissioned, so Fine had to seek a venue for its debut. On December 11, he notified Copland that the work had been accepted by the New York-based League of Composers for a music-of-the-Americas concert in February (in 1949 Fine would join both the League and the American Society of Composers, Authors and Publishers). The *Partita*

---

awfully tired of that middle name of mine. Verna is responsible for its appearing on this stationery and elsewhere." Nevertheless, he used it all his life in professional correspondence. (Bernstein and Copland sometimes called him "Oiving" or "Oiv," to which he did not seem to object.)

had its world premiere on February 19, 1949, in Times Hall, New York, played by the New Art Quintet. Fine was on hand to acknowledge what one observer described as an enthusiastic reception by the audience. Two days later, his friend Arthur Berger's review appeared in the *New York Herald Tribune*. "Irving Fine provided the all-around success of the evening, a Partita for wind quintet that would easily be an asset to a much more distinguished program. [Other composers represented were Claudio Spies, Roque Cordero, Ellis Kohs and Paul Des Marais.] It has affable melodic threads, expertly fashioned along thoroughly unpedantic contrapuntal lines, and it is alternately lively and personally tender."[4] The critic of the *Musical Leader* magazine also used the word "affable," noting skillful instrumental writing in the *Partita* that "gave one the desire to hear it again."

Fine's *Partita* is a substantial work of about fifteen minutes duration. There are five movements: Introduction and Theme (*Allegro moderato*); Variation (*Poco vivace*); Interlude (*Adagio*); Gigue (*Allegro*) and Coda (*Lento assai*). The composer provided a brief program note for the first performance.

"Described in the most general terms, the *Partita* is a set of free variations, although only the second movement bears any marked resemblance to the formal and tonal scheme of the 'theme.' Actually, the technique employed throughout is closer to what is usually called thematic metamorphosis. The material for the entire work is evolved out of two melodic fragments.

"The titles of the various movements or sections should indicate their character. Hence, the first has the character of a

---

4. Berger was a professional critic who occasionally reviewed Fine's music, but the only time Fine seems to have written about Berger's was in 1950, in a review in the *Music Quarterly* of a record of American piano music. Berger's *Partita*, he said, "originates from the same esthetic impulse as does the work by Harold Shapero [*Piano Sonata No. 1*], but reveals certain striking differences in style and personality. While Berger may seem to have less flair and a more limited range of expression, his is the more delicate sensibility." Fine further noted that the music was "completely without pretension" and that its qualities were those of "awkward charm and genuine innocence."

Classical theme to be varied in the Classical manner. The second movement is clearly a variation of its predecessor. The short meditative *Interlude* presents the basic material in its simplest form, but accompanied by warmer harmonies. The *Gigue* occupies the central portion in the entire work and is, at the same time, the most extended movement. It is in sonata form, but has an abridged recapitulation, which ends abruptly in a foreign key. The movement entitled *Coda* has the character of an epilogue and solemn processional.

"In writing this piece, I have consciously avoided the rather stylized, playful, contrapuntal idiom that is commonly associated with the woodwind medium. What I hoped to achieve was something perhaps more reflective; certainly more intimate in expression."

In 1956, Fine would mention "the grand line and atmosphere" of the *Partita*, an enigmatic reference because, with the exception of the final movement, the music tends to be short-breathed melodically, even when it is continuous and set in imitative polyphony. There is also a certain amount of thematic fragmentation à la Stravinsky. Perhaps Fine was thinking of the *Coda* where, somewhat startlingly, a personal voice finally emerges, with no hint at all of pastiche. At that point, an essentially lighthearted and witty work surprises by turning somber. Initially, this music seems to suggest pastoral Copland, but that impression is quickly dispelled by the emphasis on repeated notes and trills within a dulcet harmonic web. After the deft and attractive preceding movements, well conceived but lacking a distinct stylistic profile, the effect of this melancholic, romantically lyrical closing section is quite extraordinary. As Harold Shapero put it, "That's not Stravinsky, that's Irving."

In June 1949, the *New York Times* announced that Fine's *Partita* had been nominated, along with works by Paul Bowles, Babbitt, Hindemith, Kirchner, Karol Rathaus and Wallingford Riegger, for a chamber-music award by the New York Music Critics Circle. As it turned out, no award was given that year in that category; instead, the *Partita* received a citation. Although still in manuscript, the piece quickly became popular, performed at the Juilliard School of Music in New York in December, at an International Society for Contemporary Music concert in Chile in September 1950, at a further League of Composers concert that November and at the Coolidge Auditorium of the Library of Congress in Washington, D.C. that December. Reviewing the November concert in the *New York Herald Tribune*, Virgil Thomson cited the *Partita* for "great suavity and sweetness." He thought it "a little stiff as to form, as if it were somehow afraid Stravinsky might be looking," but concluded that "this music has nevertheless fluency in the counterpoint, imagination in the harmony, excellent tunes and a real personal poetry."

After the *Partita* was published by Boosey and Hawkes in 1951, it became a favorite of woodwind ensembles. That same year, a recording was issued on the Classic Editions label, by the New Art Quintet, the group that had given the premiere. In a record review in the *Boston Sunday Globe*, Cyrus Durgin pronounced the *Partita* "clean and logical, solidly made and stylistically individual." Also reviewing the record, Arthur Cohn concluded that "the five movements establish a specific unit in one stylistic groove, essentially in the neoclassic manner, refined (if one may be permitted the pun) with crystal-clear workmanship and a neutral (black-white) viewpoint of instrumental colors." Following a 1952 Boston performance, Klaus George Roy wrote in the *Christian Science Monitor*: "One does not hesitate to call it one of the finest contemporary works for the woodwind medium." Today, the *Partita* has achieved repertory status and stands as the most frequently performed and recorded of Fine's compositions.

Along with looking for a new teaching job, in early 1949 Fine was busy advising Koussevitzky and composing a small *hommage* to mark the conductor's impending retirement from the Boston Symphony after twenty-five years at the helm.[5] On March 15, after a request from Koussevitzky, he wrote candidly to him about his friend Leonard Bernstein's new symphony, *The Age of Anxiety* for piano and orchestra, a work dedicated to Koussevitzky. The letter is worth quoting in

---

5. At the end of his last tour with the Orchestra, at Carnegie Hall on April 16, 1949, Koussevitzky addressed the audience thus: "I know that all of you have not liked the new music I have played. But it was necessary to play it, for the good of the art and of the young new artists, the composers."

detail, not only for its acute observations but because in it Fine accuses Bernstein of one of his own problems as a composer, eclecticism. "The overall impression I have received from the first four movements is that it is music of great effectiveness and of remarkable feeling for dramatic pacing. It is also the work of an extraordinarily gifted composer who knows the orchestra inside and out, but is also haunted by unconscious reminiscences of his most recent enthusiasms—Shostakovich and Bartók." He cited the work's "undeniably eclectic flavor," noting, also, "some Stravinskian touches": one of the motives of the waltz variation, he said, "has an uncomfortable resemblance to one of the variations in Stravinsky's *Octet*." He felt that the *Dirge* movement "has great intensity" but that "the expressiveness seemed somewhat forced (acted out rather than really experienced inwardly)," although that music "gives plenty of evidence of having been composed with conviction." Fine thought the jazzy movement, entitled *Masque*, "genuine Bernstein. The jazz is by no means flippant, but is expected to convey a fantastic quality, and, it seems to me, succeeds in doing so." He added, "My own personal feeling, however, is that this movement in particular belongs more properly to the theatre than to the concert hall." He listed the work's positive qualities: "an overall dramatic effectiveness, an excellent sense of continuity, skillful contrasts, surefire orchestration, and probably considerable audience appeal"; and the negative: "the obvious eclecticism in style, a dearth of really memorable or significant melodies, and the fact that the [*Masque*], brilliant as it is, does seem more appropriate to the ballet." Despite Fine's mixed review, Koussevitzky gave the world premiere the following month, with Bernstein, his foremost conducting protégé, at the keyboard. (Copland, also, clearly had reservations about the work, writing to Fine in 1950: "The Age of Anxiety has come and gone. The piece pleased 'le public,' but I haven't been able to find any musicians around town who really went for it.")[6]

---

6. Years later, Fine described to Richard Wernick how one day as he was driving in his car he turned on the radio in the middle of a symphonic work. "He heard some Stravinsky, some Prokofiev, some Hindemith, some jazz, and he couldn't figure out what the piece was. It was driving him crazy! At the end, the

On May 2, 1949, a gala farewell dinner was planned at Symphony Hall, Boston, to honor Koussevitzky. For that occasion, Leonard Burkat asked six composers, all Tanglewood alumni—Lukas Foss, Gardner Read, Allen Sapp, Daniel Pinkham, Herbert Fromm and Fine—to write separate sections of a commemorative cantata. No fee was involved. The text was by Fine's friend, the Boston poet David McCord, one of whose poems he had previously set in *The Choral New Yorker*, and to whom he would turn in the future for a choral cycle. The title of this collaborative effort was *In Grato Jubilo*, with the subtitle, "An Occasional Cantata." Appended to the score was a Biblical quotation: "And they sung a new song" (from Revelation: V, 9).

The scoring was for a chorus of women's voices (SSA) with soprano and contralto solo, and a small orchestra consisting of single winds, one horn, three trumpets, two trombones and doublebass. Fine provided the first of the six movements, *Hymn* (*Moderato*), seventy-five bars long, lasting about five minutes (labeled "Koussie piece" in the initial sketches). Adapted from the Bible, the text throughout this unusual cantata is so ostentatious and anachronistic that one can only describe it as silly. The words to the *Hymn* are as follows:

> Symbol, symbol, symbol! Symbol in the sky:
> The light of stars, the gravid sun, the watchful eye.
> Sound, sound, sound! Sound of the trumpet: blow
> The sound as when a time of singing will it so.

Fine's music is pleasingly neoclassical: lyric and dramatic. It tends to treat the text's pomposity lightly and even playfully. A mellow, atmospheric opening in B minor in the winds is followed by an ear-catching passage in muted trumpets; the chorus enters on a syncopated figure and proceeds in stately quarter-notes. Then comes a brightly rhythmic instrumental section, beginning in Copland's Western-prairie mode but, amusingly, continuing with Baroque-like trumpet flourishes. The chorus joins in on the words "Sound of the trumpet:

---

announcer said it was Leonard Bernstein's *The Age of Anxiety*. Irving thought Lenny was one of the most unbelievably talented people he had ever met, but he also thought that his borrowings as a composer never got channeled properly."

blow," and the animated music becomes increasingly dramatic, leading to a return of the dignified choral writing of the opening. The *Hymn* ends with a striking effect: a sudden, unexpected modulation to a held F-sharp-minor seventh chord, rising from *subito piano* to *fortissimo*. The choral writing is, of course, expert; and, all in all, this unknown, never-published score is a worthy and attractive bagatelle.

Fine finished his contribution on April 7, and the collaborative cantata was premiered at the May second testimonial dinner for Koussevitzky. Lukas Foss conducted a pickup chorus and orchestra (not consisting of Boston Symphony players, who were guests at the event, but of former Tanglewood students); the vocal soloists were Phyllis Curtin (in Pinkham's movement) and Eunice Alberts (in Fromm's). The title-page of the score[7] describes the work as "A musical offering from the Boston Chapter of the Tanglewood Alumni Association." According to *Newsweek* magazine, "1000 civic leaders in Boston and New England" had gathered "for a gigantic dinner (at $8 a head)" to honor Koussevitzky. The seats on the floor of Symphony Hall were removed and replaced by tables, with Koussevitzky's table set on the stage. The general public was admitted to the balconies "at $1 each." Among other things, "Koussie" was given a huge laurel wreath inscribed "Musical architect of the future," a key to the city and a scroll with the names of "the 3000 contributors to the Serge Koussevitzky Anniversary Fund, now standing at $159,000," which was to be used to support the orchestra. Daniel Pinkham remembered Koussevitzky's reaction to *In Grato Jubilo*. "We composers greeted him afterward, presented the score to him and shook hands. He had a sort of beatific smile, like a Cheshire cat." Koussevitzky's cantata had only one further performance, at Tanglewood that summer, again in his honor.

As for Fine's fourth summer at Tanglewood, on March 5 he had written Copland with a proposition for a joint lecture series. "How about doing a retrospective survey of the wild and woolly twenties? Since you were right in the thick of

---

7. Koussevitzky's copy of *In Grato Jubilo*, signed by David McCord and all of the six composers, is in the Rare Book Collection at the Harvard University Library. The work as a whole was never published.

things at that time, you ought to be able to do some entertaining lectures on the background of the period. I think the whole thing could be quite stimulating—especially to old reactionaries like myself who need a few monkey gland injections!" A few days later, Copland replied: "I like your idea about music of the 20's. Let's do it!"

Meanwhile, aware that the 1949-1950 academic year would be his last at Harvard, Fine was putting out feelers for a teaching job: to Vassar College, Columbia University, Indiana University, Washington University in St. Louis and the newly founded Brandeis University. The latter had been "sounding him out," said Verna, since it had opened the year before. "But at that point Irving didn't know if he was going to get tenure at Harvard."

January 1949 found Fine "groping about for ideas for a new piece" and having "the usual difficulties," he wrote to Copland. "Maybe if I did a few harmony exercises or a fugue or two, I could get going. I have a few pretty themes but am resisting them for the nonce." His home life was boisterous but happy: "Verna and the baby are fine. Verna complains about fatigue but bustles about with more energy than ever before. Claudia is in the monosyllabic jabbering stage. She has been having some difficulty with her biscuspids [sic] and, as a result, has reverted to her early nocturnal yowling."

The previous month, just before the New York premiere of the *Toccata Concertante* and the same month tenure was denied, Fine had applied for a Guggenheim grant. This was at the suggestion of Koussevitzky, who had written to the Foundation: "Irving Fine is not yet widely known, though he is highly appreciated at Harvard and Boston. Being extremely conscientious and active in his Department, he does not have the time he needs to compose. [If given a grant,] I feel confident that he will produce a composition of true value and importance." That spring, Koussevitzky sent his "highest recommendation" for Fine, describing him as "a gifted composer [and] a person of unusual cultural standing, competence, seriousness and integrity."

Fine was not awarded a Guggenheim grant that year. However, he had also applied for a Fulbright grant, which he termed "as silly and futile an act as I have committed in recent years." As part of that application, he submitted an ambitious-sounding list of "plans for work": "Completion of a String Quartet, commissioned by The Koussevitzky Music Foundation (if it is not completed this winter)"; "Cantata for chorus and orchestra commissioned by Boris Goldovsky for the Worcester Festival"; "Ode for orchestra"; and "Shorter works: Sonata for piano [and] Ballade for violin and piano." The initial work on the list was Fine's first mature attempt at a string quartet. It was never finished, but forty-two pages of undated score survive, labeled "Old quartet sketches." (The Koussevitzky commission would eventually be fulfilled in 1952.) The cantata turned out not to be an original piece, but rather an orchestration of the *Three Choruses from "Alice in Wonderland"* of 1942. The orchestral ode and the two shorter works fall into the Good Intentions category, for no traces of them exist.

What Fine did compose in 1949, at Tanglewood and the MacDowell Colony, was a fifteen-minute work for *a cappella* mixed chorus with vocal solos: a set of six songs to texts by the seventeenth-century English poet and dramatist Ben Jonson entitled *The Hour Glass*.[8] Fine's subtitle is "A Cycle of Songs to Poems of Ben Jonson."

Aside from the expected high degree of sophistication in the word setting and the fastidious clarity of the choral writing, the most telling aspect of *The Hour Glass* is the manner in which it conveys, without instrumental accompaniment, intense emotions. This clearly was the task Fine set himself by choosing the poems that he did, for they run a gamut of feeling. Another notable element is the carefully placed contrasts between solo voices and choral ensemble, a playful reflection of the old *concertante* method surely stemming from Fine's own neoclassic roots. Harmonically *The Hour Glass* is rather more conventional than *The Choral New Yorker*, but it nonetheless suggests a mildly severe twentieth-century madrigal style. The music is inventive and spontaneous sounding within the limitations of the *a cappella* medium.

The first song, "O know to end as to begin" (*Allegro moderato*), commences in syncopation with sprightly and sonorous music. Then there is a polyphonic section on the

---

8. According to Verna Fine, the last two songs, "Lament" and "The Hour Glass," were written earlier, for the Harvard Glee Club: "They probably date from 1948."

words of the title, with solos in all four parts, followed by forceful (*marcato*) chordal writing for the full chorus. Just before the end, which is assertive ("A minute's loss in love is sin"), comes a striking bitonal buildup (A-flat major with B-flat major) on the word "O!" (Harold Shapero described this song as "a very deep piece.")

Lyrically romantic and harmonically opulent, the second song, "Have you seen the white lily grow" (*Andante*), for full mixed chorus, is simple in expression but subtle in some of its effects. Not the least of these are its modulations, but also to be noted is the rich tonic chord with added sixth that provides an ending on the words, "Have you seen?"

The third song, "O do not wanton with those eyes" (*Allegretto*), is more rhythmic than lyric. A quiet, syncopated opening, marked *dolce, legato*, in the full chorus is immediately answered antiphonally by solo sopranos and alto. That procedure continues throughout this brief, uncomplicated setting.

The last three songs are marked to be played without pause. "Against Jealousy" (*Allegro agitato*) stands in some contrast to what has come before, being spare and fairly dissonant. It begins on the words, "Wretched and foolish jealousy," accented and angry-sounding, with a jagged triplet underlining "foolish." At "I ne'er was of thy kind," Fine makes effective use of a reduced chorus for several bars, then sets it against the full group in *concertante* style. At "Seek o seek doubting men," he presents violently contrasting dynamics: *forte-piano*s promptly succeeded by *pianissimo*s. A solo soprano subsequently sings "Go get thee quickly forth" against sustained choral chords, and this is followed by chordal ranting in the full forces denouncing jealousy as "a disease." The song then comes to an unexpectedly quiet ending in the solo alto on the word "Jealousy."

The final two songs go some way to confirm critic Wilfrid Mellers' view of Fine as "an elegiac composer." "Lament" (*Lento con moto*), for four-part mixed chorus, is intensely harmonic and affectingly lyric. This poignant little *lachrymosa* also has drama, as at the sudden outburst on the words, "Woe weeps out her division when she sings," which contrasts nicely with an overall pattern of quiet murmuring.

The last song, "The Hour Glass" (*Andante semplice*), for full mixed chorus, is a sublimely simple meditation on death.

Its conventional harmonic setting and uncomplicated textures adroitly create a tone of mellow if brooding resignation ("Could you believe that this/The body ever was/Of one that loved?"), ending a refined choral set with elegant subtlety.

Although the published score of *The Hour Glass*, issued in 1951 by G. Schirmer, bears a dedication to Lorna Cooke deVaron and the New England Conservatory Chorus, that group did not perform the work until 1952. The premiere was given at Town Hall, New York City, on December 3, 1950, by the Hufstader Singers conducted by Robert Hufstader. The next day, the review in the *New York Herald Tribune*, by Francis D. Perkins, was unusually perceptive. "Mr. Fine has not tried to suggest a seventeenth-century musical idiom; the style is today's, but this gives the cycle a conflicting duality of atmosphere; the music is in accord with the expressive purport of the poems. The choral writing is skillful and effective; its details and melodic lines are lucidly revealed; the texts are flexibly treated and the music is not dominated by any particular formula." Arthur Cohn noted that *The Hour Glass* showed "the type of choral craftsmanship that is rare" and concluded: "There is brilliance here. It is never top-surface but always inwardly trenchant, which gives the music an emotive frame." Perhaps the last word on *The Hour Glass* came from the choral conductor and critic Edward Tatnall Canby, writing in 1978: "[These are] classically short, beautifully written and immensely concentrated...virtuoso works for chorus. [Here,] we have the [composer's] final word, really serious, *outwardly* serious music, free of the compulsion to clever satire and yet full of strength and lightness that this very satire brought to Fine's technique."

The summer of 1949 at Tanglewood was more than unusually enjoyable for the Fines, for they lived close to two of their fondest friends, Copland and Foss. The irrepressible Verna relished acting as mother hen, as she had done for the past two years. In 1946 Verna and Irving hadn't had accommodations near Copland, but the following year, remembered Verna, "we found a little cabin behind a guest home in Richmond owned by Reverend Cutler. I made lunches for everyone and took them over to the Tanglewood grounds. Aaron rented a suite with a separate entrance near Reverend Cutler." In 1948 Copland rented a converted barn and the Fines rented "the spacious Kelley mansion, [where] we all had our meals together. I got two helpers, one to take care of our new baby, the other to help in the kitchen. I ran a 'restaurant' every night with typed menus." Copland was unable to retrieve his barn in 1949, but the Kelley house had been remodeled and was larger than before. Verna recalled that "Aaron rented a suite in one wing, Lukas took another, and Irving and I and our young daughter had the main part of the house." Each composer had his own piano, so it was an ideal situation. Verna, especially, enjoyed socializing in the evenings. Musicians often came to dinner, among them Leonard Bernstein, Walter Piston, Harold Shapero and Arthur Berger; and, once, Copland's friend the actor Farley Granger. In addition to cooking, Verna did Fine's secretarial chores and sometimes typed for Copland.

That summer was also memorable for two special occasions, one musical, the other ludicrous. Copland was then at work on a major song-cycle, *Twelve Poems of Emily Dickinson*. As he later recalled, at Tanglewood "I played some of the songs for Lukas and Irving." Each song would be dedicated to a composer friend, and months later Copland told Fine: "I dedicated the nicest song to you." This was "Sleep is supposed to be," which begins lyrically and grows increasingly dissonant and oracular. "At the time," said Copland, "something about each song felt right for each person."

In 1953 Fine wrote a review of the published score of Copland's Dickinson songs. He rejected the idea that they constituted a cycle in the traditional sense, describing the set as "a composite yet remarkably unified picture of the poet herself and the themes that were close to her." The songs were, he said, "Copland at his very best, his most inspired and his most personal. They are frankly romantic, but their sentiment is at all times elevated and dignified." He noted that, stylistically, they were no drastic departure for Copland, but were nonetheless "all fresh and new-sounding." The Dickinson songs would become notorious for problematic word setting, sometimes involving octave displacement, and Fine duly observed that "the treatment of the voice and the prosody are both open to criticism" because of "frequent wide skips in the melodic line." He pointed out a disturbing detail: "Copland frequently sustains the last note of a vocal phrase over several beats. It begins to obscure the meaning when the final syllable ends on a consonant; and it can prove even comical when the final consonant is preceded by a diphthong." But, he concluded, "These are of course minor objections, especially in a work which is possibly the most significant contribution to the American art song up to this time."

In the first draft of his review, Fine wrote that "in view of the slenderness of Copland's output in the genre, his achievement in the Dickinson songs is little short of miraculous," but he evidently had second thoughts about the adjective. Also in this draft, and pertinent: "Stylistically, they fall somewhere between the more severe idiom of [the] Short Symphony [and] Piano Quartet and the more popular idiom of the ballet and movie scores. They contain no explicit Americana though they are completely American in feeling."

Rightly taking Copland to task for some awkward prosody, Fine then glossed over the flaw, stating that Copland's distortions, arising from his essentially instrumental approach to the voice, should provoke only "minor objections." One might well disagree with this exoneration, for the simple reason that good word-setting is basic to a good song, the music notwithstanding. In his handwritten notes for the article, Fine observed: "Tessitura often cruel" (changed to "extremely exacting" in the printed text). In the same notes, as an example of ill-considered prosody, he wrote: "as in 'incites the minutest cricket the most unworthy flow'r'. Analysis of the final word gives us flah-oor. What is [to] prevent the listener from assuming from the preceding text that the last word is fly? (analysis: flah-ee)." As none of this reached the final draft, Fine probably felt he had gone far enough with his criticism of his friend in his more general objections. Copland could not have been entirely pleased by this review, but there is no record of any reaction from him.[9]

On Sunday evening, August 14, 1949, an incident with

9. Much later, Copland wrote in his autobiography: "I sent [the Dickinson songs] to Irving before they were published, and with my permission, he played them for Koussevitzky, who (according to Irving) liked only certain ones—'Dear March' and some of the slow ones. Irving wrote me that Koussevitzky did not think that the music fit the words for 'Going to Heaven!'. But he wouldn't let Irving take the music home and insisted on keeping the score to study them better."

the distinct elements of farce provided comic relief from the pursuit of high art at Tanglewood. It was the end of the season, the night Koussevitzky gave a dinner party at the Curtis Hotel in Lenox for faculty members and their wives. Afterward, in Verna's account, "Aaron, Irving and I were driving home to nearby Richmond [in Copland's new Studebaker sedan]. In a car behind us were Arthur and Esther Berger. It was a very foggy night, so we were going very slowly. Suddenly, there was this huge cow standing smack in the middle of the road. Aaron slammed on the brakes, but it was too late. I let out a great scream, and then we all got out of the car. The poor cow was beyond help. Arthur almost fainted; but Aaron and Irving were cucumber-cool." Copland's car was damaged so badly it couldn't be driven, so Verna, Irving and Copland drove on to the house in the Berger's car, called the police and returned to the scene of carnage in Swamp Road, Richmond. "The police, who were extremely hostile, actually wanted to put Aaron in jail!" said Verna. "They took him to Pittsfield, and Irving, as a Massachusetts resident, put up bail. Aaron finally got out [of the police station] and returned home with Irving, who 'sprung' him about 2 a.m. The next morning, the news was broadcast on the radio, and the local paper ran the headline COPLAND KILLS COW!"

Actually, the headline in the *Berkshire Evening Eagle* the next day read: "Composer Copland Fined $35 After Car Kills Angus Steer." The article informed the public that the Dean of American Composers had been charged with "operating to endanger" after his explanation of the accident "failed to satisfy Judge Alberti." Copland told the court that farmer Leslie Birch's Black Angus steer "suddenly jumped in front of [my] car without any warning," and he denied he was speeding. A police constable, however, testified to finding sixty feet of brake marks and noted that the steer had been knocked twenty-seven feet. "Mr. Copland said that he had just slowed his car to avoid another cow when the steer jumped out of the 'pitch black' night. A passenger in the Copland car, Irving Fine of Cambridge, agreed with his driver that the animal had moved suddenly into the path of the car."[10]

---

10. The author, who occasionally traveled by car with Copland during the 1960s and 1970s, remembers that the composer

The marks on the pavement would seem to contradict Verna's "going very slowly" account, but Arthur Berger confirmed her description of police hostility. "The State troopers said to Aaron, 'How far was the cow from you?' and Verna squawked aggressively, 'How can he know how far the cow was from him? How do you know he even saw the cow?' The policeman snapped, 'Lady, keep out of this!' They hated Tanglewood because it was in the way—all the traffic and artists and Jews."

A few days after this excitement, Copland wrote to Verna, who was back home with Irving and Claudia in Cambridge. "When I went to pick the car up Monday at 2:30 I found a lawyer had slapped an attachment on it. Finally got it released (at 5:30) by the Insurance Co. in Springfield." He mentioned "an estimate of $200 to fix up the front of the car. Ouch! Because I had no collision insurance. Ouch again." The good news was that the insurance company would pay for the cow.

---

could be an alarming driver, given to speeding down the middle of country roads around curves.

# Chapter 11

■ FINE WAS AT THE MACDOWELL COLONY in late August and early September 1949, orchestrating his popular 1942 *Three Choruses from "Alice in Wonderland,"* and preparing to return to Harvard for his last year of teaching. As he wrote to Koussevitzky, he heard "at the very last moment just as the new school year was about to begin" that he had been awarded a Fulbright Research Fellowship for study in Paris of post-war French music. He had applied for a research grant, said Verna, "because he was too old to get a student grant, and the student ones' didn't pay well anyway." Fine left the Colony and hurried back to Cambridge. On September 18, Copland wrote to him: "Grand news about the Fulbright. How long is it for? And how does it affect your tenure at Tanglewood?" The most immediate concern, of course, was not Tanglewood but Harvard. Perhaps unsurprisingly, considering Fine's strained relations with the music department, he was quickly given a leave of absence, which meant that he was finished with Harvard and could go to France at once.

First, however, he had the pleasure of attending the premiere of his recent orchestration, titled *"Alice in Wonderland" Suite* (published in 1953 by Witmark). This had been requested by Boris Goldovsky, who conducted it with the Philadelphia Orchestra at the Worcester Festival in Worcester, Massachusetts, in early October. The scoring is for double woodwinds, four horns, three trumpets, two trombones, bass trombone, tuba, strings and percussion. Fine's orchestration is attractive, a straightforward, moderately coloristic rendering of the original piano accompaniment that effectively complements, without overwhelming, the sprightly choral writing. Oddly enough, it would never find a place in the festival-chorus repertory.

The Fulbright had the reputation of being a generous grant. Fine's stipend was for $5,000 over a period of nine months, replacing his Harvard salary. There was also a $1,000

supplemental living allowance. In addition, the grant included round-trip transportation from Boston to Paris and up to
$500 to be made available as needed abroad for expenses such
as books, music scores and records, travel and secretarial services.

"Overjoyed at the prospect of a year abroad," Irving,
Verna and their two-year-old daughter Claudia embarked for
France in the middle of October on the passenger liner *Ile de
France*, along with a contingent of Fulbright professors and
scholars. According to Verna, "Irving didn't want to teach
over there, and he didn't speak French that well. What he
really wanted was a leave of absence from Harvard so he could
compose."

Arriving in Paris, the family put up at a hotel and began
a long, grueling search for a suitable apartment. On November 12, Fine wrote to Copland: "We have decided (Verna
especially) that we like New York better than Paris. I think,
however, that after we get settled we'll like Paris better." They
had been "tramping the streets" for weeks looking at apartments; they had also investigated the suburbs, but Verna
decided that the suburbs "are insufficiently suburban and far
too rural, especially for the winter." He mentioned a miserable
week of extremely cold weather "at which time the furnace of
the hotel decided to go on strike."

But finally there was encouraging news. An apartment—
albeit one grotesquely over-furnished and over-priced—had
been found, in the Fifteenth Arrondissement at No. 22
Avenue Lowendal, near the École Militaire. This was "formerly inhabited by a nice old bag who is leaving Paris to forget it all (her boyfriend had decided to return to his wife)."
The apartment "is the sort of thing you might expect of a nice
bourgeois maîtresse. It is full of pseudo Louis Quatorze and
Seize furniture and horrible objects d'art, bibelots—in short
so impossibly cluttered up that I despair of getting a piano
into it." It was also "horribly expensive." But, "it *is* comfortable, and the rent (about $175 a month) is no more fantastic
than the rents generally obtained in Paris this year."

It was the beginning of a trying period for Fine, and one
that would not be very productive. He reported that he had
attended two concerts, one dull, the other of some interest
(string quartets by Honegger, Milhaud and Jean Martinon).

Two months later, he wrote again to Copland, apologizing for his sloth as a correspondent. "I can't plead an outburst of creative activity as an excuse, nor can I truthfully say that we have been so caught up in the Parisian whirl that we had no time to write. The fact of the matter is that we have been leading an existence of utter stagnation—no concerts, no theaters, no museums or sightseeing, and little social activity. This is all due to the fact that we have been spending most of our time and money on doctors and hospitals." Verna had been unwell in wintry Paris and had spent three weeks in hospital after an attack of acute arthritis, but little Claudia was the main problem. "Three weeks after we arrived the baby began to have what the Tribune calls 'Tourist Tummy.' Unfortunately she continued to have trouble with her bowels for a period of two months. We called in a specialist [and] the baby was put on a vigorous regime of carrots and water, soya bean extract, a constipating plant-food called Carube, and various other strange things." Claudia's condition went up and down and "we finally called in another doctor or rather I did (for Verna had already made reservations to sail home on Jan. 11th). This doctor put the baby in the American hospital for observation, put her on a perfectly normal diet without the fancy French medications, and within two days the baby's bowel movements were normal. She is now perfectly o.k. Verna's mind is at ease." In relief, he reported that "the return to the states has been canceled (for the time being anyway) and maybe we can begin to enjoy our stay, and I can get some real work done."

Despite all this domestic unpleasantness, Fine managed to write an article on Darius Milhaud and his operas, which was published in the *New York Times* on January 8, 1950, with the title "Milhaud at Home." Fine had been acquainted with the renowned French composer since 1948, when Milhaud was composer-in-residence at Tanglewood. He found him quite congenial. According to the French translator Claude Nathalie Thomas, a relative who knew him well, the obese and crippled Milhaud had "a kind and joyous personality, approachable and with a good sense of humor," even through the ill health that plagued his later years. Verna remembered that "Irving admired Milhaud tremendously and was very friendly with him. We spent a whole winter with him in Paris. He was often in bed writing music."

Her husband, she said, admired Milhaud's facility, but was of two minds about his habit of composing with a fountain pen. "He thought that Milhaud wrote too much, and that he needed to write with a pencil." Fine, the great reviser, was much concerned with detail. "Irving could be jealous of people who wrote so easily and so fast. 'I know I struggle,' he would say, 'but some of these people should struggle a little more'."

In his essay, Fine noted that Milhaud's theatrical works were almost unknown in the United States, although "they contain his most important music and some of the finest pages written in our time." Three of Milhaud's operas were being performed, sponsored by the Belgian and French national radios. The most important of these, he felt, was *Les Euménides*, the second part of the Orestes trilogy, adapted from Aeschylus by Paul Claudel and composed by Milhaud a quarter of a century before. The music, "of striking originality and eloquence throughout, is entirely apposite to the loftiness of the theme. It possesses abundant vitality, a kind of crude power and a genuine inventiveness, especially with regard to the creation of new sonorities." Fine termed Milhaud's melodic invention here "striking, though somewhat uncompromising," mentioned the "extraordinarily large" orchestra involved and cited the music's extreme polytonality: "At times, six or seven tonalities are juxtaposed in freely moving counterpoint." (The complex work had had the benefit of no less than sixty-five rehearsals.) Fine's rave review of *Les Euménides* contained only one, possibly tongue-in-cheek reservation: "There is the vaguest suspicion that it is overwritten, that the texture is needlessly complicated."

Two other Milhaud operas were discussed by Fine in his *Times* article. *Les Malheurs d'Orphée*, "a little masterpiece," was praised for its simple means, direct expression and "the most convincing continuity." He heard passing references to Stravinsky's *L'Histoire du Soldat*, but "the implications are quite different." The more ambitious *Médée* was "less perfect, less satisfactory as a whole" than *Les Malheurs d'Orphée*. Still, it "has more inspired moments. *Médée*'s incantation scene (scored for saxophone solo and strings) haunted this writer for days after the performance." When he had lectured on Milhaud at Tanglewood two years before, Fine had noted the composer's "great dramatic power" and the fact that he was capable of producing "music of savage intensity."

Copland had long been an admirer of Milhaud and used to speak privately of the considerable influence the Frenchman had on him. After reading Fine's dispatch from Paris, he wrote: "I was especially pleased [by it] because I felt as if I had personally won you over, even at the cost of being found out myself (at being Milhaud-influenced, that is)."

That January, Fine had begun to enjoy Paris, though suffering from frequent colds. "My spirits are much better here than they have been in Cambridge during the past few years," he wrote Copland. "I rather like it here and would prefer not to return too soon." Years later, he would recall: "Since I had no other prospects at the time, we had hopes of staying abroad for at least two years—with or without additional grants."

It was not to be. For one thing, Verna was lonely: "She has no friends and finds the language a great problem. I think she wants us to return at the end of June." Then, Fine had asked Koussevitzky for a leave of absence from Tanglewood, and Verna's mother, whom he considered a sensible woman, had written to urge him to return because "I'll never get a job while staying here [and] Koussy will not let me have a leave of absence this summer." Further, there was Claudia, whose illnesses began to seem chronic. Fine's mother had become so alarmed about the child's condition that she flew to Paris in late January. But, Fine informed Copland on February 26, "shortly after her arrival she too was laid low with the grippe, bronchitis, etc., with the result that we are now taking care of her instead of vice versa. This is bad luck since we had all planned to take a short trip. Traveling with the baby is difficult and it doesn't look as though we can gad about Europe much with her in tow." Nevertheless, the family did manage a car trip to Belgium, Holland and Austria. Not long after, Claudia contracted tuberculosis, and "we were persuaded by our French pediatrician to take [her] back to the Children's Medical Center in Boston." On April 7, Verna did just that. Fine decided to stick it out alone for a couple more months.

There were three events in Paris that winter that featured his music. The first was on February 6, 1950, at the theater of the American Embassy, when the composer Charles Jones presented a program of recordings of works by American composers. At the same hall a couple of weeks later, on the twenty-third, there was a program of music by Jones (Fine to Copland concerning Jones: "That mask of amiability and old world courtesy that only thinly conceals a certain anxiety and a rather consuming ambitiousness"), Noël Lee ("Noël's 'Song of Songs' has very good things—including some very original ones") and himself. Luise Vosgerchian played *Music for Piano* and Fine accompanied his *Sonata for Violin and Piano* ("I rather hashed up the last movet. of my fiddle sonata, but on the whole the concert was successful"). Then, on April 26, he appeared on a broadcast of American music on Radiodiffusion Française. This had been arranged by avuncular Darius Milhaud, and Fine was paid 4,000 francs for his participation.

Besides Milhaud, Fine had visited various other musicians in Paris. There was Olivier Messiaen, who had been Tanglewood's guest composer the year before: "He seems if anything a little more strange in Paris than at Tanglewood. He is the most elusive man in Paris. He refuses to use the phone or perhaps to pay the twelve francs for the phone call."[1] René Leibowitz: "His book on the technique of twelve-tone composition is finally out and I have dipped into it from time to time whenever my nerves seemed steady enough to cope with it." David Diamond: "He is said to have disappeared into the steppes of Asia." Paul Bowles: "whom I met once at Lenny's apartment but who did not remember me." Ned Rorem: "[He] is in from that mythical paradise in Fez Africa du Nord. He was completely alone [there] and out of sheer desperation wrote a symphony, a two piano sonata, a fiddle piece and other things." Fine also had a brief visit with Nadia Boulanger and was introduced to Henri Sauguet. And he

---

1. Messiaen's gargantuan, intensely ambitious and, some would say, intensely vulgar and pretentious *Turangalîla Symphony*, a work influenced by the rhythmic characteristics of Hindu music, had its world premiere in January 1950 by the Boston Symphony Orchestra conducted by Leonard Bernstein. Soon after, Copland wrote to Fine: "The Messiaen Monster produced various reactions—more illuminating as to the person reacting than as to the piece itself. Kouss was mad for it; L.B. cold, in spite of a brilliant job of conducting. It wasn't my dish of tea—'tho I can see its attractions for others."

became friendly with two avant-garde pioneers, Pierre Schaeffer and Pierre Henry.

On March 18, Verna and Irving had attended what was billed as the first concert of *musique concrète*, sponsored by the French national radio at L'École Normale de Musique in Paris and introduced by the musicologist Serge Moreux. The program featured two works by Schaeffer—three *Études de Bruits* ("Noise Etudes") and extracts from the *Suite for Fourteen Instruments*—and one collaborative effort by Schaeffer and Henry, *Symphonie pour un Homme Seul* ("Symphony for a Solitary Man"). "The building material of Concrete Music is sound in its indigenous state," wrote Moreux. By building material he meant various sounds and noises instead of musical tones. Working during 1948 and 1949 at the Paris radio station, Schaeffer had been the chief fabricator of the new genre. As Arthur Jacobs put it in his *New Dictionary of Music*, in *musique concrète* "musical and other sounds are recorded and, if desired, electronically distorted, and then assembled into a time-structure—the 'composer' thus working with recorded sound only, and the final work similarly existing only as recorded sound." He noted that the process would eventually be incorporated into electronic music.

Verna recalled the Paris concert. "It was just a man on the stage wiggling dials," she laughed. Her husband, however, took it more seriously: "He was very open, always looking for new ideas."

Fine's first reaction to *musique concrète*, as quoted in a newspaper article, was that it was "humorous, frightening and visceral," although he quickly realized that its purpose was to free "the music inherent in concrete objects." So great was his interest that he lectured on the subject that year at Tanglewood. His description in his notes, which is rather more speculative than Jacobs', is worth quoting. "Musique Concrète is a rearrangement and manipulation of sounds and noises in their natural state to bring about a kind of musical free association. The evocative qualities of these sounds are harmonized and juxtaposed to bring about something quite new, which is auditory but not exclusively so; and certainly not musical as we understand the term. The impact of this is in a sense more literary and it is possible that this new type of expression may mean more when added to visual techniques of the screen and the drama, and the radio. Its fascination lies in its pull on the layer just below the conscious—on the memory." To Copland he remarked that *musique concrète* "is a kind of renaissance of the early Italian futurism with Messiaenic implications. Some of the results are quite exciting." But Fine's most specific explanation was given a few years later in a letter to an interested music publisher. "Musique Concrète is essentially an attempt to liberate the music imprisoned in concrete objects by the utilization of all of the recording techniques available to sound engineers: i.e. play-backs at different speeds, filtering out of either low or high frequencies, echo chambers, montage-like effects, etc. The resultant sound effects, which also include fragments of music, conversation, radio signals, noises of all kinds, etc. are arranged by the composer in a sequence that strives for some kind of abstract coherence. Superficially, Musique Concrète bears some resemblance to the Italian futurism of 1913 or 1914; to some of the musical experiments of the '20s (carried on by Varese, Antheil and Cowell); and some of the sound effects used in radio and film sound tracks. However, the movement seems to have greater pretensions than the aforementioned predecessors, and possibly greater implications. In many ways (and this is my opinion only) it represents the first genuine example of musical surrealism." He added: "I believe that I was the first person to report on Musique Concrète in this country."

In 1952, Fine would arrange for the American premiere of Schaeffer/Henry's *Symphony for a Solitary Man* at Brandeis University; and Verna noted that "when we came back from France he made quite a good living for a while, going around lecturing on *musique concrète*." (The latter reference was to illustrated lectures at Tanglewood, the Philadelphia Art Alliance, Brandeis University and a Boston radio station.)

Fine's unhappiness with his situation in Paris is apparent in a gloomy letter to Copland dated February 26, 1950. "The days go by here with discouraging speed. I have never been so completely barren as far as composition is concerned. I sit me down at the piano or at the desk every day and nothing comes. In three months it will be time to return to Tanglewood with nothing to show." Further: "I am starved for good music—also for a few new ideas. I have heard very little music here that really appeals to me very much. There is a big new

Dutilleux piano sonata that has very impressive moments, but also rather poor ones. Nadia is telling her pupils that Boulés [i.e., Pierre Boulez] has something and that he is a young man to be watched. Meanwhile, I have been fluttering about with my tongue hanging out for an opportunity to meet this fabulous young man."

A month later, he made some interesting comments about Olivier Messiaen and the general situation in France. "I have come to the conclusion that you are a pretty smart cookie about sizing up developments in music. I remember your saying once that what was important about Messiaen was his impact on the younger musicians [which is], I feel, a much healthier one [than] that of the 12 tone business. Messiaen's pupils never become infected with his naive 'Sacre Coeur' sort of mysticism. More serious is the false mysticism which infects many of the composers of my generation here, and which derives from Honegger and to some extent from Schoenberg via Leibowitz. Talented fellows like Dutilleux are caught between Ravel, Honegger and Messiaen and seem to have one helluva time in keeping their equilibrium." Other composers, he added, "are trying the old game of reconciling Debussy with Schoenberg." He concluded: "As you see, I am sufficiently wound up to give a lecture on the contemporary French scene at Tanglewood this summer—maybe even two."[2]

On June 4, 1950, Fine's second article from Paris appeared in the *New York Times*. It was titled "Composers in France: Younger Generation Uses Complicated Means," and

---

2. Fine did give such lectures, and on August 6, in the *New York Herald Tribune*, Arthur Berger noted that Tanglewood was the first major musical format where *musique concrète* had been introduced, and that "the news of it was brought by Irving Fine of the faculty. An etude for casseroles and a symphony for one man at phonograph controls were cited by Mr. Fine as among its best manifestations." He reported that Fine had stated that its inventor, Pierre Schaeffer, was fascinated by isolating "the sound of the resonating substance from the percussive impact of the sounding agent." A few years later, Fine described Schaeffer as "a professional radio engineer, a skillful amateur composer and a kind of philosopher-poet."

began with the observation that "Paris seems to be becoming once more the center of the most radical tendencies in modern music." He stated that certain older composers—Honegger, Messiaen, André Jolivet—still had their followers, that Schoenberg, Bartók and Berg were "in vogue," and that Webern had his "passionate admirers." He cited the influence of Messiaen as composer and teacher, which had "reached fantastic proportions" after the Liberation but was on the decline because "the younger men now find serious limitations in Messiaen's harmonic vocabulary and are even more distrustful of his kind of mysticism." Dodecaphonic music, due to the proselytizing of René Leibowitz, was, he said, "one of the burning issues of the day."

Fine mentioned several of the younger French composers as "brilliant talents" worth watching: Maurice Leroux, Serge Nigg, Pierre Boulez, Pierre Henry and, especially Jean-Louis Martinet. He noted a certain pomposity in the young men, who were "often inclined to puritanical moralizing and to the cultivation of the serious at all costs," and he felt that for many of them the attraction of the twelve-tone technique "resides in its intellectuality, which they are prone to regard as synonymous with seriousness and a more elevated morality." That technique and Messiaen's rhythmic theories "hold out the illusion of the universal, the foolproof, the encyclopedic or the absolute musical system." He wondered why Hindemith's theories were ignored, theorizing that it might be "because the strong German-Burger quality of so much of Hindemith's music is repellent to the French temperament." Surprised by the popularity of Brahms with both audiences and musicians, he was "almost dumbfounded to hear the extravagant praise lavished upon the music of Bruckner and Mahler by some French composers." Concluding his survey, Fine observed slyly that "not a little of the music being written by French composers today possesses qualities that we would normally consider rather typically German." Copland's response: "Read your piece in the Times—apparently you're coming home with the real low-down."

Before he went home, Fine thought he should see some more of Europe. He was going back to Tanglewood at the end of June and in May he had been invited to lecture and be co-director at a music seminar at the Center for American Studies in Salzburg, a two-week stint. For the latter activity, he had to have the permission of the Fulbright commission, which was duly granted. In mid-April 1950, he drove his Renault from Paris to Rome. There, he planned to join Harold and Esther Shapero, who were in residence at the American Academy. His trip, on which he was accompanied by a couple named Gilbert, took him through northwestern Italy, to Genoa, Pisa and Florence. Verna was staying with her mother in her suite at Boston's Lafayette Hotel, and on April 20 Fine sent her a postcard describing his visit to the historic sites of Pisa, including the famous leaning tower. "Naturally we climbed the 294 stairs and looked around the countryside. The cathedral next to the tower is really wonderful, especially inside. The outside is too ornate for my taste." When he arrived in Rome, he was entranced. "I don't think I have ever stayed in a more wonderful place. If you can afford it this is the place to spend the rest of your days." The jazzman Benny Goodman was there, practicing Copland's new jazz-inflected *Clarinet Concerto* with Shapero at the piano, and Fine met and was photographed with him.[3] A Mr. Roberts let Fine use his piano "in the little theater on top of his huge villa," and he had put down a few measures of music, but, he wrote Verna, "I don't see how I can get anything accomplished until I return home. Please don't be disappointed. Just think of how I feel." The Shaperos had decided to go to Salzburg with Fine, and on May 7 he informed Verna that "we are leaving this Wednesday for Salzburg directly. I had wanted to see Venice before going to Salzburg but connections are poor and it would have been too hectic. Actually, I am now in a rather homesick frame of mind."

Harold Shapero remembered that "we didn't have a car,

---

3. Alexei Haieff was also there. Ned Rorem wrote the following concerning a group of American neoclassicists living in Rome in 1950: "It's all a closed little successful clique living off the various American foundations to which letters of recommendation have been written by older members of the same successful clique. (Alexei's music is dedicated to Arthur Berger, whose music is dedicated to H. Shapero, whose music is dedicated to Stravinsky, whose *Symphony of Psalms* is 'dedicated to the glory of God and to the Boston Symphony.')"

so we drove with Irving to Salzburg for the seminar, and I gave a little talk." Fine wrote to Verna from Salzburg on May 15. Referring to his *New York Times* article on French composers, which he had sent off from Rome, he noted that finishing it had "blighted my stay in Italy" and continued: "Now that I am in Salzburg giving lectures I am going through the same agony all over again. I have managed to get through two already, though not in an inspired manner. Sonny analyzed my reaction as a panicky anxiety brought about by the realization that my mind is absolutely empty when I sit down to prepare a lecture or write an article." At Salzburg, he thought the weather "wonderful," the scenery "superb," the atmosphere at the Center "stimulating" (he noted the presence of the modernist composers Boris Blacher and Gottfried von Einem). But the food at the school was unpleasant—"heavy and rather greasy"—though it was excellent at restaurants. He was depressed because "as far as my composition is concerned, it's no go. I can't write here and I am not going to delude myself that I can write in Paris before returning home. There is no sense whipping myself or driving myself. It only leads to more anxieties."

Fine missed the companionship of his wife. "Being separated is a terrible hardship on both of us," he wrote to her from Salzburg. "I can't confess to having had much pleasure out of this trip thus far."

Some of his anxieties (perhaps frustrations is a better word) seem, however, to have been relieved by a brief but eventful trip to Vienna with the Shaperos. As Harold told it: "After our part in the Salzburg seminar was over, we decided to drive to Vienna, because I wanted to see all the Beethoven houses. Irving had a car and I figured he was going to be useful, because we could drive around in it, but as soon as we got to Vienna he garaged it. I was mad as hell." Esther explained that "the car was a hassle because gas was rationed and hard to get." Harold continued the story. "After Irving beached the car, he and I were walking back to the hotel and we saw a bar and decided we'd stick our noses into it. This was 1950 and Vienna was a very sexy place. A gorgeous girl with a sweater divided into black and blue stripes came out on the top step, swung her hips and said, 'Hello, Joe!' Irving said, 'Let's not go in,' but I said, 'I want to see what's inside,' so we peeked through the door. It was a bar with booths with little partitions and the girls were working the GIs; you went into a booth and they performed oral sex. I don't know whether or not that charged up Irving, but we had separate rooms at the hotel and didn't see him again that night." The next morning, Harold and Esther discovered that Irving had booked a bus-tour of Vienna for the three of them. They got on the bus but he never appeared. They left the tour at the Sigmund Freud house and went to the Prata to ride the giant ferris wheel, familiar from Orson Welles' film *The Third Man*. At the park, Shapero found something that amused him far more than a mere carnival ride. "There was a store wholly devoted to Victorian nudes and Victorian sex-things. You turned a crank and watched these little stills go in sequence like a movie. I was delighted. There were fifty machines and I went to every one of them. It took hours." Esther spent the time looking at art books. Finally, the Shaperos returned to the hotel to have dinner, at which point Irving showed up. "He was all stressed out," said Harold. "What had happened was, that morning a chambermaid had seduced him. I said to him, you have to be out of your mind; you're going to get every kind of disease. The girls liked him. He was cute: had a pretty face, blond hair, blue eyes. He was the type who couldn't deflect sex with auto-eroticism. He had to *have* it. So the chambermaid got him, and she was disgusting: a blowsy German broad with a puffy face. I don't know how he could get it up with her." There was a farcical coda. "That night at two o'clock," recalled Esther, "there came a banging on our door. We opened it and saw Irving, looking nervous. He said, 'Can I sleep with you tonight? She's after me!' She wouldn't let him alone. So he slept on a couch in our room." Fine's behavior with the chambermaid was, Shapero insisted, "just an anomaly. I don't think he was a real womanizer." Fortunately for what was an anachronistically happy marriage, that Viennese incident seems never to have reached Verna's ears.

After their adventures in Vienna, the trio of friends returned to Salzburg, where they went their separate ways—the Shaperos back to Rome and Fine back to Paris, arriving on May 21. There, he had to "get rid" of his car and to buy scores and records for that summer's lectures at Tanglewood. He also arranged for Radiodiffusion Française to send recordings of recent French music, including *musique concrète*, to the Berkshire Music Center. On his way home the third week of June, Fine stopped in London. He called on Copland's friend Jack Henderson at the British music publisher Boosey and Hawkes, a visit which may have led to the publication the following year of his *Partita for Wind Quintet*.

Months before, Fine had applied for and received a Guggenheim grant for 1950-1951, during which time he was supposed to do nothing but compose. In the interim, at the urging of Leonard Bernstein and after sending an agent to Paris to conduct an interview, Brandeis University had offered him a teaching position. As he later wrote, "having already been awarded a Guggenheim Fellowship for musical composition for the following year, I began to receive a few tempting and insistent offers from other schools. One of these, from the newly founded Brandeis University in Waltham [Massachusetts], seemed sufficiently challenging and attractive to warrant the postponement of my fellowship."

In March 1950, he confided to Copland about the Brandeis situation. "They have offered me a job at Brandeis, again at the rank of asst. Prof. If I were sure of staying at Brandeis indefinitely I wouldn't worry about the rank, but other places might consider the whole business in the nature of a demotion. I have suggested a face saving device—appointing me as university lecturer and composer in residence or some such fancy non professional title." On July 16 both the *Boston Herald* and the *Boston Globe* announced that Fine had been appointed Composer-in-Residence and Lecturer in Music at Brandeis, beginning that fall.

This meant resettling in the Boston area. The task fell to ever-practical Verna, who was on the scene. In May Fine wrote her from Rome: "Just received the wonderful news from Guggenheim re postponement. I think everything is working out marvelously. Trust you completely re car and house." And from Salzburg: "As to the question of living quarters for next year, do as you see fit. I don't like the idea of Everett St. again—anything else in Cambridge is o.k., though I prefer something more suburban myself."

In September, after Tanglewood and a stay at the MacDowell Colony, Verna and Irving were still looking, but for a house rather than another apartment. On the twenty-second, Copland wrote: "Keep your courage up and find a good house." Not long after, they found an ideal one in a semi-rural area of East Natick, only a short drive from Waltham and Brandeis. The catch was that it was not for rent but for sale, and the price was beyond the means of an untenured college professor. But when Florence Rudnick heard of their plight, she stepped in with an offer to make the down-payment, which was gratefully accepted.

Joanna Fine observed that "my father was very tradition-al. He supported us. He felt you must not touch your wife's money. Still, he did let her mother help them with the house in Natick." This was a sizable two-storied, barnyard-red frame building at 29 Rathburn Road, set in several wooded acres replete with a pond: suburban and idyllic.

Although the rooms were small, the Natick house was well designed for family life. In addition to a studio for Fine, the ground floor had a living room and dining room con-nected by an open archway, a country-style kitchen, a play-room for children and, down a short hallway, a master bed-room and bathroom for himself and Verna. On the second floor were bedrooms with eaves, for children and a live-in maid. "The house felt very big and grand to us when we were young," said Claudia, "but in fact it was quite cosy. In the winter the little pond—which was more like a swamp—froze, and we all ice-skated on it."

For Fine, the most attractive aspect of his new home was his low-ceilinged studio, off the living room and closed in by sliding french doors. It was just large enough to hold his two grand pianos (though he had to have a beam installed under the floor to carry their weight), a desk, his green easy-chair, a couch, file cabinets and shelving for his books and sizable col-lection of music scores and recordings. Emily remembered her father's studio as being so dominated by the pianos that "there was almost no walking space."

On Fine's desk was a small portrait of Mozart as a boy. "He had an identification with Mozart," said Joanna. "That was because he felt that he, too, would die young." Emily remembered seeing copies of the magazine *Daedalus* in the bookcases. "It was the journal of the intellectual elite. My mother was proud of the fact that his favorite reading was

*Daedalus*. When we used to talk about religion, she would reminisce, '*Daedalus* was your father's bible'." In addition to a large collection of poetry, his books were mostly on philosophy, psychology, sociology, anthropology and politics; like Copland, he had no great interest in fiction. Fine's studio was his *sanctum sanctorum*. Esther Shapero noted that "at the Natick house they made a big deal about it being shut off from the living room and from the children."

Verna stressed that her husband had "very sensitive ears," and that the living room served as a sound-barrier between the noisy playroom and Fine's studio. She noted wryly that "Walter Piston always used to say about his house in Belmont that he had his studio, his painter-wife had her studio, and that the living room, which was the middle room, was the battleground. But there were no children, and I don't think they had a happy marriage. We never had a battleground in the Natick house, but we did keep the kids in a faraway place so that Irving could work in peace."

In October 1950, Fine had informed Copland of their about-to-be-improved domestic conditions. Not long after, they received an enthusiastic reply: "Congrats on the new house. Of course I'll be glad to be an overnight guest. Five acres—think of it—why, you're landowners." On November 1, the Fines and their black cocker spaniel Stinker moved into their new home. Two weeks later, on the fourteenth, they were in New York to attend Copland's fiftieth-birthday dinner and a gala all-Copland concert afterward at the Museum of Modern Art.

The previous March, in a letter from Paris, Fine had given Copland an indication that his long creative hiatus might be ending. "Have begun writing pretty music again," he said. "Took a three-day trip and upon return found I had a few ideas to my great surprise." The piece which eventually resulted, the *Notturno for Strings and Harp*, was labored at sporadically throughout 1950 and into early 1951, at Tanglewood, the MacDowell Colony and the new house in Natick, and finished on March 4 of the latter year. Three weeks before completing *Notturno*, Fine had written to Copland that he was having "one hell of a time" composing a fast movement: "Last night I crossed out five pages and began again from the opening section, this time determined to write a minute and one half intermezzo in my best bitter-sweet manner. Perhaps I can succeed in being charming if not important." A few days later, he wrote again to Copland concerning *Notturno*. "According to Harold [Shapero] it has quite a few Stravinskyisms. This is unfortunate—since I tend to agree. But it's a piece, anyway, and I think it has a few nice things."

The *Notturno* is a transitional work, deeply felt and well made—and, although only fifteen minutes in duration, an ambitious score. There is some relationship to the manner of two of Stravinsky's classical-subject ballets which Fine loved, the early *Apollo Musagetes* and the recent *Orpheus*, albeit Fine's melodies are generally less fragmented than Stravinsky's. Despite the *Notturno*'s considerable attractions (elegant tunefulness, colorful instrumental writing, lack of pretension), it stands as a valiant but oddly flawed attempt at style expansion. The expression is far more romantic than before, with remnants of the previously omnipresent neoclassicism confined to the fast middle movement. As noted earlier, Wilfrid Mellers once described Fine as "in toto, an elegiac composer," and even if this is something of an exaggeration, the *Notturno* certainly provides an illustration of that dictum.

The work's chromatic harmony (the prevailing tonality is that of B-flat minor) and occasional large intervallic leaps and wide-ranging melody (for instance, in the third movement's viola solos) have misled some critics to sense a derivation from twelve-tone technique ('modified twelve-tone method," said one), but this music is no more dodecaphonic in concept or detail than that of Gustav Mahler, a composer by whom it is sometimes mildly inflected.[4] A singular aspect of the *Notturno* is the inescapable fact that its concise structuring is in conflict with its strong romantic impulses. Still, that Fine managed to convey something of the effect of a compressed romantic-era symphony in such a brief score is no small achievement. He was clearly pleased with the result,

---

4. Nevertheless, Verna Fine noted in a 1994 talk that her husband told her he had been "playing around with the twelve notes" in the *Notturno*. Further: "I said to him, Irving, that second movement is wonderful. It belongs on television. There's a program called *The Twilight Zone*, and that movement is perfect for it."

referring to it in a 1952 letter to his wife as "the nocturne which I suspect is my favorite piece among my few works."

Fine explained his intentions in a brief program note for the first performance. "The term *Notturno* here is used in the sense of an evening serenade. It aims at a certain romantic effect and perhaps it may not be too farfetched to imagine the over-all character as a blend of Chopin and Mozart expressed in present-day idiom. The three movements are thematically connected."

The format is slow-fast-slow, ideally played without pause, although not so marked. The first movement (*Lento*) begins impressionistically in string quartet and harp: "pretty music" *par excellence*. This placidity ends with a four-note rising figure that will generate much of the rest of the piece. The ensuing *più mosso* is played by the full string complement and initially strikes the ear as subtly Mahlerian, with its rising and falling melody (*Espressivo, Cantabile*) over gentle *pizzicati*. Repeated notes bring on a climax with ascending harp chords, followed by a new and contrasting section propelled by harp *ostinati* that is quickly succeeded by more neo-Mahlerian romanticism. After a *crescendo*, a dramatic pause heralds a brief coda with affecting viola solos and a harmonically ambiguous cadence. Even taking into account its memorable moments, this succinct, sectional movement leaves an impression of formal meandering.

The tiny scherzo (*Animato*) that follows is perfectly conceived, replete with lively syncopations and Bartókian repeated notes. Melodic fragments over a humming moto-perpetuo background provide a compelling sense of forward movement. The string ensemble (harp *tacet*) is muted throughout, an unexpected effect that, along with the seductive gliding nature of much of the melodic material, produces that rare musical animal: an elegant scherzo. Also unexpected is the quiet dissonant chord at the end.

The concluding *Adagio* is the heart of the *Notturno*, and perhaps its most evocative music. This is lyricism of some intensity, unequivocally emotional, melancholy and elegiac. The moderately dissonant chordal opening is solemn and rather suggests a similar moment in Martinu's *Concerto for Two String Orchestras, Piano and Timpani*, but the expressive viola solos that resonate through these dense chords are pure

Fine (they were written especially for the Boston Symphony's principal violist, Joseph de Pasquale, who played in the premiere). The most gripping music begins at bar 23, with atmospheric harp arpeggios that accompany the rising motive from the first movement and its countermelody, in the first and second violins. Such luxuriant, ultra-romantic expression had never before appeared in a Fine score and never would again. This is the voice of a master lyricist, and the music disappoints only by its brevity. The *Adagio* has one climactic passage, a *crescendo* to the work's sole *fortissimo*, which lasts for a mere five bars and prefaces a quiet ending in a slightly ambiguous B-flat minor.

Fine himself conducted the first performance of *Notturno*, at Jordan Hall, Boston, on March 28, 1951. The ensemble was the Zimbler Sinfonietta, for which it had been written, consisting of members of the Boston Symphony and their founder and conductor, Josef Zimbler, a cellist from the orchestra.[5] In May the work won the first cash award ($100) of the newly formed, Boston-based Friends of Chamber Music, and in 1952 the score was published by Boosey and Hawkes.

The newspaper reviews were respectful but reserved. The most perceptive was by the composer and critic Klaus George Roy, writing in the *Christian Science Monitor*. He noted that Fine had "competently conducted the premiere of his *Notturno* for strings and an *obbligato* harp. This night-piece or evening serenade is a thoroughly neoromantic composition, filled with quiet and sincere emotion and much real beauty. Quite different from most of Mr. Fine's other works, which tend to be witty, bright and crystal clear, the *Notturno* is rich and warm in its outer movements." In the scherzo, he heard "some of the transparent brittleness" and "Stravinskian stops and starts" which he found "a delightful feature" of Fine's style. "The harmony [throughout the *Notturno*] is surprisingly conservative, the texture largely homophonic and a bit too consistently the same. Mr. Fine's remarkable melodic gift is

---

5. A few years later, Fine described Zimbler to Copland as "a maddeningly vain popinjay (English euphemism for 'potz')," adding: "and I am probably equally vain—or at least vain enough not to want to pay court to him."

given too brief a play [and] the expressiveness of the entire work seems to suffer from a certain hesitancy in an idiom new to the composer himself." The *Notturno* "made a very pleasant impression," said Rudolph Elie of the *Boston Herald*. "I found the last movement particularly attractive, the other two containing interesting material of a graceful melodic character but a little lacking in force." He thought Fine had not fully exploited his materials, "for he no sooner established a mood than he dropped it for another," but cited the music for "its distinguished substance." The *Boston Daily Globe*'s John William Riley reported that the *Notturno* had "a very warm reception," and that it gave "ample evidence that the composer speaks well in modest, compact forms. He speaks softly and has his say with quiet intensity, relying more on richly expressive content than on obvious *sturm und drang*." The *Boston Post* critic, Tucker Keiser, was unimpressed. "Mr. Fine's *Notturno* is a curious work. There are evidences of great craftsmanship throughout, but the music just never seems to catch fire. Each movement ends with an incomplete cadence and there are no real climaxes. This gives the music a rather pallid aura." Harold Shapero also criticized aspects of the *Notturno*. "It's a pretty piece, though very Stravinskian. It has some formal problems, goes astray a little bit, doesn't quite work. He wasn't perfect and he made mistakes sometimes. But the *Notturno* is still a handsome piece: it's modest, it plays well and it has good sound."

All such reservations aside, the *Notturno* was to become Fine's most popular orchestral score.

At eighteen, Irving Fine had completed an extra year of high school by attending the Boys' Latin School in Boston in order to qualify for admission to Harvard, which he entered in the fall of 1933.

Irving Fine, Harvard Yearbook, 1938.

In the summer of 1939, the twenty-four-year-old Irving Fine sailed to Paris to continue his studies with Nadia Boulanger. She had been so impressed with him when he worked with her at Radcliffe earlier in the spring, that she got him a fellowship to return with her to Paris. Irving's father, George, has his arm over his son's shoulder while Irving's mother, Charlotte, sits in front of them.

Irving Fine's class at Fontainebleau, August 1939. Fine, in striped tie, stands behind Nadia Boulanger, seated at the piano.

Irving Fine at the piano at home, Cambridge, Massachusetts, 1940.

Irving Fine, Aaron Copland, Nadia Boulanger and Walter Piston at Child's Restaurant, across from Symphony Hall, Boston, in 1945.

Tanglewood, summer of 1946. From left: Claudio Spies, Lukas Foss, Harold and Esther Shapero, Verna and Irving Fine, Leonard Bernstein.

Tanglewood, summer of 1946. From left to right: Lukas Foss, Verna and Irving Fine, Harold Shapero

Verna and Irving Fine,
Tanglewood, 1947.

Irving and Verna Fine (foreground) with Serge and Olga Koussevitzky at Tanglewood during the summer of 1948. The Fine's relationship with Koussevitzky was
professionally and personally close: Koussevitzky called Irving "mein son."

Aaron Copland (right) was, with Tanglewood founder Serge Koussevitzky, at the center of the legendary music camp's performing and teaching activities, and lived for three summers with the Fine family. Verna Fine caught this unposed picture of her husband, Irving (center), and visiting composer and teacher Darius Milhaud (left) during the summer of 1948.

Irving Fine and Serge Koussevitzky, Tanglewood, August 1948, at a rehearsal with a student orchestra of Fine's *Toccata Concertante*.

Irving Fine in the mid-1950s.

Darius Milhaud receiving an honorary degree from Brandeis at its commencement in 1955 from Brandeis's first president, Abram L. Sachar. Irving Fine, standing between them, described Milhaud as "one of the great Jewish composers."

Harold Shapero, Arthur Berger, Lillian Hellman and Irving Fine at Brandeis on January 13, 1955. Hellman was there with Leonard Bernstein to give a seminar on their musical-in-progress based on Voltaire's *Candide*.

Aaron Copland and Irving Fine at Brandeis, 1961.

Irving Fine examining the score of his *Symphony (1962)* just before its premiere with the Boston Symphony Orchestra in March 1962. From left to right: Irving Fine, Charles Munch and Eleazar De Carvalho.

Irving Fine with the score of his *Symphony (1962)* at Tanglewood, August 10, 1962, the day after he learned that he, not Charles Munch, would have to conduct the August 12 performance of the work with the Boston Symphony Orchestra.

Irving Fine conducting the Boston Symphony Orchestra in a performance of his *Symphony (1962)* at Tanglewood on August 12, 1962. Charles Munch, who was scheduled to conduct, had to cancel two days before because of illness. One critic remarked: "It is clear that Fine needed no apologies as a conductor of his own music."

One of the last pictures of Irving Fine, taken with two of his daughters, Claudia (left), Joanna (foreground), and his wife, at Niagara Falls, August 13, 1962.

First page of Irving Fine's *String Quartet*; the composer's manuscript is in the Irving Fine Collection, Music Division, Library of Congress.

Manuscript of row chart for Irving Fine's *String Quartet*, also in the Irving Fine Collection, Music Division, Library of Congress.

# PART TWO

# Chapter 12

■ BRANDEIS UNIVERSITY OPENED ITS DOORS in 1948. Harvard University was founded by Methodists, Yale by Congregationalists, Columbia by Episcopalians, Princeton by Presbyterians, Brown by Baptists, Georgetown by Catholics and Bryn Mawr by Quakers. But until 1948 no college or university in the United States had ever been founded by Jews.

In his book *Brandeis University: A Host at Last*, Abram L. Sachar, Brandeis' first president, took note of the fact, writing that while "every denominational group could point to colleges it had founded and sustained[,] astonishingly enough, the Jews, the People of the Book, whose sons and daughters sought opportunities in higher education in greater proportion than did any other group," had never established such an institution. Brandeis advertised itself as secular and thus nondenominational. Still, although it had no "Christian quota" to correspond with the restrictive Jewish quotas of other East Coast universities (which Sachar understandably termed "a galling outrage"), for at least the first several years the great majority of its students and faculty were Jewish.

Brandeis had been built on the site of Middlesex University, in Waltham, Massachusetts, a Boston suburb. Standing on nearly 100 acres of rolling, wooded countryside near the Charles River, the privately sponsored institution was founded by a Boston surgeon, Dr. John Hall Smith, in 1926, and gave degrees in medicine, veterinary medicine and liberal arts. Smith, a Protestant of decidedly progressive views, would not allow restrictions due to race or religion at Middlesex, so that many Jews who had been rejected elsewhere enrolled there. This seems to have displeased the American Medical Association, which continuously threatened to withdraw accreditation, provoking Smith to angry accusations of out-and-out anti-Semitism. When he died in 1944, his son maintained Middlesex for the next two years with difficulty, forced to sell parts of the campus. Then, the Massachusetts legislature suspended Middlesex's medical program, allowing only the veterinary and arts schools to continue, and the end was near.

At that point, a group of New York Jews, headed by a contentious Zionist rabbi, Dr. Israel Goldstein, entered the picture. Disgusted with the quotas in effect at many medical schools, they sought a suitable campus for a Jewish-sponsored university. Negotiations with near-bankrupt Middlesex were quickly completed in early 1946, and the grounds and charter were turned over to the New Yorkers with, wrote Abram Sachar, "no purchase investment, a better bargain therefore than the acquisition of Manhattan from the Indians for twenty-four dollars in beads." Because the associates had no financial resources, money for the new institution had to be raised. For this purpose a committee called the Foundation for Higher Learning was formed, and Dr. Goldstein sought well-known figures willing to lend their names. The first person approached, the renowned scientist Albert Einstein, was enthusiastic, writing: "I would approve very much the creation of a Jewish college or university, provided that it is sufficiently made sure that the Board and Administration will remain permanently in reliable Jewish hands. . . . Such an institution, provided it is of a high standard, will improve our situation a good deal and will satisfy a real need." His support (Einstein was, said Sachar, "a magnetic asset") stimulated other prominent personages to join the committee, which subsequently decided that America's first Jewish-founded university should be named after America's first Jewish Supreme Court justice, Louis Dembitz Brandeis (1856-1941).

On March 19, 1947, the *New York Times* reported that ten million dollars would soon be in Brandeis University's coffers. Not surprisingly, most of this came from Jewish sources. A few months later, following a certain amount of internecine squabbling (for instance, a furious Einstein had resigned from the committee after Dr. Goldstein invited New York's ultra-reactionary Francis Cardinal Spellman to give the invocation at a fundraising dinner), the announcement was made that Brandeis would be purely a liberal arts university. This abandoned one of the original goals of having a school of medicine that continued Middlesex's refuge tradition for Jewish medical students. The plan had been to open Brandeis in the fall of 1947, but the old campus was discovered to be in such a state of deterioration that the opening was postponed for a year, until September 1948. At that time, 300 students were enrolled, about eighty-five percent of them Jews.

When Brandeis' incipient School of Creative Arts began in the fall of 1949, its faculty consisted only of Erwin Bodky, a German-born harpsichordist and musicologist of no great distinction who was, however, friendly with two of the University's major donors. He had also been recommended by Serge Koussevitzky, whose official Brandeis title was University Consultant in Music. At a planning conference the following year, Koussevitzky supported the fledgling university's high ideals with a bold statement: "Brandeis must create the very finest of musical education, else it is better that we do not start."[1] In 1951, an Advisory Committee on Educational Policies in Music, headed by Koussevitzky, included Aaron Copland, Leonard Bernstein and the distinguished musicologist Alfred Einstein.

Fine became the second member of the music faculty in September 1950, with the title Lecturer in Music and Composer in Residence. According to President Sachar, he had been "winkled away" from Harvard. That, of course, was hardly the case, and it is difficult to imagine Sachar's being unaware of the Harvard tenure denial. Fine's appointment came about through the urgings of his influential friend Bernstein, who had written to Sachar in June 1949: "I would like to repeat, at this time, the first piece of advice I gave when the University was in the process of forming, which was to get in touch with Irving Fine of the Department of Music at Harvard. If Mr. Fine's services could be secured to head your new School of Music,[2] it would be an invaluable asset to your Uni-

---

1. Sachar's book misattributes this statement to Bodky.

2. Consulted about the history of music at Brandeis University, former faculty member Caldwell Titcomb observed: "I am uneasy about the term 'School of Music.' There was no notion of setting up a conservatory, which it implies. In the University's early years, there was an avoidance of departments. We had just four Schools: Humanities, Science, Social Science and Creative Arts. It was only after several years of growth that one spoke of 'the department of X'."

versity, since he has had not only a wide experience at Harvard, but also the experience with more informal classes at The Berkshire Music Center at Tanglewood."

Only one full course in music had been offered at Brandeis during 1949-1950, but the following academic year saw three full courses and three half courses. The highlight of spring 1951 was an extraordinary survey course in contemporary music with lectures by such visiting luminaries as Copland, Roy Harris, William Schuman, Lukas Foss, Marc Blitzstein and René Leibowitz, while that fall Fine and Copland jointly taught a class entitled "The Anatomy of Twentieth Century Music." Largely due to Fine's initiative and connections, music at Brandeis was off to a flying start.

Remembering those early days, Sachar described Fine as "a driven young man—in the sense that Mozart and Schubert were driven." He noted that "the perfectionism that he expected from others was imposed as rigidly upon himself. One would have liked to put up a hand and say, 'Irving, there is plenty of time.' But for Irving there was never enough time—for teaching, composition, performance."

In 1951, Fine helped persuade Bernstein to commute one day a week from New York to lecture on modern music. It was a highly successful course that was, according to Sachar, "anything but a conventional introduction to music appreciation [because] Bernstein's eloquence was phenomenal." Fine said that "when [Bernstein] talked on the modern symphony or on the opera—and incidentally, he would go through it, singing practically all the roles—the hall would be jammed with students enrolled in the course, other students, faculty members, everyone who could possibly squeeze in. It was always a brilliant performance." Naturally, this helped increase enrollment in the Brandeis music division where, said Fine, echoing his old Harvard bugaboo, the ideal was "to maintain a precarious balance between scholarship and performance. You can't talk about music without experiencing it, whether by listening or performance and preferably by performance." He noted in 1955 that the performing arts had traditionally been undervalued at American colleges and universities. "What do you do about such necessary evils as singing, playing, acting, directing? Do you give them academic standing? Do you give them credit? The answer at places like Harvard, Radcliffe, Bryn Mawr, Swarthmore and Princeton has been no." He stressed that "music on paper is merely a blueprint, as is the printed drama. Performance is needed to complete the experience. Music has too often been taught as if the act of musical performance did not exist. Music is something to be made and played [and] in this area at least I am proud to say that Brandeis has taken a position in advance of many of its distinguished sister institutions."

In the University's first years, its campus facilities were minimal. The main building, known as The Castle, was a large, rather hideous Gothic edifice inspired by a medieval Irish castle. It had been built without benefit of architect by Middlesex's founder, Dr. Smith, and came complete with tower and crenelations. The Castle had had to be internally remodeled to provide classrooms, dormitories and a cafeteria. Smith's own residence, a small house of white stone, became Brandeis' administrative center, and the one existing classroom building was transformed into science laboratories and a lecture hall. As the 1950-1951 General Catalogue put it, the campus "presently consists of six major buildings and several smaller units which are connected by wide, curving walks, landscaped areas and vistas of rugged, unbroken foliage."

The tiny music domain got the short end of the Brandeis stick, being initially housed in a woefully substandard structure called The Shed. Harold Shapero remembered that this was "a little curved thing, which I think had been an old barn or gardening hut they plastered up." Richard Wernick noted that "it was shaped like a banana, and it was yellow." After a few years, the music department moved into Roberts Cottage, which, said Wernick, "seemed a palatial mansion by comparison. There actually were rooms for classes." Roberts Cottage was a moderately sized, three-storey clapboard house located slightly off campus, with classrooms on the first floor, offices on the second and a small apartment on the third. For a while in the mid-1950s, some music classes and rehearsals were held in the basement of the new Ullman Amphitheater. Then, in 1956-1957, music education at Brandeis finally came into its own, with the opening of the Slosberg Music and Arts Center, a quarter-of-a-million dollar project, complete with recital hall, faculty offices and studios, classrooms, practice rooms and a library with recording and transcription alcoves.

Fine had fought hard for a music building and thus had a great feeling of accomplishment. He described it as "very pretty," "small but nice and attractive and certainly adequate to our present needs. True, the recital hall is small (250 seats [240, actually] with a provision for overflow into the adjoining art gallery). But the stage area is flexible enough to accommodate a little symphony orchestra or a large chorus or even dance concerts." He praised the auditorium's acoustics, as well as those of the classrooms.

In a speech delivered in 1952, at the time of the first graduation ceremony, Fine had charmingly recalled his initial visit to Brandeis four years earlier, when he discussed "ways in which a modest music program might be introduced" to the University. "I remember very well and with agreeable nostalgia the way the campus looked. It was spring recess and there was nobody to be seen on the grounds. Brandeis seemed particularly attractive to me on that day, coming as I did from the bustle and gasoline fumes of Harvard Square. Not only were there no teachers or students, but there were hardly any buildings to be seen. I was shown around the grounds. We left the administration building, which was then even smaller than it is now, passed by the stable that had been converted into a library, passed a temporary dormitory (still temporary!) on our way to lunch at The Castle. With the exception of the classroom building, Ford Hall, I had virtually completed the tour." When Fine inquired as to where music classes might be given, he was shown "a strange banana-shaped building that had formerly been a kennel. At one end was the campus store, at the other the speech and psychological counseling clinic. It was proposed that music classes and rehearsals be held in the middle." He discovered that the suggested music room had "the most treacherous acoustics, [and was] probably the most resonant chamber I have ever been in. A solitary violin possessing the feeblest of tone sounded like the entire string section of the Boston Symphony Orchestra. A whispering bass crooner sounded like Chaliapin. Two years later when I joined the Brandeis faculty I conducted choral rehearsals in that room. What a sense of power one got: our twenty-voice choir sounded like massed combined choruses of an intercollegiate choral festival."

Fine had managed to postpone his Guggenheim grant

for a year, to 1951-1952. "I rather suspect," he wrote to Copland in February 1951, "that I shall take my Guggenheim at home—unless we sell or rent the house before that time." He was by then the de facto head of the still-minute Brandeis music division. "Brandeis," he continued, "is beginning to take up a great deal of time. Much more teaching and more demands in administrative and promotional schemes." The following month, mentioning that his obligations at Brandeis were "mounting sharply," he declared to Copland: "All we need is money—about a half a million—or at least enough for a classroom, a lecture-rehearsal room and six studios plus some pianos." He added, "Have recommended Shapero for half time job teaching harmony and counterpoint."

This was the beginning of Fine's drive to enlarge gradually the Brandeis music faculty and to fill it with unusually talented, often colorful people, rather than the usual academics. Harold Shapero began teaching in the fall of 1951, and Arthur Berger and Caldwell Titcomb in 1953. Shapero recollected that he had been happy to join the Brandeis faculty, even at a disappointing salary. "It was a peanuts job: take-home pay $2,700, very little even in those days. But I had no experience and didn't deserve anything better." At that point he felt that having to teach rather than to be a successful composer was "a great defeat. Everything shallow, like Lenny Bernstein, made it big. I was discouraged because I obviously wasn't going to make it artistically or financially, so I was thrilled to have the lectureship Irving arranged for me." Looking back, Richard Wernick reflected that "I'm sure Irving brought Harold in because he felt sorry for him, but he kept him around because he turned out to be a first-class teacher. We would sit with a blackboard he had filled with the most incredibly complex counterpoint. I really learned, from him, how to push notes around." A year after Shapero's appointment, Fine had written Bernstein that he "seems to be doing very well in his teaching at Brandeis. His students are both impressed and charmed."[3]

---

3. Part of Shapero's charm was his quirkiness. Wernick remembered, for instance, his unusual ear-training method. "In the 1950s, a lot of people drove convertibles; either that, or they'd park their cars on the campus and leave their windows down. Harold

In 1954, Klaus George Roy would enthuse about Brandeis in the *Christian Science Monitor*: "How remarkable and promising is the fact that the very young Brandeis University at Waltham, Massachusetts has on its music faculty not only [Arthur] Berger but also Harold Shapero, Irving Fine and— by remote control—Leonard Bernstein!"

Fine, of course, had high academic standards and was intolerant of mediocrity. Brandeis was a challenge. Verna Fine remembered that some colleagues "were amazed that Irving was bringing in such superb people, because most administrators would hire those who wouldn't be a threat. Shapero was a wild tiger, but also a genius. Irving welcomed competition. He didn't want to hire dummies. He said, 'I want to work with people I respect, who are even better than I am. That's stimulating'." By 1955, along with himself, Bodky, Shapero, Berger and Titcomb, the faculty list included Leonard Bernstein (in a part-time capacity only), the musicologist Kenneth Levy and the choral conductor Alfred Nash Patterson. An advisory council consisted of Copland and Harvard musicologist Otto Gombosi. Undergraduate and graduate courses were offered in composition, orchestration, harmony, counterpoint, form, music history, analysis and criticism, contemporary music, twentieth-century techniques, thoroughbass improvisation and contemporary lyric theater. "Irving was very driving and ambitious, not all that self-effacing," said Shapero. "In the early days of the Brandeis music department, he used to accuse us, mostly me, by saying, 'You guys aren't helping me out.' I'd reply, 'Okay, then delegate some authority.' But he refused to. He liked being boss." Shapero sometimes teased Fine about that. "He wasn't autocratic. He was a reasonable person, pretty good, pretty kind. He always wore a tie in class, which I hated because I thought it the lowest form of bourgeois conformity. But I was glad to be at Brandeis. It was much more fun than Harvard, especially early on. The music department was a happy family. Irving, Arthur and I were buddies. We had such a wonderful time together." Fine,

---

would give us a middle C in the little banana-building, and we had to remember it. Then he and his class would walk around campus and he'd put his hand into cars, press the horns and ask us to name the different pitches."

he added, "knew all the academic ropes and really liked administrative work. He enjoyed being in charge and had plenty of ego."

During the 1951-1952 academic year, Fine's official title was shortened to Composer in Residence, a part-time position. That was the period of his first Guggenheim grant, under the terms of which he was not allowed to teach, only to compose.[4] He had, however, received permission to conduct choruses at Brandeis and do some administrative work. Upon resuming a full schedule in the fall of 1952, he was appointed Associate Professor of Music, and, the following year, Professor of Music and chairman of the Graduate Division of Musical Composition, with tenure given in 1954.

By all accounts, Fine was not only a superior administrator at Brandeis, but a superior teacher. Sachar thought he showed "genius in transmitting his passion for music. His students loved him because he gave himself to them." Arthur Berger remembered him as "an influential teacher [who] never sought to mold his students into any particular style or into his own image [and who] zealously developed their individuality." Wernick recalled that "sometimes Irving would read through a score at the piano and sometimes he would just look at it. He had a knack for sensing what a young composer was trying to do but wasn't able to accomplish. He would say, well, if you want to get from this point to that, you have several options. This is a way you can do it harmonically, and this is a way you can do it motivically." Fine's intellectual honesty was admired. Aaron Copland wrote that "his students and his fellow composers depended upon him to tell the truth about their music and, in general, about the music of our time," citing the "sureness and rightness of his judgement." He summed up: "To my mind his outstanding quality was his musical sensitivity—he had an ear that one could trust."

Fine's "sunny disposition," noted Sachar, made him "perhaps the most popular faculty man on the campus." One student, Stephen Pruslin, said that his classes "combined rigor with spontaneity [at] no sacrifice of wit and flexibility," estab-

---

4. Fine had not only managed to delay the grant by a year so as to begin his work at Brandeis on a full-time basis, but had been given an increase: from $2,500 to $3,000.

lishing "a discourse that was an uncanny cross between a formal lecture and an intimate conversation. He evinced an intense concern for his students and went far beyond the limits of his academic responsibility." Another student, Richard M. Finder, recalled that the overworked Fine "was sometimes criticized by undergraduates for being cold outside of the confines of the classroom," this because "he usually limited his greetings when passing by his students to a quick nod." Yet "within the classroom and his own office he was gracious and charming, and willing to help a student with any sort of problem—academic, bureaucratic or personal. As an advisor, he brought to people's problems the understanding of a skilled psychologist—intuitively." Milton Babbitt observed that "Irving was very generous to students, and not in any sense decisive. He always gave in to them, would never challenge them, even the nutty ones. He didn't want any student to feel intimidated. Copland would say: 'You're on the wrong track. That's no way to write music.' But Irving was offended that anyone should take that sort of godlike position with a student."

Finder affectionately remembered some of Fine's mannerisms. "He was always terribly busy, and never quite caught up with himself." Arriving at his office, he would toss his hat onto "some handy object" and then "start the first of his uneven chain of cigarettes." On one occasion, Fine was so preoccupied with the day's correspondence that he forgot he was due to teach a class. "It is typical of the esteem in which we all held him that for over an hour not a student of his left the building," said Finder. When Fine eventually realized the time, he rushed off to the waiting class, made a brief apology, opened his capacious briefcase, pulled out several scores, and "plunged immediately into a complex musical analysis." At the end of a class, Fine often would remain to answer questions: "Staying after class was not an unusual practice for him." As for Fine's teaching method, Finder reported that he instructed "with the easy informality of one who explains rather than unveils mysteries. He was always quick to grasp the idea behind a student's composition and the problems encountered in putting the musical idea across. 'Let's see what Haydn [or Mozart, or Beethoven, or Fauré, or Copland, or almost any composer who might have encountered a similar problem] did here,' he would say, and then with consummate keyboard skill, with his students grouped at his back, he would proceed to the fundamental similarities and differences between the student's work and the approach of the Masters together."

Sachar was especially impressed by an incident from Brandeis' early days, when Fine fostered a young man "whose general talents were quite pedestrian" but who seemed to show considerable promise as a composer. "Irving by-passed every conventional admissions rule until he brought the boy in. He encouraged and nourished the still unripened talent and he was prouder than if he had personally completed a symphony when his protégé won a double Fulbright and made a meaningful contribution to the world of music." Fine, said Sachar, "was not a simple character," but he "found real joy in the success of others. He did not dilute by one iota any of his own high standards, but the law of kindness was on his tongue." Jack Gottlieb, who studied composition with Fine, thought him "the real definition of a gentleman. He struck me as a tweedy guy: genial, kind, sweet, soft-spoken." Berger stressed that Fine "was genuinely interested in his students," and that that interest "also extended to his energies as administrator," where his ideals "were always governed by his own high standards as a composer."

Fine's most important Brandeis appointment had come in 1952, when he assumed the position of chairman of the Council of the School of Creative Arts, a post he would hold until the end of his life. This meant that he had authority over not just the music division but also those of fine arts and theater. Berger thought that he was "a dominating person in his career, managing all those things at Brandeis." The School of Creative Arts, he said, was "vastly expanded under his guidance, often threatening his speculations as composer." According to Verna, "Irving's main job at Brandeis was creative administration, planning. He did that very well, although he hadn't known he had the talent for it. That's where he put all of his energies." Fine, said Richard Wernick, "was very well organized. He was absolutely terrific at dealing with people and getting them to do the work."

President Sachar remembered that Fine was "ever worrying over curriculum and faculty, over festival and concert. His calls came through for more pianos, more classrooms, more secretarial assistance, and above all, for more funds to encourage graduate students, for more help to perform the compositions of gifted young people." Fine found persistence to be a necessity. He had no hesitation about bearding the president in his den, banging his fist on his desk and demanding money for a pet project. "That was done as a matter of principle," said Wernick. "Irving had his vision of what the Creative Arts program should be." Sachar himself noted that Fine was "most resourceful in his administrative battles, and when one door closed because of practical difficulties, he came in through another, and when this door also closed, he came in through a window. He usually got what he wanted—rarely for himself, primarily for his colleagues and students." He was a member of "our unofficial cabinet," which "would take lunch informally, not only to discuss problems but to spin dreams."

Fine, however, was no dreamer. He was a practical planner, and his vision of the function of the Brandeis Creative Arts program can be found in two speeches, delivered in 1952 and 1955. In the first, he quoted a maxim: "In the Arts, learning is bound up with doing," and stated that the Creative Arts faculty believed in it "profoundly." In the second, he declared that "we wish our students to have a liberal education, but we should also like to avoid the pitfalls of scholarly dilettantism." He noted that, in the music program, "undoubtedly our curriculum bears some resemblance to the one I helped set up ten years ago at Harvard, but the spirit is substantially different by virtue of the Koussevitzky/Tanglewood overtones." A university music department, he said, must not only teach appreciation, history and composition, but must realize that "not all music was written by dead composers" and that "even the music of dead composers could only come alive in performance." He continued: "Performance by students must be stimulated by the presence of a performing faculty; and if we wish to stimulate musical creativity, we must also give the creators a chance to hear their music." With some satisfaction, Fine observed that in the first few years of the School of Creative Arts, "our progress has been remarkable."

In a 1954 letter to Fine, Sachar warmly acknowledged that progress. "You loom large in the pioneering of our curriculum and in the development of the School of Creative Arts, which has now a very honored place in the American academic scene. It ought to be a matter of great pride to you as the first Chairman of the School to note how strongly anchored it has become. You laid the foundations, and what the School will ultimately become will be permanently influenced by these early years."

Fine had strong opinions on the role of liberal arts education. At a 1954 Brandeis forum, he noted acidly that in America as in England "the arts have always been considered synonymous with the social graces, more specifically the feminine social graces. Art education was a kind of conspiracy directed at maintaining a chivalric ideal of the woman and at the same time dramatizing the intellectual and cultural differences between the sexes." Consequently, art education "has continued to be considered as peripheral, feminine, frivolous, non-essential, and in general unworthy of consideration beside the more austere mental discipline traditionally found in an academic institution." But, he argued, "at the highest level, art has value in that it makes us continuously aware of the *ideal of perfection* [Fine's italics] and the possibility of perfection in man-made things." The most perfect art works "confront us with that higher order and introduce us into a realm of perfected forms. I have had the feeling in listening to the purest works of music (a symphony of Mozart or an opera such as *Così fan tutte*, or a late Beethoven quartet or the *Symphony of Psalms* of Stravinsky) of a kind of an idealization of a previously existing harmony." Fine felt that if students had "continued contact with quality and with perfection at that level" they were bound to be ennobled, and would rise "into an area above that of vulgar individuality." The arts, he declared provocatively, "are a weapon against the Russian and American enthronement of mediocrity—the product of commercial advertising in America and of political and cultural mass propaganda in Russia."

Caldwell Titcomb stressed that, as the chairman of the School of Creative Arts, Fine "did an enormous amount of work and made tremendous decisions at Brandeis. But although he handled positions of terrific authority, he had a great sense of humor and was not at all a forbidding person." Of necessity, much of Fine's time had to be spent overseeing the workings of the three Creative Arts departments, but he still managed to conduct composition seminars. Sachar thought him "the ideal teacher," because "he helped to mold talent and then worked hard to place it, to gain hearings for it, to link it with opportunity and position. I trusted implicitly his judgement in the creative arts. He was fair. He was sensitive. He was balanced." Fine's standards, he said, were "impeccable."

Those standards were never more apparent than in the four Festivals of Creative Arts presented by Brandeis University between 1952 and 1957. Because of the strong support of President Sachar and the élan and intellectual vigor of Fine and some of the brilliant pedagogues he had assembled, Brandeis had quickly developed into an innovative institution vis-à-vis the arts. The festivals emphasized that fact in a grand manner and provided Brandeis with an abundance of welcome publicity. Insofar as was known, no other American university had ever sponsored such ambitious celebrations of the arts.

According to Verna Fine, the first festival was the brainchild of her husband and Copland. "After Koussevitzky died in 1951, Irving and Aaron got the idea of putting on a festival at Brandeis in June 1952 as a Koussevitzky memorial, one that would also honor the initial graduating class."[5] Both men thought their friend Leonard Bernstein, by then a renowned conductor, the ideal choice to direct the festival, and they found him willing to take on the job. Sachar, who constantly sought ways to publicize Brandeis so as to raise money for its improvement and expansion, was delighted. As he wrote, "Bernstein's presence made it possible to plan creative arts festivals on a most ambitious scale." Jack Gottlieb noted that "those were wonderful festivals, and Bernstein was the celebrity brought in to give them panache."

The 1952 Creative Arts Festival, designed by Bernstein in consultation with Fine and Clarence Q. Berger, Sachar's executive assistant, was impressive. Bernstein was billed as director, Fine as "University Advisor to Mr. Bernstein." From June 12 to 15, there were six events—as an advertisement put it, in "Opera, Art, Jazz, Poetry, Concerts, Ballet," omitting scheduled film screenings and a film symposium.

A portentous statement by Bernstein in his best rabbinic

---

5. Mrs. Franklin D. Roosevelt delivered the first commencement address, June 16, 1952.

mode opened the program book. "This is a moment of inquiry for the whole world: a moment when civilization looks at itself appraisingly, seeking a key to the future. In this spirit we shall examine the creative arts during our four-day Festival—examine them by performance, by asking questions, by the answers we receive. We cannot pretend to wisdom; but through performance we can provoke thought and free discussion; through discussing we can learn; and through learning we can rediscover our culture and ourselves." "It was Lenny's show," Harold Shapero reflected half a century later, noting that because of the festivals and Bernstein's occasional classes and seminars, "to this day the Jewish community thinks he founded the Brandeis music department."[6]

The festival events were quite splendid. On Thursday, June 12, the evening began with a symposium entitled "An Inquiry into the Present State of Creative Arts." Bernstein was the moderator and the panel consisted of experts on writing, art, theater music, jazz and dance. This was followed by the world premiere of Bernstein's "little opera in seven scenes," *Trouble in Tahiti*, finished just in time for the occasion and conducted by the composer. The next day was devoted to discussions and screenings of five art films, along with a jazz symposium and concert with such famed performers as Miles Davis, John Lewis and Max Roach, among others.

---

6. Verna Fine claimed that the idea that Bernstein founded the music department was started "by the Brandeis public relations department, in a coffee-table book about the story of the university. It's such a horrible lie. Irving founded all three departments [of the School of Creative Arts] and built them up." In December 1990 and March 1991, she wrote letters to the editors of two Brandeis publications, attempting to set the record straight. Bernstein, she said, "taught only in the two academic years of 1952-53 and 1953-54, coming up sporadically about one day a week." Further, he "came to Brandeis University in June 1952 to direct the first Festival [, but] he never had any direct involvement in designing or shaping the arts program (music, theater, fine arts) at the University. It has always been my late husband (until recently) who was credited with the building of the three departments of the School of Creative Arts from scratch." She concluded: "It is really sad that a young university like Brandeis feels impelled to alter its short history." Both letters went unanswered.

Saturday afternoon saw poetry readings by Karl Shapiro, Peter Viereck and William Carlos Williams. Afterward, there was a remarkable evening of theater, combining elements of music, dance and opera. Excerpts from the *Symphonie pour un Homme Seul* by the Frenchman Pierre Schaeffer were played on tape, accompanied by dancers choreographed by Merce Cunningham (which, thought Bernstein, would render the avant-garde offering more acceptable to the public), advertised as the first presentation of *musique concrète* in the United States.[7] Next was a danced performance of Stravinsky's choral ballet *Les Noces*, again with choreography by Cunningham, the singers (among them Phyllis Curtin and Eunice Alberts), chorus, pianists and percussionists conducted by Bernstein.[8] After intermission came the first concert performance of Marc Blitzstein's English adaptation of Kurt Weill's 1920s hit, *The Threepenny Opera*, in its original chamber-orchestra version, with the composer's widow Lotte Lenya in the role of Jenny, Blitzstein narrating and Bernstein conducting.

Three events on Sunday, June 15 closed this initial Brandeis festival. In the afternoon, Bernstein conducted a string orchestra comprised of members of the Boston Symphony in a concert dedicated to the memory of Koussevitzky, with a spoken introduction by Copland. This program, which constituted the festival's climax, contained works by four American composers (all of them Jews) and one British: William Schuman's *Symphony No. 5* (listed as *Symphony for Strings*), the premiere of Ben Weber's *Two Pieces for String Orchestra*, Benjamin Britten's *Serenade for Tenor, Horn and Strings*, Fine's *Notturno for Strings and Harp* and the first Boston-area performance of Copland's *Clarinet Concerto*.[9] That night

---

7. The unusual offering had been entirely arranged by Fine, who met Schaeffer in 1950 during Fine's stay in Paris. On November 30, 1951, when the festival was still in the planning stage, Fine had written to Bernstein: "It would be nice, as a stunt and for its shock value, to have some short work of Musique Concrète."

8. Bernstein had asked Fine to be one of the four pianists in *Les Noces* but Fine had refused.

9. The previous December a Brandeis faculty committee had offered repertory suggestions for this concert: Leon Kirchner's

there was a film symposium and then a closing forum on the arts, with the same panel of experts from the first evening, Bernstein again serving as moderator (and foolishly announcing that the concert hall was very likely a thing of the past).

The newspapers had near-universal praise for the festival's inventive programming and excellent performances, although some reservations were expressed about aspects of the format. For one thing, it was felt there had been too much talk. In an overall favorable review of the festival, Arthur Berger, then a critic for the *New York Herald Tribune*, wrote that "in an attempt, perhaps, to make the programs of music, opera and ballet more worthy of academic auspices, they were heavily interlarded with panels on art and 'discussants' who replaced printed program notes. This was a pity [because] talk rarely mixes well with music." He noted that an audience of 3,100 people had to wait until 11:00 p.m. for the beginning of Bernstein's opera because of an extended preliminary symposium.[10] "Is discussion to dwarf the music?" he asked. He also called attention to acoustical problems inherent in Brandeis' outdoor amphitheater and criticized Bernstein's planning as being plagued by "indecision and over-ambition." And Berger did not fail to cite the most glaring lapse in a creative arts project: no new works had been commissioned.

The *Christian Science Monitor* termed the festival "a conspicuous success [with] much of the unusual, much of the significant." The *musique concrète* offering "did not leave the audience tearing its hair, as had been humorously predicted [and] was absorbingly interesting and occasionally funny." Weill's *Threepenny Opera* had "a captivating performance" and Fine's *Notturno* was "a gem of subdued emotion and clarity of statement." The *New York Times* noted "a vivid per-

---

recent *Sinfonia*, Shostakovich's *Piano Concerto No. 1* (with Bernstein in the dual role of soloist and conductor), Britten's *Serenade*, Copland's *Clarinet Concerto* (with Benny Goodman; the actual soloist would be David Oppenheim), Harold Shapero's *Serenade for Strings* and an unspecified piece by Lou Harrison. Bernstein, however, had the final decision on programming.

10. Richard Wernick remembered that the opera was also delayed because of loud hammering from another area of the then-incomplete building.

formance" of the Weill, described Fine's piece as "deeply felt and sensitively wrought" and denounced the *musique concrète* as "an unmitigated bore."

In retrospect Sachar could state that the consensus of the country's leading critics was that "Brandeis had given enduring significance to its first commencement." As one of them put it, "Not in our time, in this part of the country, had there been any such comprehensive and knowing attempt to appraise and stimulate the arts in America."

A week after the festivities ended, Bernstein wrote to Fine from Tanglewood. "Darling Oiving: How to thank you for all you've done and meant to the Brandeis Festival? It seems rather odd for me to thank *you*, since, in a way, I have been your employee in this thing: but I am impelled to anyway: for your taste and your enthusiasm and your love of art and your joyful person—and for getting me into it to begin with. . . . Thanks from the bottom of my heart."

The scope of the second Creative Arts Festival, in June 1953, was somewhat less ambitious. Once again, Bernstein directed, with Fine in advisory capacity. But that year's subject was lighter. In October 1952, Bernstein had written to Fine, "Your idea of 'Classicism and the Comic Spirit' appeals to me, but, God, under another title. That one would scare any audience away except an academic one." He noted that the previous festival had made clear "that we are not living in experimental times: that our times are cautious in the extreme: that we are not producing real tragedy." Real satire was not apparent either: "the caution prevents it." Bernstein felt that the concepts of Good and Evil still had validity in art works, "but since our time doesn't major in this field, let's be amusing, or pretty, or diverting. That is, I think, a theme."

So it was that the 1953 festival, the last in which Bernstein would participate, came to be dedicated to "The Comic Spirit." Bernstein again provided a printed introduction, this one with the title ". . . And a Time to Laugh," its tone less ostentatious than before but still basking in the shadow of the Cold War. "I sometimes think that Man's capacity for laughter is nobler than his divine gift of suffering. Laughing cleanses a man: it restores his sanity, and balances his sense of values. Now in a time of caution and fear, in an atmosphere turgid with non-direction and non-expressivity, let us laugh and let laugh, lighten the air we breathe, and feel clean."

Perhaps inevitably considering its theme, this festival emphasized theater, poetry and film over music. At least one of its events, an academic symposium on "the cultural significance and artistic qualities" of the American comic strip, with Al Capp (creator of "Li'l Abner") and Milton Caniff ("Steve Canyon"), flirted with pretentious absurdity. In addition, there were readings of comic poetry (with Ludwig Lewisohn, Louis Untermeyer and Fine's friend David McCord, among others), a lecture on "Classic Comic Film Sequences" followed by a screening (including Charlie Chaplin, Harold Lloyd, Robert Benchley, Walt Disney, W. C. Fields, the Marx Brothers, Myrna Loy, William Powell and Buster Keaton) and an art exhibit, "Three Centuries of the Comic Spirit," with more than 100 paintings, sculptures, drawings, prints and posters by Tiepolo, Toulouse-Lautrec, Daumier, Alexander Calder, Ben Shahn, Saul Steinberg and Fernand Leger, to name a few.

The principal events, however, were in theater and opera. Louis Kronenberger's play *The International Set* had its first performance, directed by Eric Bentley with a cast including Ian Keith, Mildred Dunnock and Felicia Montealegre, Bernstein's wife. A symposium entitled "A Survey of Comic Techniques," moderated by Fred Allen and S. J. Perelman, prefaced a staged student production of Pergolesi's little eighteenth-century opera buffa *La Serva Padrona* (The Maid as a Mistress), with Erwin Bodky at the harpsichord and an orchestra conducted by Fine (who was listed as "Musical Director"). On the festival's final evening a program of dance and opera was presented, beginning with Morton Gould's populist *Concerto for Tap Dancer and Orchestra*, danced by Danny Daniels with members of the Boston Symphony and Boston Pops Orchestra conducted by Bernstein. Then came the musical highlight of the 1953 Creative Arts Festival: the American premiere of Francis Poulenc's controversial transsexual comic opera *Les Mamelles de Tirésias* (The Breasts of Tiresias), to a libretto by Guillaume Apollinaire. This was performed by New York's Lemonade Opera Company, with a cast that included James McCracken and Phyllis Curtin, the orchestra under Bernstein.

Despite the obvious merits of this second festival, once

again there was a plethora of the besetting sin of academia: talk. And once again nothing was commissioned. Bernstein had raised the subject in an October 1952 letter to Fine— "Let's not forget to commission; and let's do it soon, so as to have the work on time"—but the idea evaporated. Odd that, because Bernstein was then becoming a champion of new music, particularly by American composers; and Fine was always on the lookout for young talent and interested in the recent efforts of his colleagues. Perhaps a commissioning project had been vetoed by Brandeis' president, although it is not clear he was ever consulted.

In 1954, the festival, originally conceived as an annual event, was postponed until the following year. The reason: the campus entrance had been blocked by a road-building project.

Fine was the moving force behind the themeless 1955 festival, which he described to Copland as "an artistic success and a financial flop," despite the fact that an opera-ballet event had sold out. "We had bad luck with the weather," he said. "It was rainy and/or cold and we didn't have Bernstein as a drawing card." A Koussevitzky protégé, Izler Solomon, was this year's director and conductor. Fine had arranged to present several works of his friend Darius Milhaud (whom he considered "one of the great Jewish composers"), and to bring the Frenchman to Brandeis for an honorary degree that he had sponsored. "Milhaud turned out to be the star of the festival, which was no more than fitting" and he "was thoroughly delighted with everything." It proved to be "a kind of Milhaud festival." Works performed included the *Cantate Nuptiale*, in its U.S. premiere with Adele Addison as soloist, the percussion concerto (both with Milhaud conducting), the "sung ballet" *Salade* (seven singers, eight principal dancers) and the opera *Médée* (Medea). "Not a clinker in the four and all designed to show Milhaud at his best and in all his variety," was Fine's assessment. Reviews were laudatory, especially in the *New York Times* (the opera had a "strong dramatic impulse" and Phyllis Curtin sang "superbly" in the title role; the ballet "bubbled with frivolity") and the *Boston Globe*. Other orchestral music heard was Hindemith's *Concerto for Woodwinds, Harp and Orchestra*, the U.S. premiere of Michael Tippett's *Divertimento on Sellinger's Round* (which score Fine appraised as "interesting but not quite there"), Arthur Berger's

172

*Serenade Concertante* and Mozart's *"Haffner" Serenade.* An afternoon concert featured works by four Brandeis students: Halim El-Dabh, Jack Gottlieb, Mary Sadovnikoff and Charles Jones. A lavish production of a previously unperformed play by Maurice Valency, *The Thracian Horses* (with incidental music by Richard Wernick), consumed "so much money that we seem to have jeopardized the future of the Festival (chiefly because of the stage people)." Fine concluded: "It's a bloody shame the money and effort [that] gets blown away on single performances."

The fourth Brandeis Creative Arts Festival, in 1957, was, according to President Sachar, "dedicated to an appraisal of six art forms—chamber music, dance, jazz, poetry, orchestral and *operative* [Sachar's italics; obviously, the adjective should be operatic] music, and the fine arts," and "represented a kind of climax." Arthur Berger had charge of music programming and casting of singers. There was an extensive art exhibit and a symposium on poetry led by Richard Wilbur and Robert Lowell. And, at long last, Brandeis had given commissions: six new works from, said the *New York Times,* "jazz and long-hair composers." The review's headline was "Brandeis Rocks to Beat of Jazz Played at Fete of Creative Arts." Milton Babbitt contributed a twelve-tone jazz piece titled *All Set.* The *Times* critic thought Gunther Schuller's *Transformation* "the tautest and most authoritative" of all the new scores, "and the one that blended the idioms most convincingly." Harold Shapero's *On Green Mountain,* the title a pun on the name Monteverdi, was "an attractive arrangement of one of that composer's chaconnes that managed to preserve its baroque character and yet sound quite deliriously impudent with its jazz instrumentation." Charles Mingus' *Revelations,* although it "reached furthest into concert music," seemed "the least successful piece in finding a convincing middle ground." *All About Rosie* by George Russell "was exhilarating in its swift sections," and *Suspensions* by Jimmy Giuffre was "the most original in sound of all the works." The unusual event ended with Duke Ellington's *Reminiscing in Tempo* from 1935, and "for many it was the real hit of the evening."

At a chamber music concert, Fine's 1956 *Fantasia for String Trio* (played by members of the Juilliard Quartet) and Berger's recent *Duo for Clarinet and Piano* had their New

England premieres. On the festival's last night, Copland (for whom, like Milhaud, Fine had arranged an honorary degree) conducted a concert of his own works, consisting of the jazz-inspired *Music for the Theatre*, the ballet suite *Appalachian Spring* and excerpts from the Americana opera *The Tender Land*.

Decades later, referring to the Brandeis School of Creative Arts' diligence and stimulating festivals, Sachar would proudly write: "The momentum of the early exciting years never slackened."

# Chapter 13

■ NINETEEN FIFTY-ONE HAD BEGUN WITH FINE reviving his
pianistic skills for a concert at Brandeis with a young Israeli
violinist, Zvi Zeitlin, on February 25. He accompanied his
own violin sonata, Mozart's *Sonata in G Major*, K. 301 and
Stravinsky's *Duo Concertant*. A few months later, at Tanglewood, he appeared with the Boston Symphony under Charles
Munch as one of the pianists in two Bach concertos for three
keyboards and strings: the *Concerto in C Major* on July 7 and
the *Concerto in D Minor* on the eighth. A photograph published in the *Christian Science Monitor* on July 10, shows
Munch and his pianists (Fine, Ralph Berkowitz, Bernard
Zighera) in rehearsal. Fine, elegant in a bow tie and white
sport-jacket, is bent over the keyboard, immersed in the
music. According to the newspaper's critic, the trio "gave a
performance marked by clarity, control and musicianship."
The following month, on August 10, two Fine works were
heard at a Tanglewood student concert: the *Alice in Wonderland Suite* for chorus and orchestra, with the Department I
orchestra conducted by Robert Mandell; and four selections
from *The Hour Glass*, sung by the chorus of Department II
under four student conductors.

That year, for Fine, Tanglewood almost didn't happen.
On February 15 he wrote angrily to Copland: "Am having
salary difficulties with that frozen volcano, that bastard of an
evil spirit, George E. Judd."[1] Fine had asked for extra money
for extra work (assisting in a music teachers' program and taking over some of Leonard Bernstein's analysis classes for conductors, all at the request of Koussevitzky), but "so far, no
dice. If he [Judd] persists, I am afraid I shall have to give up
the idea of Tanglewood this year and begin the Guggenheim
in June instead."[2] Then, five days later: "Brace yourself for this

---

1. Judd was the manager of the Boston Symphony.
2. Fine had recently told Copland: "I once remembered your

one. I am afraid that the Berkshire Music Center and I have come to the parting of the ways." Tanglewood officials had refused compensation for the expanded work load. "I have turned the offer down," said Fine. "I feel badly about the business but I couldn't have done it any other way." He noted that he would miss his personal associations at Tanglewood, especially with Koussevitzky and Copland, "but I refuse to allow those feelings to be exploited." On March 1, an alarmed Copland replied from Rome: "Your 'brace-yourself' letter naturally put me into a state. Try as I may, I find it hard to believe, at any rate, until Kouss is heard from. So I'm sitting on pins, until he *is* heard from. In the end, *some* compromise solution must be found." Evidently Koussevitzky intervened on Fine's behalf and the problem was resolved, for at the beginning of April Copland would write: "I'm enormously relieved. Couldn't get my mind to accommodate itself to any other outcome."

It was the last thing Koussevitzky did for Fine. On June 4, while on vacation in Arizona after exhausting concerts in Israel, he suddenly died. When Copland heard the shocking news, he wrote Fine from Rome: "At this distance it seemed unreal and impossible. I felt sorry that neither Lenny, nor Lukas, nor I myself were around at the end. Poor Irving—I suppose you got the full brunt."

Verna once described Koussevitzky as a father-figure for her husband, so Fine's grief at his death can be imagined. She remembered that the two men were always on affectionate terms. Koussevitzky would call Fine "mein son," and tell him: "Some day I vant to play your music with music of Vincent D'Indy, and then ve vill have a concert that is Fine and Dandy." Smiling, he would poke his protégé's shoulder and declare: "That's a joke, son!" But if there was to be no "fine-and-dandy" concert, the conductor had, after all, grandly launched Fine's career with his performances of the *Toccata Concertante* with the Boston Symphony. Verna recalled that "Koussevitzky always said, 'My name is going to last as a promoter of new music, nothing else. And that's what I *vant* to be known for'." At Koussevitzky's funeral, Fine served as an

---

saying that you were still trying to find out how to say 'no' to Koussy after twenty-five years. I have given up in ten."

usher, along with Nicolai Berezowsky, Arthur Fiedler, Randall Thompson and G. Wallace Woodworth. The church service for this former member of the Jewish faith, at Boston's Church of the Advent, was unusual: a combination Russian Orthodox and Episcopalian ceremony. The honorary pall-bearers included four composers championed by Koussevitzky: Leonard Bernstein, Walter Piston, William Schuman and Howard Hanson (Copland, conspicuous by his absence, was still in Italy).

In addition to his teaching duties at Brandeis during the first months of 1951, Fine gave a lecture at the Philadelphia Art Alliance Auditorium on May 14, "New Trends in French Music," a subject on which he had become expert, and participated in a Brandeis education forum on June 18. On the twenty-third, at a gala event called "Brandeis University Night," he conducted the student orchestra in a performance of Mendelssohn's *Capriccio Brilliant*, with Erwin Bodky as piano soloist.

That summer, on commission from Boosey and Hawkes, he began arranging for chorus Set I of Copland's *Old American Songs*, originally for solo voice and piano. This version would not be completed until 1952. Copland had never felt entirely comfortable with choral writing, and when asked by the author in a 1986 interview why he had recommended Fine for the project, he replied: "I thought it would be a good idea. After all, Irving often conducted choruses, and he felt more at ease in that area than I did." (In 1954, Fine also arranged the last song of Set II, "Ching-a-ring Chaw," and Copland wrote him: "What a pleasant surprise to receive the Ching arr. They [?] look ducky. How do you think up all those things?") According to Verna, Copland insisted on Fine's having two percent of his ten percent royalty for the *Old American Songs*, a far better deal than the standard flat fee given for arrangements.

A considerably more important commission had come in June, from the Rodgers and Hammerstein Foundation through the League of Composers, specifying "a major work." There is, however, no evidence that Fine set about complying with it until well into the following year. Two years before, in May 1949, he had been given a $500 commission for "preferably a string quartet" by the Koussevitzky Foundation. He had worked sporadically at it ever since. In February 1951 he informed Copland that he was suffering "creative constipation." Nonetheless, he had "inflicted" a portion of his quartet on Harold Shapero "and he seemed to be impressed." This was at the time when Fine was putting finishing touches on the *Notturno*, and it proved a false start. On March 26 Fine told Copland: "The Quartet is still-born. Kouss says to give it up, but I keep coming back to it. Your suggestion that the transition from the first and second themes in the first movement was too short led me to scrap all but the first two pages. But I have no regrets; sometime I may save the piece."[3]

During the 1951-1952 academic year, Copland delivered the prestigious Charles Eliot Norton Lectures at Harvard University. At the end of November, a delighted Fine wrote to Bernstein: "Aaron's lectures have been triumphantly successful. I now know what you meant when you said he was an intellectual. He makes all academic musicians seem like pigmies by comparison."

Nineteen fifty-one ended musically for Fine with a Brandeis student-and-faculty recital on December 15. He conducted the University Glee Club in works by Heinrich Schütz, Britten and Schuman, among others, and accompanied on the piano two student violinists in Bach's *Concerto in D Minor* for two violins, strings and continuo. On the same program, he and Shapero performed Mozart's *Sonata in B-flat Major* for piano, four hands.

The next year began with a family vacation in Miami Beach, followed by a performance of Fine's *Music for Piano* at Boston's Gardner Museum, by the brilliant young pianist Seymour Lipkin, on January 27. In early March, Fine himself played the work at another Boston museum, the Museum of Fine Arts. On the same program he and Shapero joined forces again in the latter's four-hand sonata, and Shapero performed his own *Piano Sonata No. 1* and Stravinsky's *Ragtime*. But the big event of that month for the Fines was the birth of their second child, Emily Alison, in Boston on March 11.

During this period, Fine worked diligently at his Koussevitzky-commissioned string quartet. He had begun it the

---

3. He never did. The music exists only as forty-two pages of pencil score, labeled "Old quartet sketches."

previous September and would finish it, except for revisions, in May 1952. In November he told Copland, "What [notes] I have, I sometimes like and sometimes detest," and much later Copland would write that, at that time, "characteristically, Irving was mulling over his notes."

Probably inspired by the example of Copland's masterly *Piano Quartet* (1949-1950), which is based on an eleven-note row and which he had heard at its New York premiere in November 1950, Fine was now involved with dodecaphonic, or twelve-tone, technique.[4] Verna remembered that "when he was working on this piece he had a [row] chart on the piano for about four or five months." The chart contains the standard forty-eight variants of Fine's row, in transposition, inversion, retrograde and retrograde inversion, carefully notated. Here, Fine had a system which could almost automatically generate material. As the British composer Alan Rawsthorne once noted: "A serialist has forty-eight ways he can handle his tone row; he can put them down on a piece of paper to keep him on the rails. Less fortunate people can't do that."

Serialism, as defined by Arnold Schoenberg, the system's inventor, is a "method of composing with twelve notes which are related only to one another," all notes of the octave being treated as equal. It is a method that, in its most rigorously applied form, avoids tonality and had been originally developed as a criterion for atonal music. Copland's *Piano Quartet*, however, postulated unequivocal tonal centers and was at the same time imbued with a compelling lyricism. Fine seems to have wished to emulate his friend's example rather than the more forbidding Teutonic rhetoric of Schoenberg. (As an aside Verna mentioned that "we never knew Schoenberg, who lived on the West Coast. We had heard unpleasant things about him from Aaron Copland. But Irving used to play Schoenberg on the piano, especially in the 1950s.") Inevitably, even a loose application of twelve-tone principles would result in a more chromatic, more dissonant music than before.

Fine told his wife on several occasions: "I can't follow

---

4. According to Milton Babbitt, "Irving was hurt by the notion that people thought he began writing twelve-tone music because of Stravinsky, when the fact is he did it before Stravinsky."

any strict rules. Whatever they are, I'm going to break them. Music must *sound*. The most important thing is what you *hear*. The ear is the ultimate arbiter." "Right from the start," she said, "he cheated."

Indeed, it turned out that Fine's serialism had little to do with Schoenberg's, for he ignored Schoenberg's rules about the avoidance of note repetition and doubling at the octave and, like Copland (and, later, Stravinsky, Dallapiccola and Frank Martin, among others), wrote music that demonstrated an easily heard rapport with the traditional major-minor key system. The tone-row which Fine devised is, however, rather different from Copland's, which is smooth and lyric and partly founded on whole-tone progression. Fine's is more jagged, subtly suggesting the tonality of C major-minor. It is used, during much of his quartet, in a more fragmented manner, although it has triadic implications and is capable of evolving into functional melody. As notated in his chart, the row is: C, F-sharp, A, F-natural, B-flat, A-flat, B-natural, E, G, E-flat, C-sharp, D.

In a program note, Fine stated that the *String Quartet* "is the first work in which I have employed the twelve-tone technique with some consistency. While all of the melodic material, the harmonies, and the figuration have been generated by the 'row,' the use of the 'row' technique is fairly free; and the work as a whole is frankly tonal, C being the prevailing tonality."

Copland's adoption, in a few works only, of serial technique was provoked by simple boredom with traditional harmony. "I've run out of chords! I need new chords!" he used to exclaim.[5] Fine's interest in serialism was more complex and far-reaching. Boredom, yes, but boredom with a too-derivative neoclassic style. New, more interesting chords were only a part of the reason for his conversion to twelve-tone ways. Verna recalled his worrying in the early 1950s that he hadn't

---

5. Milton Babbitt remembered Fine's joking about Copland and serialism. "Irving mentioned that Aaron had once said that twelve-tone is mechanistic and mathematical; but then Aaron stated in a public interview that, with it, he could find new chords. Irving laughed and said, 'Well, since Aaron had gone to a Boulangerie, where chords were sliced, packaged and labeled, what do you expect?'"

produced any "important" music. Clearly, by late 1951, his former exuberant neoclassicism not only had lost its allure but had become a straitjacket. Fine's *String Quartet*, his most ambitious chamber work, was his first attempt at style expansion by means of a new technique.

The twelve-tone system, though it can be elastic and invigorating in the right hands (Stravinsky's and Copland's, for example), is a potentially deadly procedure, at its worst productive of mechanical, academic writing replete with mathematically calculated pitch-sets that have little if anything to do with musical expression. (Rawsthorne also warned that "distortion is a process common to all art. This is impossible in serial music, which is tautological.") Fine, who was, after all, an extremely "musical" composer, certainly knew the pitfalls. Although more methodology is apparent in the quartet than in his subsequent serially inflected scores, and the music is perhaps less tonally focused, Fine's overall approach to serialism was never to be doctrinaire. Rather, he utilized it in conjunction with a tightly controlled romanticism. As Howard Pollack wrote, "the idea of achieving melodic and harmonic unity through a predetermined arrangement of the chromatic scale was quite consistent with Fine's general principles."

In a 1960 letter to Vincent Persichetti, Fine admitted that in his *String Quartet* he "often use[d] serial techniques in a fairly consistent way though far removed from Schoenberg, Webern and post-Webern practices." He added: "I am often apt to use new series derived from the basic row by the use of alternates (1,3,5,7,9,11,2,4,6,8, etc., or 1,4,7, etc.). In the Quartet I occasionally use chords derived from the series and embellished in various parts with some row derivation."

If his twelve-tone music occasionally approached austerity, as in portions of the quartet,[6] it never veered into Webernesque abstraction as did Stravinsky's in his *Movements for Piano and Orchestra* and *Requiem Canticles*; nor did it become as chromatic as Copland's late orchestral pieces, *Connotations* and *Inscape*. Richard Wernick has perceptively noted that "the

---

6. Introducing her husband's *String Quartet* in San Francisco in 1994, Verna Fine termed the music "quite austere," and warned the audience: "I tell you, you will not go out whistling the tunes."

so-called twelve-tone works of Stravinsky, Copland and Fine are where their music sounds the least similar." The fact is, the intellects and temperaments of the three men were quite different, and of them Fine was by far the most inclined to romantic expression. "I think," said Wernick, "that Irving found the idea of generating harmony from the bass line, the main principle of Western tonality, could be accomplished within a loosely and musically applied twelve-tone technique. He understood that within the framework of serial writing you could nevertheless have a functional harmony that produces tension and relief of tension. We frequently talked about the capacity of the ear to be constantly fooled."

One of the most noteworthy aspects of the *String Quartet* in comparison to previous Fine scores is its broader emotional palette, which takes on expressionistic overtones in the brooding moments of the second movement ("undeniably morbid at times" was the composer's appraisal). But, romantic as the rhetoric may be in this piece, the neoclassic aesthetic is still present, especially in the agitated first movement, evidenced by the careful manner in which motives and phrases are constructed, the striking rhythmic energy,[7] the melody-cell repetition, the reiterations of a single pitch and the predilection for ostinato-like patterns. Additionally, the pronounced contrapuntal element, the formal balance and the clear instrumental textures within a dissonant framework all hark back to the work of Fine's fastidious neoclassicist teacher, Walter Piston. Wernick thought the quartet intriguing "because, compositionally, it is full of experiments using twelve-tone regulated pitch, but then it will back off from them with what would be considered, in context of a lesser composer, a trite cliché: repeated notes or Classically derived stackings of sonorities, more by thirds than fourths." Milton Babbitt, a foremost exponent of rigorous serialism, noted that "in Fine's quartet, the twelve-tone aspect is on the surface a great deal." Nonetheless: "I think of that piece as being, above all, elegant, like all of his music." An assessment Fine once made of Roger Sessions' music, that in it "intellectuality coex-

---

7. This aspect represents a further distancing from Schoenbergian serialism, for, as Virgil Thomson once noted, rhythm is the weakest factor in that style.

ists with extraordinary intensity of emotion," could equally apply to his own quartet.

Fine's *String Quartet* is cast, unusually for the medium, in only two movements. The turmoil à la Bartók of the first movement's outer sections encloses a slow chordal central part embellished with arresting recitative passages. The second movement, constructed contrarily as slow-fast-slow, features intensely melancholic lyricism. This is reflected through instrumental discourses with sustained, near-mesmeric melody set against ruminative cello *pizzicati* that are contrasted with dissonant eruptions. Embedded in the center is a tiny driving scherzo that seems almost like a separate movement, but that soon gives way to the closing section: dark-hued, musing rhetoric founded partly on implacable treadlike motion, followed by repeated viola unisons, at the point of the bow, that bring the work to an emotionally chilly end.

Fine himself gave a capsule description of his *String Quartet*. "The work is approximately nineteen minutes in duration and consists of two movements (*Allegro risoluto* and *Lento*), each of which is essentially tripartite in form. The first movement's fast exposition and recapitulation are separated by a quieter contrasting middle section. In the second movement, the outer sections are slow and the middle section more agitated."

The above is a remarkably modest and inadequate account of one of the most impressive string quartets by an American composer—unquestionably, "important" music. It is truly, as one critic wrote, "a substantial contribution to string literature." Fine's quartet is a score that not only illustrates his lifelong attachment to romantic expression but also displays high seriousness in a quite personal application of serial technique. For twelve-tone derived music, the rhetoric is amazingly direct and thus readily comprehensible. Still, this is a work filled with subtle details, and they tend to emerge only with repeated hearings.

The only extant correspondence from Fine regarding the *String Quartet* is to his wife in June and July 1952, when he was at the MacDowell Colony revising and copying the piece. Some extracts: "In copying the last pages of the 1st movement of the quartet I have run into some trouble with the revision of those passages which never pleased you or me. Everything is now cleared up tonight except the last tune in the cello, which you hate but which I find less offensive." "Spent the whole day on the quartet. Will it ever be done? I've finally copied the whole first movement after making the changes that I mentioned. As usual these were agonizing to do—they're still not ideal—but it's the best I can do at this time." "The slow movement has so many black notes my eyes are beginning to suffer." "The damned nuances and bowings etc. are a pain in the ass. I change my mind about them every day." "Have been driving myself to finish revision and copying of quartet. It is now all done—52 pages of score—and I am so fatigued with it that I have no real sense of what the minor changes are like. In any event, I am taking it back to the Lodge with me tonight, where I expect to do all the editing. If I were to keep it in the studio I should be tempted to keep making changes."

Fine's *String Quartet* had its premiere at Brandeis University on December 10, 1952, played by the Juilliard Quartet. "Irving never had trouble about getting performances. The Juilliard couldn't wait for him to finish the piece," Verna recalled. The same group gave the first New York performance (erroneously billed as the "first performance") at the Museum of Modern Art on February 18, 1953. The occasion was an evening of American chamber music presented by the Juilliard Quartet in honor of the thirtieth anniversary of the League of Composers, and the concert also included string quartets by Virgil Thomson, William Schuman and Bernard Wagenaar (all composed in the 1930s) and a recent (1951) piano quintet by Wallingford Riegger. The program listed the title of the Fine as "Quartet No. 1 (1952)".

The new score received respectful reviews. Ross Parmenter, in the *New York Times*, termed it "a beautifully sustained, deeply thoughtful string quartet" and "outstanding work." Writing in the *Saturday Review* magazine, Arthur Berger noted that "Irving Fine brought Gallic contours and a general amiability into a new relation with Stravinsky's angularity until recently, when he surprised us by reaching into Schoenberg's stock of twelve-tone implements to give his music new strength." In his *New York Herald* Tribune review of the premiere, Berger observed that "for Fine, dabbling with themes and chords from twelve-tone patterns is something quite new" and admitted he found Fine's retreat from "his customary amiable and melodious style" startling. But he also detected "remarkable strength, invention and atmosphere" in the quartet. Berger then provided an astute capsule description of the score that is worth quoting. "The first of the two movements combines, in an unusual way, somewhat chromatic elements with what may be described as the more symmetrical rhythmic asymmetries which occur in the music of Stravinsky's most vital American disciples. The second movement is more liberated and the arresting, tenuous atmosphere of the close makes one look forward with great interest to what will come of this new turn in his creative evolution."

Retrospectively, nearly half a century later Berger stated: "Irving was trying to do bigger things. At that point, he was a little concerned about the personality of his music, not happy to be the small, intimate composer of his previous works. His early romanticism is very gentle, and I think he wanted to do something stronger—Germanic and dramatic. He felt his music was too lightweight and he wanted more recognition. He used serialism thematically, as in traditional music. It was an intuitive thing with him, not the rigid twelve-tone system." But Berger had reservations. "I think the *String Quartet* is a manufactured piece, a little too stiff. It wasn't quite himself."

Conversely, Leon Kirchner thought the quartet "a beautifully conceived work." He remembered that "Irving and I never talked about his past music or what he felt about it. But he was aware that something had changed." Harold Shapero said that, previous to writing the quartet, Fine had thought of himself as "a minor figure, but then he composed that piece, with its beautiful, poignant and sad second movement." Noël Lee observed that "the quartet is a fantastic piece—twelve-tone, but at the same time very rhythmic and American."

In early 1954, a recording of Fine's *String Quartet* by the Juilliard Quartet was released in Columbia Records' second set of six discs of contemporary American music.[8] Not long

---

8. Kirchner's *String Quartet No. 1* was paired with the Fine, and, not long after the record was issued, he remembered encountering Fine at a gathering. "Irving asked me whether I had heard his quartet on the other side of the disc and I replied: "Not yet. But I

after, the work received the prestigious Society for the Publication of American Music Award for 1954. Verna recalled: "When the *String Quartet* got the SPAM award, Irving simply couldn't believe it. It was as if he was getting the extra piece of candy but didn't really deserve it. He had a fragile ego." Also in 1954, the quartet was given a citation by the New York Critics Circle. The score was published the following year by SPAM, dedicated "to the memory of Serge and Natalie Koussevitzky."

Fine was fortunate in that the recorded performance by the Juilliard was superb, revealing much detail that might not so easily be perceived in a live performance. Reviewing the album in the *Christian Science Monitor* on March 2, 1954, Klaus George Roy noted appreciatively that "Fine's Quartet is an impressive, deeply felt work of impelling motion, a clear departure from the bland neoclassicism of his earlier days." That same month, a critic wrote in *Musical America* magazine: "When the first twelve-tone works began appearing, the common complaint was that this music was rhythmically inert and impossibly rigid in plan. Now, with the emergence of such works as Fine's Quartet, we can see that this apprehension was unnecessary. Rhythmic energy and expressive freedom are two of the outstanding characteristics of this quartet." Writing many years later, Arthur Cohn observed that Fine's use of dodecaphonic technique "takes on new meaning, for his twelve tones are clothed with the royal purple of classic design. And within his music there is the necessary freedom that must be enjoyed by good art. Fine's quartet has clear positiveness; it is his own music, exhibiting a codification of rare sensibility and sensitivity."

---

know that the Kirchner is a 'fine' quartet." It was a joke with a little tension in it, but Irving was very amused and laughed."

A laudatory review of the set appeared on March 14 in the *Washington Post*, and Copland sent it to Fine with the inscription: "Pass this around and everybody take a bow." Along with the Fine and Kirchner, the Columbia collection included works by Harold Shapero, Henry Cowell, Roy Harris, Robert Palmer, Peter Mennin, Andrew Imbrie, Paul Bowles, Norman Dello Joio, Arthur Berger and Edward Burlingame Hill.

Fine spent June, July and a part of August 1952 at the Mac-Dowell Colony. It was an extremely active period for him, musically and, as will be seen, otherwise. In addition to making final revisions in the *String Quartet*, he had begun an orchestral piece, evidently meant to be a symphony, seemingly in fulfillment of the previous year's Rodgers and Hammerstein commission. He was also hard at work on what would be his only "serious" song-cycle. On June 1 he had written Verna: "Don't worry about me. I am sure that this will be a productive stay."

Fine was happy that Copland was also in residence at MacDowell, for the month of June. After showing him his virtually complete *String Quartet*, which had clearly provoked a positive reaction, Fine's pleasure was evident in a June 19 letter to Verna. "Aaron tells me that he is now beginning to get a real picture of me as a composer—which is his way of saying that I have begun to make a real impression on him as a composer." (But Copland would always have reservations about his friend. David Diamond recalled that in 1962, "Aaron said to me that Irving had a lot of talent but didn't work hard enough and hadn't yet found himself"; and the author remembered a similar comment by Copland about Fine's derivativeness years later. In a 1967 essay on Fine, Copland noted that "his problems as composer concerned matters of aesthetics, of eclecticism, of influence. These limitations he recognized; they made him modest to a fault.")

Copland left MacDowell for Tanglewood in early July, and on the eighth he sent a postcard. "One week gone. We miss you. All goes well. A lively crowd of composers. Hope you're working well. L.B. turned thumbs down on Sonny's choruses [Harold Shapero's *Two Psalms* of 1952], and Lukas agreed. Poor Sonny. I tried to protect him."

That year, Fine had obtained a leave of absence from Tanglewood, and on June 22 Leonard Bernstein wrote: "I am going to miss you sorely this summer: it is already difficult to think of the season without you. I think it is a mistake that you are not here: but if you can come out of the Colony with more works as moving and as 'wrought' as the Quartet, then it is better you stay there. You are a large personal loss, though, for all of us."

Howard Taubman announced Fine's Rodgers and Hammerstein/League of Composers commission in the *New York Times*, on June 8, as follows: "a score by Irving Fine, which Charles Munch and the Boston Symphony will play for the first time next season." That September, the *Christian Science Monitor* would refer to "a new symphonic work by Irving Fine" and in October the *Boston Globe* would report that Fine was composing "a Sinfonietta, still unfinished," for the 1952-1953 Boston Symphony season.

The aforementioned symphonic piece seems never to have been finished, and was possibly an early attempt at the work that eventually became the *Symphony (1962)*. It is probable, however, that Fine was engaged concurrently on two orchestral scores that summer, for in a July 28 postcard to Verna, he wrote: "Looked over my little orchestral pieces and found them o.k. to use. Symph. moves as expected [a] few measures a day."

Thirty-two pages of full orchestral score, marked "B.S.O. Commission," are extant, along with fourteen pages of condensed score of the same music with the title "Orchestral Preludes" written over the roman numeral one, both manuscripts undated. The unfinished work opens with dramatic, discordant gestures in brass and winds, proceeds with motoric writing and busy passagework, comes to a *tutti* climax and continues with a short-winded second subject featuring a minor-second clash in English horn and muted trumpet set against string-and-woodwind triplets. This recedes gradually, and then heavily accented ostinatos, in which the piano is prominent, lead to pages of brisk running sixteenth notes in various instrumental choirs, eventually devolving into a canon based on the opening subject—which is where the piece peters out. Although there are no tempo marks, the music suggests an energetic allegro, one not unlike that of the *Toccata Concertante*, though more dissonant. There are occasional hints of possible thematic twelve-tone writing, but no real themes; rather, rhythmic motives abound, often with an emphasis on a dropping minor second. As far as this music goes (about two minutes' duration), it is potentially powerful: still Stravinsky-inflected, but effective. One suspects, knowing of the stylistic crisis Fine was experiencing at the time, that the lingering ghost of neoclassicism may have caused him to abandon this nonetheless interesting score.

As for Fine's symphony, so-called, he had evidently begun it before arriving at MacDowell. On June 1, he wrote to Verna that "material for the new piece is accumulating. I think I've got the character and an inkling of the form of the first movet. All I need is a slightly less corny opening than the tentative one I've sketched." (There followed two-and-one-half notated bars of triadic fanfare music, the like of which occurs nowhere in the "Orchestral Preludes.") Two days later: "Copied four pages, wrote beautiful contrasting theme in slow mvt (in oboe and accompanied by violas and cello). Also some striking material for 1st mvt. All in all, this has been about my best 'first day' at the colony."

In July, Fine's letters to Verna contained numerous intriguing references to the symphony. "In spite of sticking at the desk and piano all day I have accomplished virtually zero, beyond discovering (maybe) how to continue the opening phrase of the symphony. The idea of working on the slow movement is a good one." "The stuff I have for the slow mvt. falls into place suspiciously easy—so easy that it results in far too short a movement—about three and a half minutes. This is with a simple A B A form—with your favorite theme coming back accompanied by a more elaborate orchestration and texture." On July 15, Fine described the first movement as "more like a 1st movement of a concerto for orchestra than a symphony." On the seventeenth, he noted that the formal outline of the beginning of the symphony's opening movement seemed to be assuming definite shape, and added: "One thing is sure—it is *not* in sonata form and the entire movement will be short—no more than four minutes. If only I can keep it strong and free from easy pattern and formula." Further: "I think I see progress on the first two movements. The slow movement is right pretty and I have written a closing section (about 1 minute long) which is positively luscious and which has the great virtue of having been almost completely conceived in its instrumental form."

On July 18, came a mention of serialism. "The opening is now set (except for orchestration). Also decided to write a complete chart of rows, though I do not know whether it is absolutely necessary in this piece." A week later: "As usual, am having difficulties with phrase rhythm and rhythm in general. You were right—I can't really write a short movement. The first movement seems to be growing in size and probably length and the more I work on it the more panic stricken I get—it comes so slowly and there's so little time. I should know by now that it is always difficult to write in large forms." "Symph moves as expected, few measures a day." "I had a good day on the symphony (1st movement). Finally wrote down 45 bars of continuation and transition to the second theme. Am beginning to revise my estimate of the length of the movement upwards." "So drowsy and relaxed I took two or three catnaps and spent the rest of the time copying and extending the numerous bits of material I had for the 2nd mvt. There is almost enough for the entire mvt. But whether I can assemble the jigsaw pieces is another question. Feel much better already about the piece, however—at least the 1st two movements." "Tomorrow back to the Symph, to see what's cooking in the subconscious."

Two years later at MacDowell, Fine seems still to have been wrestling with this symphony, having destroyed most of the "little scraps of music from the R&H piece." "[I am] tidying up all of the ideas that might work on the development of the 2nd movement. To hell with the last movement for the time being." As none of this material can be located, the chances are that it was either lost, destroyed or incorporated into *Symphony (1962)*. Because Fine seldom dated his sketches, the mystery must remain.

There is, however, no mystery involved in the composer's personal behavior at the MacDowell Colony in 1952. The fact is, while writing his only major song-cycle, Fine was sleeping with the author of his texts.[9] Irene Orgel was a young, unmarried English poet of Jewish extraction whom he met at the Colony. Several years before, she had published a "Sonnet to Lise Meitner" and presently was completing a set of poems called *Mutability*. Subsequently best known for her 1966 book *Odd Tales*, Orgel would also publish articles in a British journal of Judaism, including one with a title drolly appropriate to her romantic summer of 1952: "Sex in the Jewish Tradition." (It should be noted that the author was unable to

---

9. The information came initially from Verna Fine, who told the author that she felt it was pertinent to this biography because of the song-cycle.

determine absolutely whether the Irene Orgel who wrote for that Judaism journal was in fact Fine's Irene Orgel.)

Which appealed more to Fine, her poetry or her person, can only be surmised. But the song-cycle seems consequent to the affair, for his composing agenda was already excessive (two orchestral pieces, string quartet revisions) and he appears to have had no binding request for a vocal work (in September, the Creative Concerts Guild of Lexington, Massachusetts would offer a $300 commission for the just-finished cycle).[10]

Verna and Irving had been married for more than a decade, and perhaps the boredom factor was coming into play, at least on his side. Too, colony life provided a respite from family pressures. Fine's friend Arnold Modell remembered that "Irving told me Verna was inhibited and wouldn't go along with his sexual desires, which involved doing it often and in different ways. He was definitely a sensual man, and he once said that Verna wasn't very sensual and was not very interested in sex. I think Verna was quite a difficult lady to live with, fairly brittle. She could be patronizing. She admired Irving's talent, but would sometimes say so in a kind of baby voice, which I thought a bit humiliating for him." Modell added: "My firm impression is that he was pretty active with other women, although he never told me he was having affairs. I recall that when my wife became increasingly ill, Irving was very sympathetic and encouraged me to find sex elsewhere."[11] Joanna Fine stated that "my mother was penis-phobic. I remember her telling me as a child: "Penises are ugly. Stay away from them'."

---

10. It is probable that a commission, though not yet formally confirmed, was in the wind, for the word appears in a postcard to Verna dated July 14: "Wrote another song today. Only need two or maybe three more to complete the commission."

11. Claudia Fine noted that Modell's wife had multiple sclerosis. "One time, they came for a visit and Arnold was more interested in being with my father than in attending to his wife. He ignored her and didn't physically support her and she actually fell down. My mother was furious. After the Modells left, my parents had a big fight because my father defended Arnold. He said, 'How much can you expect of a man who has been living with a woman who is dying slowly, and it's not a good marriage anyway, so don't be so hard on him.' That brought some of their differences to the forefront, and I remember them screaming at each other."

Claudia Fine reminisced: "The impression I got from Mom was that my father had a fairly good sexual appetite and, although because of her somewhat Victorian upbringing, she could take it or leave it, she was always accommodating. She loved him and felt it was her duty. They were very affectionate." Arthur Berger noted that Fine "would joke about the sameness of his life. 'I lead such a quiet life,' he complained. He used to be jealous when we talked about other people having affairs, and I think he envied some of his homosexual friends, because they carried on and he didn't."

Fine's intimates, Esther and Harold Shapero, were privy to the Irene Orgel affair. "The thing is," said Esther, "Irving was attractive, very cute. He didn't have to work hard to get girls because they were always after him." Still, said Harold, "Irene Orgel was one of the few he actually *did* it with. As they say in law courses, penetration occurred." He continued: "The problem in that marriage was a simple one: Irving hungered for an artistic companion and Verna didn't supply that. That's what led to the Irene Orgel affair." Orgel, he recalled, "was a chunky little girl, dark hair with ringlets. Irving used to call her a cute little cupcake, but I had contempt for him for getting such an ugly girl." Esther disagreed: "She was very attractive and had beautiful skin."

Harold stressed that "Irving was not gross in any way. Rather, he was refined. The affair was probably a catastrophe, because he would instantly be full of guilt and complexities. I know those affairs at artists' colonies. You climb into bed and can't get it up and it never works and is a mess. It wasn't real love—that affair lasted about three weeks. She was artistic and a nice, sympathetic girl, but she didn't have any style, and Irving was full of style." Esther said: "When Verna found out about that affair she was not happy. She was hurt." Harold: "She wasn't that hurt. Verna was practical and matter-of-fact. When she heard about it, she made a sensible remark on the order of, 'Well, *I* wasn't there and he had to have something.'"[12] Perhaps. But Leon Kirchner remembered Verna

12. Further comment on this subject—Esther: "I know of one other affair Irving had, with a Brandeis student. I was told by a relative that it was serious enough so that the girl nearly committed suicide when she realized Irving wasn't going to leave Verna and

telling him "that she was pretty angry with Irving because he had gone off with some woman at the MacDowell Colony."

Fine's only documented comment about Irene Orgel came in a July 9, 1952 letter to Verna, while he was at work on the songs. She "has quality but is very neurotic," he declared. In the same letter, he sent his wife "an excruciatingly titillating kiss for you on your left nipple, thousands of others for the nape of your neck, your eyes and mouth, and a deliciously snug fit inside some other place." After twelve x's, he signed off: "Yaaaahvungh."

During the first two weeks of July, Fine's letters and postcards to Verna contain occasional references to his progress with *Mutability*. "[I] wrote a very powerful beginning (a tone row) to another song [No. 6]. It's a pity to waste it on a song. Moreover, the song I completed yesterday (with the words beginning 'I have heard the hoof beat[s] of happiness close in the night") [No. 1] is full of romantic longing and tenderness. The new idea seems somewhat grandiose by comparison." "I also wrote a very pretty melody for another song but ruined it and lost the original conception in trying to work it out." "Despite a rather low state of mind have written another song [No. 5] for the cycle. (It needs to be extended somehow but that is not difficult.) This number leads into the final number for which I have the best material (next to the opening of the symph) that I have written here. It's too good for the lousy song cycle."

On July 2 Fine had made a revealing observation, possibly referring to his work on *Mutability*. "I have been noticing that whenever I write something romantic and lyrical in a major key I get tense and rather depressed but that when I discover material of a powerful yet rather impersonal nature [serial writing?] I feel quite elated. Don't know which comes first—the music or the mood. In the end I usually prefer the impersonal music."

Perhaps because of a certain expressive inhibition combined with a rather idiosyncratic mixture of the diatonic with the chromatic, *Mutability* seems weighted toward the impersonal side of Fine's art. It is, nevertheless, a persuasive if not

---

marry her. But that idea is ridiculous. He never would have left Verna."

completely unified work, one notable for meticulous clarity. This is "pure" music, with no straining for effect. The cycle as a whole has a dry, neoclassical veneer occasionally decorated with serial detail (octave displacement, progressions of non-repeated notes), and the carefully conceived, often arresting piano accompaniment contains little chordal writing until the final song. Unmistakable is the overall influence, melodically, harmonically and in the spacious angularity of the vocal line, of Copland's Emily Dickinson songs, although Fine's prosody, unlike Copland's, is seldom awkward.

The six poems that Fine set so professionally in *Mutability* are romantic and peculiarly symbolist. The first song, "I Have Heard the Hoof Beats of Happiness," begins with skittering piano passagework that seems serially inflected because there are so few repeated notes (eleven different tones in the first two bars). The text suggests a satyr, and so, surely, does the mercurial, fresh-sounding piano accompaniment. The vocal line (for mezzo-soprano) is lyric and lively. There is a lovely moment of pure Copland near the end, at the words "with quiet eyes."[13]

"My Father," also partially Coplandesque, is more conventional music, with a relatively diatonic vocal line and freely chromatic accompaniment.

"The Weed" is strikingly declamatory and dissonant. Especially effective is the exchange of triplets between voice and piano at the words "Get you indoors!"

"Peregrine" is the most straightforward of the poems image-wise, and Fine's arpeggiated accompaniment in the first section reflects that fact. The octave displacement in the voice at the utterance "It was no canary" is telling, as is the fast "soaring" music that comes a little later.

"Jubilation" initially features a lyric vocal line set against odd stuttering accompaniment marked "quasi guitarra." In the *allegro* second part, the brilliant keyboard passagework is in Fine's best neoclassic manner, and the vocal part is joyously austere. The song ends with a repeated and alarmingly dis-

---

13. The rising major third and dropping fifth is a prominent motive in Copland's Dickinson song "Sleep is supposed to be," which is dedicated to Fine. Perhaps a little homage was intended.

cordant piano chord. There is no pause between the fifth and sixth songs.

"Now God be Thanked for Mutability" is, as the composer himself was aware, the gem of the set. The twelve-tone piano introduction is dramatic and memorable, setting the scene for moody romanticism expressed in music fairly dissonant but sometimes triadic. Within a serial context, the appealing lyricism of the vocal line comes as something of a surprise (there is one notable moment of clumsy prosody at the words "jack-o'-lantern moon"). A ruminative piano coda brings this distinguished cycle to an end.

Fine left a brief commentary on *Mutability*. "Four of the songs in *Mutability* were composed at the MacDowell Colony, Peterborough, New Hampshire, during the month of July 1952. Two of them (numbers two and six) were begun there and completed in the following September. The texts are by a young English poet, Irene Orgel, who was resident at the MacDowell Colony at the same time. The songs were commissioned by the Creative Concerts Guild, Inc. for the mezzo-soprano Eunice Alberts. They are essentially romantic in conception and employ a variety of harmonic techniques. Numbers one and three utilize a relatively free modern chromaticism; number five a rather stylized diatonic classicism; number six (an epilogue to the set) employs the twelve-tone technique, but within the framework of a clearly defined tonality."

After a tryout at Kirkland House, Harvard University, in early 1953, Eunice Alberts and Fine gave the premiere of *Mutability* on April 7, in the Dorothy Quincy Suite at Boston's John Hancock Building. The duo gave further performances that November: on the twenty-third at a MacDowell Colony Composers Festival at Hartt College of Music in Hartford, Connecticut; and on the twenty-eighth at a Composers Forum at Columbia University (Fine's *String Quartet* was also played, by the Juilliard).

After the premiere in Boston, Klaus George Roy reported in the *Christian Science Monitor* that the audience included "many of the leading musicians in this area." He noted that "as sung with technical assurance and the finest understanding by Eunice Alberts, the composer assisting expertly at the keyboard, the cycle confirmed Mr. Fine's steadily growing stature as a creative artist." Roy felt that, despite the "variety of contemporary techniques," *Mutability* attained unity in its "manifold attractive patterns." He found flowing lyricism "conspicuously absent" and thought that the piano accompaniment "seems at times to be moving on a separate plane." Roy criticized some word repetitions, "particularly in restating the first lines at the end, where they nullify or at least divert from the climaxes inherent in the poems"—this in reference to the second and fourth songs. The cycle was "complex and highly subtle" but nevertheless communicated "a good deal of the imaginative poetry even at first hearing." It was "a fascinating product [and] Mr. Fine does not stand still as a composer—he is experimenting and inventing, seeking and finding." Warren Storey Smith, in the *Boston Post*, pronounced Orgel's poems "distinctly odd, though not devoid of meat or meaning." Their brevity, he complained, "has tempted [Fine] to resort to the dubious practice of repeating words and even whole lines." In setting these texts, "the resourceful Mr. Fine has made use of various modern techniques. The voice part is in the nature of recitative and Mr. Fine, who played the accompaniments, had given himself plenty to do." The *Boston Herald*'s critic, Rudolph Elie, described *Mutability* as cast "in a strong, individual idiom notable for its lack of eccentricity and its abundance of emotional force." The vocal line, he said, "occasionally overdid the jagged intervals," but "they underlined the poetic sensibility of the words."

In 1955, Alberts and Fine recorded *Mutability* for CRI Records. Verna explained that "that year Irving and Henry Brant [and Adolph Weiss] got the first American Academy of Arts and Letters awards, which included money [$1,000] and a recording, one side of an LP. His half was *Mutability*." Because the song-cycle lasted only fourteen minutes, Fine was asked to fill out the side with two excerpts from *Music for Piano*. The recorded performance of *Mutability* is authoritative, although Alberts' diction is not always perfect. Fine's pianism is impressive: brilliant, alert and, when necessary, subtle, although, as composers will, he occasionally ignores his own dynamics, and sometimes holds chords beyond their specified durations. Minor quibbles, these: it is a magnificent document.

The year 1952 had ended with a gratifying review of the

*Partita for Wind Quintet* in the *Christian Science Monitor* by the ever-perceptive Klaus George Roy, who judged it "one of the finest contemporary works for the woodwind medium," adding: "Stravinskian in rhythmic method and harmonic stylization, it is nevertheless strikingly original in feeling and expressiveness. Here is a civilized wit, a sure sense of form and motion, a convincing belief in the meaning of purely sonorous values."

# Chapter 14

■ "CIVILIZED WIT" WOULD BE FINE'S SOLE strong suit during the following year, for the only substantive music that came from his pen was the second set of *Alice in Wonderland* choruses. In December, he finished an additional choral piece, *An Old Song*, and he perhaps tinkered periodically with his ill-fated symphony. But, as 1952 had been artistically fertile, 1953 proved arid. In retrospect, it can be seen as the beginning of a serious writer's block.

In April, Fine's *String Quartet* was performed at Dartmouth College by the Juilliard Quartet, and during the year he gave lectures there and at Harvard University and Amherst College. At a Harvard seminar in August that included Elliott Carter, Virgil Thomson, G. Wallace Woodworth and Allen Sapp, Fine was articulate on the subject of the need for new choral music. "It is important to distinguish between contemporaneity in feeling and contemporary techniques. The problem is to achieve something fresh." He conceded that, in some ways, the medium was limiting: "You can't write for chorus as you write for instruments, or even for solo voice." But he noted disapprovingly that many composers seemed leery of setting words to music, finding something "ignominious" about the practice. "They regard the text as a nuisance, and are especially reluctant to set contemporary American poetry." He pointed out that "most singing groups are amateur and cannot cope with extreme difficulties," but that "one of the great virtues of choral music is the fact that it frankly is not dependent on an audience for its complete fulfillment. And, unlike the orchestra, which is pretty impersonal, the chorus has the tremendous appeal as a human, personal thing."

During the first two weeks of June, Fine had been deeply involved in the second Brandeis Festival of the Creative Arts, dedicated, at his suggestion, to "The Comic Spirit." Then, as usual, there was Tanglewood. That summer, the Mexican composer and conductor Carlos Chávez was the guest composition instructor, and Fine was appointed to assist both him and Copland. Ingolf Dahl directed the Tanglewood Study Group, Lukas Foss taught the analysis classes and Fine taught a third group of student composers. On August 6, he conducted his *Notturno* with the Orchestra of Department I; later, on November 29, the *Notturno* was heard in New York for the first time, performed at Town Hall by the Saidenberg Little Symphony under Daniel Saidenberg.

In September Brandeis University opened its Graduate School, with the New York editor and columnist Max Lerner as chairman. Fine was promoted from associate to full professor of music, with an attendant salary increase.

On the domestic front that year, there were three noteworthy events. During the summer the Fines built a new addition on their "rather nondescript, though not unattractive country house" (Fine's words) in Natick. Then, on August 17, their favorite pet, Stinker the cocker spaniel, died. ("That's the trouble with having pets," Fine once observed. "You get too attached to them." "Irving adored dogs—we always had dogs," said Verna). But most important, on August 27 their third daughter, Joanna Lisa, was born.

Verna recalled that, this time, Fine had been hoping for a son, but was resigned following the birth, and said something like, "I guess I'm destined to have only daughters.[1] Announcing the advent of yet another one to Olga Koussevitzky, the conductor's widow, Verna described her husband as "recovered from the initial shock," and on September 11 Copland wrote jokingly to her from Mexico, "The explanation is simple: Irving has always been much too interested in girls." (Subsequently, Copland would become so close a family friend that Fine's daughters called him "Uncle Aaron.") That month the Fines also received a handwritten card inscribed, "Best greetings to the very [new?] Joanna Lisa Fine and her parents from I Stravinsky."

A few days after Joanna's birth, Fine's mother sent him an unexpected item, a Bible. He thanked her for "the wonderful 'unbirthday' present. It's a splendid book for which I shall find much use in the future." Verna noted that "toward

---

1. In 1962, he would describe them as "three lively and mostly quite adorable daughters."

the end of his life, Irving said, 'I'm going to use the Bible for texts, because I don't need to get copyright clearance'." She remembered that he had been exasperated by such difficulties when the score of *Mutability* was published. (One might wonder whether they arose from the Woman Scorned syndrome.) "Of course, with Lewis Carroll, there was no such problem," she said.

The *Three Choruses from "Alice in Wonderland,"* Second Series, which date from 1953, are scored only for women's voices with piano accompaniment. They had been commissioned by Bradford Junior College of Bradford, Massachusetts, a boarding school for girls, to celebrate its 100th anniversary. The work was premiered there in April 1954. The first two numbers, "The Knave's Letter" and "The White Knight's Song," were originally solo songs in the incidental music to *Alice* from 1942, now arranged for chorus. The third, "Beautiful Soup," had to be newly composed, because in the theatrical production that song had been written by Allen Sapp. The score of these choruses was published in 1954 by Witmark. Texts of the first and third songs are from Carroll's *Alice's Adventures in Wonderland*, that of the second from *Through the Looking Glass.*

The chantlike "Knave's Letter" (SSA: *Allegretto*) is sardonic and mordantly witty. It is cast in simple tripartite form and has a middle section replete with brilliant running piano passagework.

"The White Knight's Song" (SA: *Andante*), a lilting lullaby of gentle diatonic lyricism, features a solo soprano. An irregular rhythmic figure, the so-called Scotch Snap, is prominent throughout.

"Beautiful Soup" (SSA: *Allegro moderato*) is set to parodistic, marchlike music, its silliness perfectly matching the words. The piano accompaniment is subtle and sly-sounding.

Howard Pollack has noted that in these choruses Fine's high craft and emotional detachment allowed him "to be tender and nostalgic without being coy or saccharine." David Diamond pronounced Fine's *Alice* music "absolutely charming, beautifully done, rather inspired in terms of spontancity and with good rhythmic interest." But Milton Babbitt failed to see the charm, referring disparagingly to the *Alice* choruses as "very cutesy pieces." Arthur Cohn perceived the same elements in the second set as in the first: "elegance of style, rich harmonic choices and the special ability to write *for* the voice without sacrificing any creative integrity," and cited this second group of *Alice* choruses for its "telling colors" and "phrased finesse."

As opposed to the popular *Alice* songs, Fine's other choral work of 1953, *An Old Song* (SATB, *a cappella*), is little known. It was written for the Harvard Glee Club as a salute to Archibald T. Davison, and the score (published in 1954 by Witmark) bears the dedication: "To Doc—a song for his seventieth birthday." Davison himself conducted the Glee Club in the first performance in March 1954, at Sanders Theater, Harvard University.

The text is by Yehoash, the pseudonym of Yehoash Solomon Bloomgarden, who was born in Lithuania in 1872, immigrated to the United States in 1890 and died there in 1927. He wrote poems and stories, co-authored a Yiddish dictionary and translated the Bible into Yiddish. "An Old Song" was translated into English from the Yiddish by Marie Syrkin (1899-1989), a prolific author and member of the Brandeis English Department whom Fine knew well. Japan is the locale of this curious poem, which contrasts militarist bravado with pastoral imagery and mother love: "In the blossom land . . . an old song ran: 'Hammer me a sword forthwith,' said a warrior to a smith. 'Make it long as the wheat at harvest song . . . Supple and swift as a snake . . . Full of lightning . . . Smooth as silk and thin as the web that spiders spin . . . And merciless as pain, and cold . . . On the sword's hilt . . . Trace for me a running lake, a flock of sheep, and one who sings her child to sleep'."

*An Old Song* is a three-minute miniature of remarkable beauty. In it, Fine displays a personal romanticism employing conventional but freshly rendered triadic harmony. Within the bounds of simple part-writing, the lyricism is mellow and mellifluous, especially in the last section, beginning with the words "A running lake"; and there is effective *fortissimo* declamation at "Supple, swift as a snake" and a striking *forte-piano* on the word "pain." All in all, a small gem.

Nineteen fifty-three was also the time of the McCarthy committee's anti-Communist witch hunts in the United States Senate. Fine, who had always been sympathetic to the

Left, was horrified by a May 27 article in the *Boston Globe* headlined "Aaron Copland Denies He Ever Was Communist." Their friend had been questioned for two hours behind closed doors by the Senate Investigations Subcommittee on Un-American Activities, directed by the Republican senator from Wisconsin, Joseph R. McCarthy. Further, McCarthy had announced that Copland subsequently would be interrogated at a public hearing concerning "alleged Communist subversion of State Department propaganda programs"—this, because he had lectured in South America in 1947 under the auspices of the U.S. State Department. The *Globe* reported: "As to permitting use of his name by various organizations and causes [Copland] said, 'I did so without the knowledge or intention of supporting Communist or Communist front organizations'."

Verna remembered Fine's response to the absurd but alarming hullabaloo. "Irving hated television, but he would cut classes to watch the hearings. He said, 'I wonder if they'll look up my history,' because he recalled performing for some group called Artists and Scientists for Peace, or something like that, and it turned out that Senator McCarthy discovered it was a Communist front. But Irving didn't personally have any trouble. Still, we were aghast when Aaron was called before the committee." Even before his May 1953 ordeal in Washington, Copland experienced political problems. Ironically, that January his ultra-patriotic *Lincoln Portrait* had been removed from President Eisenhower's inaugural ceremonies after he was denounced as a fellow traveler by Congressman Fred E. Busbey of Illinois, who stated, ludicrously: "The Republican party would have been ridiculed from one end of the United States to the other if Copland's music had been played at the inaugural of a president elected to fight Communism, among other things."[2] Although Copland was never charged with any offense, being summoned by the McCarthy committee inevitably had consequences. Thirty years later, he would wryly tell the author that there were towns in Texas

---

2. Copland once described Busbey to the author as "an ape." (He reserved the appellation "apette" for Joan Peyser, the author of unsavory books on Pierre Boulez and Leonard Bernstein that seethe with what is known, in popular parlance, as psychobabble.)

and in the South where they still wouldn't play his music.

Careerwise, Copland's hard times continued into 1954. On April 1, at his invitation, the Fines attended the world premiere of his opera *The Tender Land* in New York. For a variety of reasons but primarily because of a weak libretto, the work was badly received; the composer would ultimately make drastic revisions. When, in a 1980 interview with Copland, the author mentioned Samuel Barber's remark that he had felt like fleeing to Morocco after the failure of his *Antony and Cleopatra*, Copland's dry response was: "I'd already been to Morocco. I just went home to bed."

Fine's reaction to the debacle has gone unrecorded, but Harold Shapero observed: "Irving was elegant. He wasn't a great commoner like Aaron." Copland, he said, "was the biggest snob of all because, deep down, he was actually very fancy, very elitist, aesthetically." But, with folksy, populist works like *The Tender Land*, "he wanted to reach a big audience." Shapero recalled a startling incident. "Aaron's opera had been a flop and Gian Carlo Menotti had a success with one opera [*The Saint of Bleecker Street*, which won the Drama Critics Circle Award as best play, the Music Critics Circle Award as best opera and the Pulitzer Prize]. Aaron said angrily to me: 'That wop!' I was shocked. You rarely saw Aaron in that mood."

On March 9, 1954, Fine had written to William Schuman, then president of the Juilliard School of Music, accepting a commission to provide songs for a 1955-1956 festival celebrating the School's fiftieth anniversary. He termed the invitation "a great honor," continuing, "I am not sure at the present time whether I shall compose one or three—it all depends upon my luck in finding texts—but in any event you may count on me."

Schuman's proposal was the impetus behind the fifteen-minute cycle that would eventually be titled *Childhood Fables for Grownups*. He found his texts in the work of a friend he had met at the MacDowell Colony, the poet Gertrude Norman.[3] She had first attempted to interest Marc Blitzstein in

---

3. The initial title had been *Children's Songs for Grownups*. In early 1957, after the publisher of the score had asked for a new

setting her poems, but on December 15, 1954, she wrote Fine: "I'm so glad to know you're working on the songs. This is mostly to let you know I talked to Marc and definitely disengaged him from the project." Fine had, she said, "carte blanche on any you'd like to set."

There was no Brandeis festival that year, and in June Fine received a fellowship to MacDowell for August. There, he set to work on the songs while also puttering about with his fragmentary symphony. He seems to have felt stylistically adrift after experimenting with serialism in the *String Quartet*, perhaps not satisfied he had achieved a persuasive romantic idiom within the terms of that system. At any event, the *Childhood Fables* represents a kind of throwback, couched in a tonal and accessible idiom, one that even occasionally suggests popular music. "All of the French influence comes out in these songs," he said.

Aside from any question of a stylistic crisis, an obvious reason for the accessibility is Norman's anthropomorphic texts à la Walt Disney. These are, at times, tiresomely coy. They sport such dreadful lines as "he loves to swim and splish and splash and splash and slush," "with icicles and spicicles and other little nicicles" and "they wiggled, they squiggled, they wiggled, miggled, squiggled, wriggled." The surprising thing is that Fine managed to write a good deal of engaging and sophisticated music to such drivel. But he clearly had a taste for it, as a loving father who enjoyed baby-talking to his children (an example from a letter: "Dearest poopy doopy little Claudia"; and in a postcard to Emily: "schnick-schnack, pooh-pooh, put a wight on, cause I wove you"). And a privately made acetate recording exists of him adeptly introducing the *Childhood Fables* in an exaggerated manner calculated to appeal to children. This was made to entertain Fine's daughters after his own domestic performances as both singer and pianist failed to please them. (He had a high baritone voice that was, as with most composers, untrained and unattractive.) Subsequently, it was used as a demonstration disk that, according to Norman,

---

title, Norman wrote Fine and suggested *Fables for Voice and Piano*, with either the subtitle "Children's Songs for Grown Up Singers" or "Childhood Tales for Grownups." Or, she asked, "what about just *Psychological Fables?*"

was "going the rounds" by May 1955. A one-and-a-half minute spoken prelude, possibly written by Norman, sets the scene, and each of the first four songs (played out of the published order: two, three, four, one) is briefly introduced by Fine. The pianist is the composer and the vocalist is Ramon Gilbert.[4] Norman hoped that, if promoted properly, at least one of the songs "might be taken up, become a great hit, and we might sell a million copies."

In the *Childhood Fables*, as in the two sets of *Alice in Wonderland* choruses, Fine excelled at creating a child's world in music, with whimsical wit and with no lapse into vulgar sentimentality. If any arcane inferences are to be drawn from this special talent—aside from the evident one that Fine liked children—they must be left to the psychoanalytically inclined.[5]

Not surprisingly in a composer who was an accomplished pianist, Fine's accompaniments tend to outshine his vocal writing. Here, they show a high degree of polish, being both rhythmically intricate and harmonically fluid. The voice part, always effective, leans toward declamation rather than flowing melody, with large leaps and octave-displacement a recurring factor.

*Childhood Fables* was originally conceived in two sets, the first four songs written in 1954 and early 1955, the last two in 1955. Songs one to four were published in 1958, songs five and six in 1959, all by Boosey and Hawkes, and a later edition combines the six songs into one group. Each song was dedicated to a composer friend, and, except for one, all were intended as mild, parodying portraiture.

"Polaroli" pictures the antics of a polar bear. Dedicated

---

4. Gilbert, a Brandeis graduate who had originally come to the University on a sports scholarship, was given to singing in the showers after football practice. One day, impressed by his resonant baritone voice, his teammates encouraged him to visit the music department. There, he met Erwin Bodky, who took him to see the chairman. Fine liked Gilbert's voice so much that he arranged singing lessons at Cambridge's Longy School, financed by Brandeis. Ultimately, Gilbert became a cantor.

5. Fine was also fond of animals. Howard Pollack counted more than forty different ones mentioned in his titles and texts.

206

to Arthur Berger, it suggests twelve-tone writing in the piano introduction and has a leaping vocal line as a tribute to Berger's early proto-serialism, though the music is firmly tonal. Verna noted that this song "is, I think, more a musical joke than a text joke. The music makes fun, in a warm, loving way, of Arthur's music. It hops, skips and jumps, just as Arthur's music hops, skips and jumps. Arthur is fastidious, doesn't exercise and is not athletic, so the text is ironic."

The restless ferocity of "Tigeroo" is meant to connote the personality of Harold Shapero. There is a busy, neoclassic-sounding piano part and, at the words "I'll eat all I like," a dissonant march reminiscent of Prokofiev. Verna remembered that "Irving was going to do something very Beethoven, to make fun of Harold, but he decided that would be too obvious. He felt the text suited Harold, who can be I'll-gobble-you-up ugly, but whose bark is much worse than his bite. Like Harold, the tiger had problems and complications, and kept people at a distance." This particular song, Fine thought, "really works."

Dedicated to Leonard Bernstein, "Lenny the Leopard" invokes romanticism with triplet motion, sensitive hesitations and rolled piano chords. On January 17, 1955, Fine wrote to his wife: "Have been constantly chipping away at the songs. Am trying to keep Lenny the L. from being too sentimental." In the poem, the leopard "hated his spots" and "tied his tail in a hundred knots" and did "everything else bad leopards do," all related in Fine's mind to Bernstein's flamboyantly egocentric character. Verna recalled: "When Irving played 'Lenny the Leopard' for Bernstein, Lenny said, in his over-dramatic fashion, 'Oh my god, that's my whole life story in one poem!' He always had a problem about wanting to be loved, wanting the world to love him."

"The Frog and the Snake" is cast in Fine's best witty manner—sprightly, vivacious neoclassical music, chromatic and modulating, sometimes rather Coplandesque. The dedication is to Lukas Foss. "Irving adored Lukas," said Verna, "but there was always a side to Lukas that was a bit amoral—his little shenanigans." She related a "classic" story. "When Lukas was the Boston Symphony's pianist, Koussevitzky would get very fussy about the Bach piano concertos." Before a rehearsal, Foss sometimes erased the Maestro's markings in the conductor's score. "Koussevitzky would come to where he had wanted a *ritard*, look down at the score and say to the orchestra, 'I told you. No *ritard!*'" That anecdote, she believed, "is much related" to Fine's song. In the text, the frog, about to be devoured by a snake, saves himself by insisting that he is a golliwog, and that if he is eaten the snake "will die of a tummy ache." Verna thought that "Lukas was a little like that in the early days. He could talk himself out of a difficult situation."

"Two Worms," inscribed to the composer and writer Arthur Cohn, was the only song written with no dedication in mind. Its musical highlights are the atmospheric, slinky chromaticism of the opening, a trilling effect of sixty-fourth notes in the piano and fast triplets meant to illustrate words like "wiggle" and "squirm." With its large leaps and octave displacement, the vocal line is intentionally non-lyric. The song ends dramatically on the words "through life." According to Verna, "Arthur Cohn was a very famous playboy. Irving used to tell me about his exploits and I think he secretly admired them. Every woman that walked: it used to be a joke. But Irving thought Arthur was a lonely man, with all his Don Juanism"—thus, the lonesome worms of the poem.

The piano sets the stage for the last song, "The Duck and the Yak," with a lively and dissonant introduction followed by dry, *misterioso* ostinato accompaniment. This Slavic-tinged music, dedicated to the Russian-born composer Alexei Haieff, evokes a mock-sinister, silent-film style. At the words "sometimes you get tired of you," there is an echo of musical comedy in the Bernstein mode. The accompaniment throughout is inventive and rhythmically intricate, and the song ends with dramatic declamation set against brilliant keyboard scale passages. Verna remarked: "Alexei Haieff was very Stravinskian, and a close friend of Irving's after the War. He always seemed to live by his wits. Irving liked his music. I don't think the words have anything to do with Alexei, just that the whole sound was Russian." This song was considerably revised before its publication in 1959.

The first performance of *Childhood Fables for Grownups* (as *Three Children's Songs for Grownups*) was given on February 20, 1956, in New York at the Juilliard School, by mezzo-soprano Regina Sarfaty and pianist Robert Starer. This was at the fourth concert of Juilliard's Festival of American Music, a program that also presented songs by Mark Schubart, Theodore Chanler and Ross Lee Finney. The next day, Howard Taubman wrote in the *New York Times*: "Mr. Fine—and his verse writer, Gertrude Norman—need not be modest. Children would find their songs flavorsome and amusing, too." Fine himself often accompanied singers, both female and male, in these songs. This succinct, unpretentious cycle would become popular at recitals, both as a set and as individual numbers.[6] Nevertheless, despite its cleverness and charm, *Childhood Fables* stands as only a minor entry in the small Fine canon.

During January 1955, while Verna was vacationing in Florida with Emily, staying with her brother Spencer Rudnick and his wife Justine, Fine wrote that he was "working a bit this evening to dispel the 'miss you miss you' blues," adding: "Hope you are getting as fat as a house and are furthermore getting tips from Justine on how to become even more sexy than you are." Verna seems to have let herself go somewhat and was perhaps on her way to becoming a *hausfrau*. A few days later he returned to the subject of her appearance. "Have fun, get fat, or at least plump, and if it pleases you to dye your few grey hairs—do it." In another letter, he said, "Loved hearing your voice, and am glad to know that you are recuperating your vital resources when away from *the kvetch*—(meaning me, 'natch')."

Verna constantly worried about her husband becoming flabby, so that when he was away from home he would have to reassure her in letters that he was watching his diet: "I am at the moment eating my lunch which is minus starches (bread or pastry). Maybe I can lose a pound or two"; "Am watching my diet to the extent of eating no bread beyond a slice of toast in the morning. A year of this and I might lose five pounds." (Fine especially enjoyed herring, pickles and "jimmy frosting cup-cakes," he told one of his daughters.) Joanna Fine said that "he had a tendency to gain weight, and when he did Mother was very hard on him." Conversely, Fine wanted Verna to stay the attractive woman he had married.

---

6. In 1977 all six of the *Childhood Fables* were orchestrated by Joel Spiegelman.

Claudia Fine noted that "she never wore makeup. I remember going shopping with my father and him buying her expensive Elizabeth Arden makeup and eye-shadow. He wanted her to spruce up, but she never used it. She felt that a beautiful woman didn't have to wear makeup." He was affectionate and rather domesticated. "He would make breakfast and bring it to her in bed" ("Bet you miss my breakfasts and chocolate sundaes," he once wrote Verna).

In January 1955, as Verna basked in the Florida sun and Fine endured a bitterly cold, sunless Massachusetts winter, Leonard Bernstein and Lillian Hellman came to Brandeis to give a seminar on their musical-in-progress based on Voltaire's *Candide*. Jack Gottlieb remembered that "part of the exercise in the seminar was to write music for the same section of the show that Bernstein was writing—a battle scene, for example. He would return a month later, look over what we had produced and then, since he had already finished his own music for that scene, he'd show us how *he* had done it. That was a high-powered and certainly different way of being introduced to theater music."

On January 13, Fine had heard Hellman discuss theater music and opera, after which Bernstein played and sang several numbers from his score. "Hellman is a very impressive one might almost say austere woman," he informed Verna. "She takes the Candide book very seriously. Judging from the few excerpts I heard from Lenny's music she takes it far more seriously than he does. The numbers I heard were a curious kind of Americanized Gilbert & Sullivan. Well done, cute and very deft in their treatment of words, but not particularly original, though they have some of Lenny's tricks."

In a January 17 letter, Fine mentioned that he had spent an evening at the home of Arthur and Esther Berger, where the violinist Joseph Fuchs was rehearsing one of Berger's works. "Fuchs then asked me to play through my sonata with him. He reads like a streak." Afterward, Fine played the Columbia recording of his *String Quartet*, which Fuchs "admired very much." He continued: "It's quite a number— much more mature but also undeniably morbid at times. Much better to get that morbidity into the music, however."

Gertrude Norman wrote to Fine on March 5 regarding *Childhood Fables*. "It's very nice to have the songs. I waited till

I could get to a piano, before writing to thank you, and even from my own garbled rendition (more divined than read), they seem delightful, and the music carries out so well the feeling of the words." It is unclear whether she was referring to the first four songs, or whether Fine had completed the last two songs and sent them to her. (Later that same month, Norman informed Fine that she and her seven cats were being evicted from her New York apartment. Richard Wernick, who would have dealings with her a few years hence, remembered her as "a nutcase from Nutcaseville.")

In the April issue of *Musical Quarterly* magazine, Fine reviewed a recording of music by two British composers, Constant Lambert (1905-1951) and Lord Berners (1883-1950). Berners (Gerald Hugh Tyrwhitt-Wilson) was a kind of amateur composer who also painted, wrote novels and poetry and had been a diplomat. Charmed by his Satie-like piano pieces, Fine noted that "the man of many talents is, of course, always suspected of dilettantism," and while Berners was neither a great nor important composer, "he had more genuine mastery and creativeness than many a full-time professional composer." Lambert's jazzy *Concerto for Piano and Nine Instruments* fared less well. An obviously irritated Fine termed it "a dated composition [that] contains little else besides manner." He thought the ensemble for which it was written "rich in sonorous possibilities" but felt that the composer "has realized extremely few of these." The work contained "serious formal weaknesses," including an over-long slow movement and "an embarrassing coda" to the last movement. He summed up: "But what makes the Concerto a particularly exasperating listening experience to this reviewer is its aura of phony *chic* (its jazz sounds suspiciously like musical slumming) and its expressive ambiguity."

Somewhat earlier, Virgil Thomson had fared better. "One of the things that often makes listening to [his] music such a pleasure is the feeling that he had a whale of a time composing it." Fine was reviewing a record of Thomson's *Ten Etudes for Piano*, which were "fun to hear," and he felt that in many of them "there is a suggestion of the parlor trick raised to the level of art." Further: "All of this makes a very fascinating kind of speech, highly individual and at the same completely impersonal and unsentimental."

That June, Fine dashed off a jocular song, vocal line only, for his father. It was titled "The Mesabi Blues, A Father's Day Greeting to Papa Georgie." The words were by "I.G.F. and Papa Georgie Fine," the music by "Papa Iggy Fine alias Uncle Irving." The lyrics addressed the woes of George Fine's favorite stock, Mesabi Iron Ore of Minnesota. Harold Shapero recalled that "Irving's stockbroker father had a thing about the energy crisis in the 1950s. There was this low-grade iron ore called Mesabi, and the old man was always trying to get us to buy it. His dream was that when all the high-grade ore was exhausted Mesabi would be valuable." Papa George obsessively bought Mesabi stock, certain that it was only a matter of time before he would be a millionaire, but it kept dropping. "Irving lent him at least three or four thousand dollars to hold on," said Shapero. "The irony was that in the last years of Irving's life Mesabi was suddenly worth millions of dollars."

According to Wernick, "Irving's mother would borrow money from him to go to Florida, because his father never had any cash: everything went back into the market." But Papa George had controlling interest in Mesabi Iron and in the late 1950s it split four ways. Wernick's wife Beatrice remembered, "that was when Verna and Irving put in the swimming pool and the deck, and terraced the back yard of the Natick house. And the little daughters were getting substantial dividend checks every quarter."

In 1955, however, Mesabi stock had plummeted. Thus, the blues of Fine's little song, the lyrics of which are full of waggish Yiddishisms. Excerpts: "I've got the Mesabi blues, because the second mortgage lobby refused to buy Mesabi. Mesabi's a sure-fire thing. It ought to make one sing. But all the little litvak noodniks prefer to shtoop their kopeks in their poopiks to dancing the Mesabi swing." Another line of this mocking text read: "Papa Georgie Fine will you listen I pray. You're a hero at least on Father's Day." Years later, Verna noted that when she was selecting material for the Irving Fine Collection at the Library of Congress, she had kept back some items to avoid hurt feelings. "His father was still living, and there were some very personal remarks, some very nasty things, about how Irving felt toward him."

Fine neither taught at Tanglewood nor worked at the MacDowell Colony during the summer of 1955. As he wrote to Copland on July 10: "We are not budging this summer. Claudia and Emily are at day camp and we sit about rotting in the dampest, hottest weather in years. Started a vegetable garden and even the radishes rotted." Regarding composition, he said that "I've been trying to find out how one 'keeps it tough' (your famous injunction to me). Chiefly I suspect by keeping myself out of it or at least keep one's anxiety out of it." He continued: "You mention new discoveries in orchestration in the 'American Songs' orchestral version. I wish you'd send me a score—Please, pretty please. Suspect I could learn a lot. Haven't stolen anything of yours for a long time now. Oops, what am I saying?" (Copland had written that "it seems to me I am beginning to mix str. & w.w. [strings and woodwinds] in a way that produces a most dulcet effect.")

If the *Childhood Fables* had been one of Fine's lesser efforts, his next work, *Serious Song, A Lament for String Orchestra*, is another matter entirely. Lasting only ten minutes, it has the breadth and depth of a longer score and gives the impression of, as one critic put it, "a miniature symphonic poem."

*Serious Song* was composed at Natick during the summer of 1955. The February issue of the *Brandeis University Bulletin* had announced that three members of the music faculty—Fine, Arthur Berger and Harold Shapero—were writing works for the Louisville Orchestra as part of its ongoing commissions program, under a grant from the Rockefeller Foundation.[7] Fine's commission had come in September 1954, and specified a fee of $1,000, an additional $200 for orchestral parts, a recording on the Louisville label (which was eventually released in 1957) and a due date of September 1 of the following year.

A threnody of considerable power, *Serious Song* constitutes one of Fine's most satisfying, stylistically unified scores. It is cast in the composer's favorite slow-fast-slow tripartite format, with the tempo mark *Andante quasi adagio, molto cantabile*. The string textures are often extremely rich, at times even dense because of contrapuntal complexities. An empha-

---

7. Berger composed his *Polyphony for Orchestra*, Shapero his *Credo for Orchestra* (which was a shortened and simplified version of the slow movement of his *Concerto for Orchestra* of 1955).

sis on extreme ranges and frequent polyphonic shifts between choirs are notable elements throughout. Emotion is expressed directly and unsubtly, though the effect is never cloying. This is an expertly crafted work, its compressed length perfectly suited to its lyric materials, which progress either in 6/8 or 9/8 meter. Fine has reverted to a completely tonal idiom, ignoring the style-expanding possibilities of serialism to produce a convincing, if slightly impersonal, hyper-romantic rhetoric that is, in Leonard Bernstein's words, "in the great tradition of nineteenth-century lyricism—the tradition of the Chausson *Poème* and the *Verklärte Nacht* of early Schoenberg." Introducing *Serious Song* before an April 16, 1959 New York Philharmonic performance, Bernstein continued, "Now, Mr. Fine has usually been identified with neoclassic tendencies; that is, most of his music has been related to Stravinsky, rather dry, spare, clean, objective. So it's all the more curious that suddenly this piece emerged three or four years ago, a completely subjective statement, unashamed, passionate, out-and-out romantic. I must confess it's my favorite work of his." He concluded: "This is rich, sensitive, emotional music."

Fine's only recorded appraisal of his *Serious Song* was characteristically modest: "Not a bad piece, but so sad and *fin de siècle* in sound"; but some of his composer colleagues voiced higher opinions. David Diamond cited its "seriousness of purpose," continuing: "The *Serious Song* has a lovely elegiac quality, a very good kind of lyric flow. For me, it's probably his best piece." Arthur Cohn praised the work's "flexible lyricism and warm severity, plus a mood of demanding asceticism. It is in turn tender and serene, desperate and impassioned." Harold Shapero thought *Serious Song* "a very pretty piece, a tear-jerker."

Fine provided the following program note at the time of the premiere. "*Serious Song* is essentially an extended aria for string orchestra. There are three main sections in the composition. The first begins very slowly and quietly with a unison statement of the main thematic material in all of the violins, developing that material subsequently in a flowing, freely contrapuntal style. The tonal implications are, in the main, E phrygian.

"The second section, which is the longest, presents a contrasting theme in the first violins with accompaniment figuration in the violas and counter melodic fragments in the cellos and violins. The tonality is C minor. The internal organization of this section is essentially A B A-prime, the B sub-section being characterized by considerable development and tonal digression. The return of the contrasting theme occurs at a climactic moment, but the music goes on to achieve a main climax just before the commencement of the third main section of the composition.

"This last section is coda-like in character. The texture is simplified to melody and an accompaniment consisting almost entirely of *tremolando* and *pizzicato* effects over a fairly static harmony. The tonality is E major for the most part, but occasionally ambiguously major-minor. The ending is extremely quiet, slightly slower than the beginning, and fading away to E, *ppp*."

*Serious Song* was given its first performance on November 15, 1955, in Louisville, Kentucky, by the Louisville Orchestra conducted by Robert Whitney. Fine attended, and a few weeks later wrote to a former student: "Heard my Louisville piece played with mixed feelings." Local newspaper reviews were appreciative. The Kentucky *Irish American* pronounced *Serious Song* "pleasant, interesting and very clear in its meaning." The *Louisville Times*' critic wrote that "it is a lyrical and very sad piece of music. Segment by segment, it doesn't seem too impressive, but at the end, the cumulative effect is impressive and you realize you've given yourself, all unwittingly, to the mood." The correspondent for the *Louisville Courier-Journal* dubbed *Serious Song* "a coherent and expressive statement couched in attractive terms for string orchestra. Fine knows how to manage contrapuntal textures without losing his, or his listener's, way." The piece is "solemn and austere, but not bloodless [and] develops logically [to] a poignant and dignified close." In an article about the ongoing commissioning project, another writer hailed the work as "one of the best achievements of the entire Louisville series."

Published in 1959 by Broude Bros., Inc., *Serious Song* quickly achieved a certain popularity. It had its New York premiere on May 19, 1956, conducted by Howard Shanet at Columbia University; it was introduced to Tanglewood by the Boston Symphony under Lukas Foss a few weeks later, on July 8; it received its Boston premiere on March 23, 1958, by the Zimbler Sinfonietta conducted by the composer; and in addition to Bernstein's 1959 performances with the New York Philharmonic, it was played that same year by Eugene Ormandy and the Philadelphia Orchestra. During the 1960s, Aaron Copland occasionally conducted it, for instance, in June 1964, in Hilversum, Sweden.

The notices were uniformly positive. Edward Downes in the *New York Times* found the score "unabashedly romantic [and] written with great skill. It was stirring music." Miles Kastendieck called it "a beautifully sustained piece of melodic writing" in the *Journal American*. Howard Taubman noted in the *New York Times* that Fine "writes with an elegant ear for the textures of the strings [and] his taste is fastidious. Though he does not wear his heart on his sleeve, he manages to say moving things." Jay Harrison described the work in the *New York Herald Tribune* as "diatonic, rhapsodic, a shade bleak. It is an extended three-part statement of considerable poise and majesty."

Reviewing *Serious Song* in Boston, one critic stated that Fine was now "a mature composer [and] it is hoped that he will find time to turn out a symphony," then praised "his ability to turn out a rightly integrated score charged with ideas that communicate on the highest poetic level." Another critic noted that the audience's applause recalled Fine several times and "attested to the immediateness of [the music's] appeal." In Philadelphia, *Serious Song* was characterized as "a noble sorrowing" and as "dignified and dolorous."

Fine had, so to speak, hit the jackpot with his *Serious Song*. As he once wrote on the subject of communication: "If the composer is unwilling to give up the joys of a live audience, then he has got to stop writing as though he didn't want anybody to hear his music. Music designed for performance by somebody before a group of non-participants is a *public art*; and it is blind folly to deny this." One suspects that in this unexpectedly retrogressive score is heard the true, pure voice of Irving Fine, a voice that, rather similar to the case of Sergei Rachmaninoff, unashamedly reveled in romantic expression alien to its time—here, however, with complete success. As Fine once wrote about the American composer John Alden Carpenter, the music "was born out of date." Over the years, *Serious Song* would gain a firm place in the string-orchestra repertory.

# Chapter 15

■ ON NOVEMBER 22, 1955, just after the premiere of *Serious Song*, Verna's mother, Florence Rudnick, died suddenly in Boston. Her death came as a blow to Fine as well as to her daughter, for Florence (whom he always called "Flo") had invariably been approving, affectionate and generous toward him and he, in turn, had been extremely fond of his mother-in-law. Three weeks later, Fine wrote to Jack Gottlieb that "we are just barely beginning to get back to normal."

What might have constituted normality in Fine's life at that point is anyone's guess. For some time, he had experienced sporadic writer's block and been subject to depressions. As Howard Pollack aptly put it (in his 1992 book, *Harvard Composers: Walter Piston and His Students from Elliott Carter to Frederic Rzewski*), writings in Fine's notebooks "reveal a man haunted by insomnia, hypochondria, depression and anxiety, a perfectionist tortured by a sense of inferiority. This melancholy worsened throughout the 1950s."[1] By mid-1954 the problem had become so acute that he began analytical therapy at the Boston Psychoanalytic Institute. Verna stated that "there was a research project there and Irving was invited to join it at five dollars a session because they were studying creativity. I felt, and he did too, that his depressions were tied up with his composing, because he would have blocks. He and Harold Shapero used to call these depressions 'blackies' (sometimes they were beige or grey).[2] The funny thing was that Irving always got a little depressed when he finished a work; he said the double barline depressed him. I would laugh

---

1. Pollack further noted: "A Freudian description of Fine's character as anal would find plentiful justification in his limericks, which often joked about behinds, as well as in a bizarre fantasy [in a 1944 letter to his sister Barbara] about Nazi carrier-pigeons that defecate on a Jewish middle-class family."

2. Once, Fine even made reference to a "delayed blackie."

and ask him why and he would joke about it, saying it was because that meant he had to go on to another piece. Composing was painful for him, but he had to do it. He used to say, 'It's like a spigot: you can't turn it off. It's in your head and it drives you bananas if you don't get it down on paper'."

Fine's gloomy moods were well known in his family. His sister Audrey recalled: "My mother would tell me, 'Oh, Irving's got a blackie!' He was always looking for an answer when he was having a deep depression, and going to an analyst was the fashion then." Fine's other sister, Barbara, noted that "Irving was a perfectionist and he really worked at it. He talked to me about that. He'd say, 'Oh, I'm having a blackie and I just can't compose'; but he'd make light of it. Probably, he felt it would pass, which it did. The blackies weren't constant."

Claudia Fine remembered that her father "used to talk about his blackies, but he was careful not to inflict them on his children. My mother would say, 'He's in one of his moods, feeling depressed, can't write.' At such times, he would be quiet and disappear into his study, and we wouldn't see him for hours." She added: "He was a major hypochondriac." Joanna Fine, who became a psychiatrist, noted that "Mother told us they were studying creativity in Boston when my father had his analysis, and they wanted to study him. That's not true. He went for analysis because he was in pain. Analysis is a huge commitment, an investigation into yourself. You have to have some dissatisfaction with your life to go into it. But he was drawn to that field anyway. He felt that if he hadn't become a composer he would have liked to have been a psychiatrist."

Harold Shapero had a good deal to say on the subject of "blackies" and analysis. "In the early years, when Irving and I were very close and working together, I noticed that I would sometimes go into a terrific black mood. Then, out would come the next section of a piece I was writing. Irving experienced similar things. Blackies were what we both experienced preceding creative adventure. We had fun talking about them. They had the feeling of a depression, but you knew there was nothing particularly to be depressed about. It's as if putting life into notes involved some kind of psychic borrowing, producing a black kind of mood.

"Irving and I discovered that with the blackies the psyche feels as if it's a black negative. Then, there's light, which bursts through when you're composing, and the material forms and you suddenly get the next section of a piece. We both noticed that." Shapero compared a blackie to the flu, which attacks the central nervous system. He felt that the same system "is involved in composing music in a mysterious way that's not understood." He pointed out that "some of the things that are the most inspired don't produce exaltation in their maker until much later." He continued: "I can never compose without getting sick, and I watched Irving and saw all the signs and knew they were work-related. He would have lots of symptoms when we talked on the telephone. One of them was: 'I taste blood in my mouth'—he used to say that."

According to Shapero, Fine's analysis ultimately proved the undoing of their intimate friendship. "Initially, when he started analysis, I complained all the time. You don't *need* it, I said. Freud is all wrong, absolutely at his weakest in understanding the creative process. I went to an analyst only once. When I got to the end of my *Symphony for Classical Orchestra*—the last movement was a giant thing with a million notes that began with a chorale—it blew my head open. I didn't know what was happening to me. I was afraid to go to sleep because I thought I was going to die. I went to see Hans Sachs and listed an endless set of symptoms: I had the blackies, I was going to die, I had rings around my stomach and bands around my wrists—psychic things. Sachs listened to that dreadful recital and then said: 'That's normal. You'll get used to it.'

"So that was my one visit to an analyst, but Irving went for a long time. He was a sensitive artist but he came a little late to it and didn't realize that being an artist is a sick-making thing. I said to Irving your problem is your work, and I kept hollering at him that if he understood that he didn't need analysis. But Irving didn't make mistakes in composition very often like I did. He claimed that there was nothing wrong with his music or his technique, so that wasn't what was making him sick.

"Then I found out that I was figuring in his analysis, that I was an ego-prop; and Irving related that the psychiatrist told him to get rid of me. I didn't need Irving desperately, but I was angry that he listened to this man. So I shut him out, figuring I was doing Irving a favor by getting rid of me for him. We didn't play our music for each other anymore, we didn't discuss music or talk about anything deep after that. He later complained that I had clammed up, gone neutral and didn't offer him anything. He told me: 'You weren't there when I needed you.' I always had the feeling that when he got over that damned analysis we'd be like old times again. But that never happened, although it wasn't an unfriendly relationship. We were social and saw each other at Brandeis all the time."

Esther Shapero was fond of Fine but thought him "very neurotic—he got depressed easily." She reflected that "our relations became strained when Irving went into analysis and we could never understand why. Verna said that the analyst told Irving he shouldn't see Harold so much. They reached out for different friends. Not musicians, but all kinds of varied people." In Harold's opinion, "What happened was that Irving was ready to write some of those later pieces that are sort of twelve-tone, far from what my influence would have been. He was about to stand on his own feet, so our break was in the psychic realm."

One of the Fines' new friends, their Natick neighbor the psychiatrist Arnold Modell, noted that "Irving was certainly prone to depression, but overall I didn't see him as really ill. I imagine he could be depressed at times about his work or his status or about competition with colleagues. And the kind of music he was writing was not quite in fashion. But he was very open with me emotionally, and demonstrative. He was somebody who elicited love in other people."

Richard Wernick believed that Fine had "a strong desire to get rid of his inhibitions, because he felt his music was too inhibited. I remember him talking about Rachmaninoff in very positive terms when he would bring up the question of inhibition. The thing he admired about Rachmaninoff was that there was a composer who could let it all hang out, who could write these great big works that let the melodies flow and who did not worry about details of harmony.

"Irving had gone through a long period of creative block. Perfectionists don't write a lot of music because they get involved in detail. Part of the block derived from the fact that he wanted to use that elegant aesthetic passed down to him from Stravinsky through Copland, but he wanted to do something different. He didn't want to rewrite Copland and, although a lot of Stravinsky appears in his music, he certainly didn't want to rewrite Stravinsky. It may be that he used his busyness at Brandeis as a rationale for not composing, but he never complained about being overloaded. The early to middle 1950s was a low time for him creatively, and it was a period when everybody was running off to have Freudian analysis. I think his analysis messed him all up." Joel Spiegelman often saw Fine at Brandeis in the late 1950s. "Irving had an outgoing personality, but occasionally he could be distant and cool, quite unresponsive. I found out later that he was in analysis at the time." Beatrice Wernick said, "I seem to recall, before he wrote the *Symphony (1962)*, that he wanted to compose a big piece and was having trouble doing it. That was one of the reasons he was in therapy."

Some of the handwritten notes Fine made during his therapy (comments he termed "spiritual dredging") have survived and make for fascinating, at times revealing, reading. Excerpts follow, edited for spelling and punctuation. From a list of "disturbing things" in July 1954: "sound of baby's crying in sleep; newspaper story of murder of divorcee; story of [William] Schuman's ballet [*Undertow*];[3] the old anxiety about finishing the articles comes after a day of emotional upsets; fear of domination!" In the category "Impulses of the day": "Very hungry after leaving [home] and anticipated going to the Red Bell [restaurant] on the way to Brandeis. Thought of ideas for Slosberg building. Why the anxiety (tightness in gut)? All a form of hypochondriasis. As I write, I think I should read this to Verna. Why? For reassurance." A section of free association: "What should I call this: a night journal? Quite a title. A contradiction. Day piece in the night. Again the idea: what about showing this to Verna? What good

---

3. In a review of a recording of *Undertow*, published in the *Musical Quarterly* that October, Fine praised Schuman's "original and highly insistent music," and called the ballet itself "a shocker." He continued: "It describes in Freudian terms the career of a Transgressor, doomed by infantile frustrations to a life of torture culminating in murder." He termed *Undertow* "shock art," noting that when he saw a production in Boston during its first season (1945), "I found it quite unpleasant."

is this literary free-wheeling? Can you make anything of it? This is the problem of dealing with quickly written criticism."

Several months later, Fine was concerned with "*sympathy, empathy*" [his emphasis], which led to more free association. "Why does one weep for somebody's sufferings? Why does one say 'poor Audrey,' 'poor Claudia,' 'poor Dr. Nemiah' [Fine's analyst], etc.? And at the same time why does one feel here a sadness but not a despair and not a loneliness, almost a relief? Because one is living through somebody else and has in a sense got out of one's self by the identification of one's self with another. This is an acquired habit—in my case, through constant sympathy with my mother. Eventually, however, there must be a point at which one frees oneself from all such identification to this extent: we are like each other but we are also different. In my case, why am I so afraid of being different? My fear is that difference means queerness, eccentricity, even insanity. Whereas in a certain sense eccentrics and the insane, especially the latter, are less different from each other, progressively so, as they regress to infantile states. Why, in the last analysis, must we please ourselves first in our work? I'm thinking primarily of my composition but the idea has far-reaching manifestations—because the more we do so the less dependent we are and conversely the more selfish and less dependent we get the more we can give from our surplus."

Because Man spends a quarter of his life asleep, his mind free to roam unrestrained, Freudian analysis lays strong emphasis on the interpretation of dreams—never mind that modern science has determined that dreams are the product of random electrical impulses in the brain, the adjective arguably rendering them meaningless. Fine was asked to transcribe his dreams upon awakening. One, about playing golf, might appear to reveal insecurities in the social and sexual realms. "There are young men and women in this [dream]. I am schlemiel at golf. A talented couple follow me. They think little of me. I have singular lack of success. I attribute it to my clubs. The young woman says this is unlikely. I point out that my putter can be bent in two; certainly it ought to be rigid. She agrees at least with this. [in the margin, Fine wrote: "obvious sexuality; impotence?"] I think that I begin to feel that my general disability is due vaguely to madness. The first woman is very tender. I want her to stay with me—or, rather, I want to date her." [In the margin: "Shapero," followed by "character . . . poignant harmony."] Another dream concerned a memorial concert for the Welsh poet Dylan Thomas, who had died in 1953, at which "I am ignored." Waking from that dream, Fine wrote the details on music paper, "then turned to musical sketch to add ctpt. Anxiety lessened slightly while writing dream but returned when I turned to music. Earlier, upon going to bed, had noticed the extraordinary amount of musical activity in my mind." A third dream was analyzed by Fine as a "wish-fulfillment type": "Received the package, then another, both of which indicated that I had won a first prize. From England? As I associate with this—quartet [publisher's] proofs came to mind." At one point in his notes, he mentioned an "attack" of anxiety that left him with a "spooky feeling" and provoked him into taking a drug: "had half dex. tablet."[4] Summing up, Fine asked: "Why do I write all of this? As a desperate act to drive out myself from my thoughts? Because writing music brings no relief."

The following lines were probably written sometime in 1955. They stand as Fine's most acute and philosophical meditation on the enigmatic elements involved in musical composition. "The initial musical impulse must be strengthened by practice. It must be freed of anxiety. Only then can it leap forward. *Music is only notes.* Only by working at it with a playful, constructive attitude can we provide groundwork for inspiration. *God helps those who help themselves.* Outside help is a bonus. Let the mind attach itself fully, completely and without reservation, and without thought to self, to that which is outside of it. Complete and total surrender—complete commitment is necessary. The presence of self in music is a flaw. That music which concerns itself least with self-expression contains the richest personality."

Fine's analyst, the distinguished Harvard University psy-

---

4. According to Joanna Fine, her father often used Dexedrine, also known as "Speed," while at the MacDowell Colony. "Harold and Esther Shapero told me that when they were at MacDowell together they all drank heavily and took 'Speed.' We had a long conversation about the drugs they used there. It was part of the artists' environment."

chiatrist John Nemiah, consented to speak about his involvement as a young practitioner with the composer. He felt, however, that to reveal specifics about Fine's problems, even many years after his death, would be a violation of professional ethics. Thus, Dr. Nemiah understandably limited his remarks to generalities.

"Like all of us," he said, "Irving Fine had moments of anxiety and depressions. The difference is that he was a genius. He was a very sensitive person with the capacity to back off and look at himself honestly. But that goes with an artist or genius who has great depth and, fortunately, can sometimes get in touch with it and produce art for the rest of us.

"He was the first person I did analysis with, and there was really nothing unusual about his conflicts and problems, nothing perverse or shocking, nothing Barbara Walters would like to talk about. There was also nothing dramatic about his analysis process. His problems may have been a nuisance—for whatever reason, he was having difficulty in producing—but there certainly was no major mental illness of the sort that needs hospitalization."

Fine underwent analysis with Dr. Nemiah at the Boston Psychoanalytic Institute at Massachusetts General Hospital for four years, from July 1954 to the spring of 1958. "There was a kind of clinic at the Institute where people could be referred for analysis who couldn't afford high, exorbitant fees, and if they seemed good candidates they would then be referred to candidates-in-training, like myself, who would do the analysis under the supervision of a senior training analyst. I saw Mr. Fine five days a week for at least two or three years, and then it tapered down to three or four days a week. The sessions lasted for fifty minutes and took place either in the late morning or early afternoon. Classical Freudian psychoanalytic analysis is a long procedure. The thing you look for in people is essentially the capacity for self-observation, the ability to stand back, to relate. That implies a certain amount of intelligence and emotional development. Mr. Fine had a very complicated personality, intellectual in a good sense and rich in knowledge of music and literature. He was a psychologically minded person who certainly had the capacity to do analytic work. He was also a cultured, distinguished man, and there was no problem that I remember in his talking to me.

"Creative people are in a different class from the rest of us. Unconscious creation is a marvelous mystery, beyond pathology. It is a wonderful gift, but it can be hampered by conflicts. His pattern of dealing with anger, disappointments and frustrations was, however, like that of many other people: rather dime-a-dozen, garden-variety."

Dr. Nemiah recalled an amusing incident. "I had an office in the decrepit old Bulfinch building that dated from about 1816. It was a little closet with huge water pipes running across the ceiling. During one session, a pipe began to leak and a drop would come down about every ten seconds. I vividly remember poor Mr. Fine on the couch, rolling from side to side to avoid those drops. We both found it rather entertaining, and that said to me that at least he had a sense of the comic." As to Shapero's complaint that Fine's analysis had damaged their longtime friendship, Dr. Nemiah responded: "Every man is entitled to his own fantasy of interpretation."

He continued: "The analytic process is not so much advice-giving as helping the person to realize his conflicts and how he is dealing with them. If one's problem is diffidence, insecurity, trying to be a good guy, and suddenly one could get over that neurotic toe-stubbing, of course that would affect the writing. It would make good sense that a composer would be bolder, more secure and confident in expressing the kind of music that was in him, that previously he might have felt was too aggressive. That could well have been part of being freed up internally by the analytic process."

In André Gide's distrustful view of psychiatry, the maxim "know thyself" is as malign as it is inelegant. A person who studies himself, said Gide, obstructs his own development. Then, there is the funny story about the man who declared, "How wonderful! Today, after fifteen terrible, painful and expensive years of psychoanalysis, I can finally say shit to M-o-t-h-e-r."

But let Dr. Nemiah have the last word, for he was certain that Fine's analysis had proved beneficial. Referring to the composer's magnum opus, *Symphony (1962)*, he remarked, "After all, he did go on to do some wonderful work."

# Chapter 16

■ THE YEAR 1956 SAW PRODUCTION OF three trivial piano pieces and a major chamber score. The former all date from the spring. *Homage à Mozart* (the title carelessly mixes English with French) was described by Fine as "a perfectly innocent sort of bagatelle more or less Mozartian in character" and was inspired by the Mozart bicentennial (1756-1956). Set mostly in 6/8 meter, it was composed for his daughter Claudia, then eight years old, but "it got beyond her technical capacities." Fine thought that the piece, for intermediate pianists, "ought to be of some use in student recitals or in piano recitals, either as part of a modern group or as an encore." Despite his claim of Mozartian character, the music does not, to these ears, even remotely suggest Mozart, never mind the dry scale passages. In fact, its would-be harmonic cleverness and mannered hesitations seem far removed from the Viennese master. An odd tribute this, from one who admired Mozart and played his music well.

Harold Shapero, the adamant Classicist, recalled being irritated by Fine's bagatelle. After humorously noting that "the worst thing Irving ever did to me was to come for a visit and stamp out his cigarette on my front sidewalk," he declared: "But the thing for which I disliked him most was for publishing *Homage à Mozart*. To me, that was a revoltingly pretentious thing to do. I remember thinking, who the hell does he think he is, titling something like that? You can only do that if you're a great composer yourself. And it isn't even a very good piece."

Dedicated "For Claudia," the two other little piano pieces that Fine wrote at the same time, *Victory March of the Elephants* and *Lullaby for a Baby Panda* (for beginning pianists), are harmless trifles, not at all pretentious. Their editor, Isadore Freed, termed the first a "vigorous and jolly march" and observed that two closely related modes, the Ionian and the Lydian, are employed and that the music ends in

227

a semi-cadence, "as if it could still go on for a long time." The rather pretty panda-lullaby is, he said, "delicately tinted," with a "purposely vague" key-center.

*Homage à Mozart* (duration, one-and-a-half minutes) was published in 1957, *Victory March* and *Lullaby* (combined duration, two minutes) the following year. The circumstances of their first performances are unknown. (There is extant a typed program from a piano recital given at the Natick house on June 18, 1961 by all three Fine daughters at which Emily played *Lullaby for a Baby Panda.* As decoration, and apropos of nothing, a lyric twelve-tone row is notated at the bottom, in Fine's hand.)

On August 24, 1956, Fine sent a postcard to Verna from the MacDowell Colony. "Worked very hard yesterday but still have not got to the climactic place in the development. Discovered I needed more little notes in the earlier section that you liked—an occasional flash of them—but without changing the quiet and scattered sound with which the development begins." The reference was to a recently begun chamber work, the *Fantasia for String Trio.* This had been commissioned in December of the previous year by the Fromm Foundation and the University of Illinois, for a fee of $400. The score was completed at Natick in January 1957.

In the same card, Fine noted that Louise Talma had played her twelve-tone piano etudes for him. "They're terrific," he enthused, "at least the 1st three or four are." With the *Fantasia,* Fine turned once again to serialism, and, said Verna, "he felt he was making progress with the twelve-tone method. Not that he wanted to write twelve-tone-ugly music, but he was experimenting."

Brief and compressed though it is, the *Fantasia* impresses as one of Fine's most noteworthy, and personal, pieces. It is highly organized, rhythmically vital and intensely harmonic within a freely serial scheme with tonal ramifications, its slow music memorably imbued with elegiac romanticism that is expressed through highly chromatic writing and sustained sonorities. Elegance is the word that comes to mind throughout, even in the lightfooted yet volatile, slightly Bartókian scherzo that dominates the work, with its cross-accents, buzzing ostinatos and quickly shifting tonal centers; and this elegance is achieved mainly through elusive harmonic detail. Richard Wernick confirmed that Fine's principal preoccupation here, and in the later symphony, was "discovering a way in which he could write so-called twelve-tone music in an elegant manner." He added: "I think that a reason why Irving may not have been interested in the Second Viennese School was that he probably did not consider it to be terribly elegant. He didn't like ugliness in music."

The *Fantasia* proved a significant step away from the constraints of Stravinskian neoclassicism. David Diamond observed that Fine "got caught between Stravinsky and Schoenberg, those two big influences, as did so many of the young composers at that time. Those Boston-Brandeis neoclassicists were a strange, isolated group. I don't think they cared very much what was going on in other parts of the country." Harold Shapero remembered that "I might have joked to him that we were all second-rate Stravinskys, which was true."

Wernick recalled that during his studies with Fine in the early 1950s, the twelve-tone system might as well not have existed. After 1955, however, "we had a lot of discussion about the adaptation of twelve-tone technique, a system inherently atonal, into tonality, which manifested itself in the *Fantasia*. It was important for him to find a new language on which to support his musical impulses, which always were neoclassic. He agonized over that, inside. Irving wanted to break out of the hermetic Boston neoclassical scene, and I think he felt that, with the *Fantasia*, he was really on the right track. For everything it owes to the neoclassic aesthetic, it is a very original piece. I don't know of another like it, harmonically." Wernick cited the *Fantasia* as a more integrated serial work than the *String Quartet*. "At that point, Irving had figured out how to do it, whereas, the quartet is more a study in how to do it." Shapero thought the *Fantasia* "a handsome piece, very successful."

The *Fantasia for String Trio* is cast in three connecting movements, slow-fast-slow, the brief outer movements surrounding a fully formed scherzo. As Fine stated in a program note, "all of the melodic and much of the harmonic materials of the entire work derive from the opening statement in the viola at the beginning of the first movement." That generative and highly lyric viola passage contains a twelve-note row (C,

D, F-sharp, D-sharp, C-sharp, B, G-sharp, A, E, F-natural, B-flat, G-natural), that violates strict method by the repetition of one note (G-sharp), as the "thirteenth" in the series, a subtle indication of the freedom in which the dodecaphonic system is to be treated (additionally, the twelfth tone appears only in a grace-note that leads to the repeated note). In Fine's terse description, the first movement (*Adagio ma non troppo*) is "a kind of fugato, and lyrical in character," one supplied with six thematic statements. The second movement (*Allegro molto ritmico*) is "a scherzo, fairly extended and developed, but without formal recapitulation or contrasting trio." The final movement (*Lento assai, tranquillo*) is "of more varied character [and] opens with a freely imitative section, followed by a rhapsodic or declamatory middle section, and concludes with the same quiet, reflective quality of the beginning of the movement." The formal design of this ternary finale places dramatic focus on a *fortissimo* violin solo in the central portion.

Dedicated to the contemporary-music patron Paul Fromm, the *Fantasia* had its first performance on March 3, 1957, in Urbana, Illinois, during the University of Illinois' Festival of Contemporary Arts, played by members of the Walden String Quartet. There was a repeat performance on March 29. Fine had been unable to attend the premiere, but on the twenty-seventh he wrote to Jack Gottlieb, who was in Illinois: "Thanks a million for sending me news of the trio. It's the only news which I have received; and in fact, I had begun to wonder whether or not it had even been performed!" A recording made at one or the other of the concerts was subsequently issued in the University of Illinois Custom Recording Series. Reviewing it in 1961, Arthur Cohn concluded that the performers "do not master this work as it has been mastered by others." However, he pronounced the *Fantasia* "a refreshingly inventive work," noting that "analysis of Fine's score shows a textbook of possibilities for tone-row technique applied to the paradoxical relationship of tonal diatonicism. The exterior is beautiful, but the interior of this trio structure is just as exciting." He also praised Fine's "impeccable clarity." Writing elsewhere, Cohn stated: "Fine's *Fantasia* represents a hybrid of dodecaphonic technique applied to freed tonality; the twain meet successfully."

On March 11, Fine had written to Copland, "Got check

for my trio from Fromm and a nice letter telling me that I shall hear it at Tanglewood this summer. Had a reading recently . . . and it wasn't bad at all." Two weeks later, he told Copland (revealingly, considering the dichotomy that plagued him), "It's paradoxical, here I am—just having completed a kind of intellectual work—something that's certainly not going to make anybody's hit parade—and yet my tastes in the music I want to hear are essentially conservative. I still like tunes and catchy rhythms and clean sounding instrumental effects."

Fine got to hear his *Fantasia* performed in concert June 1, on the opening program of the fourth Brandeis Creative Arts Festival, and on July 23 he heard it at Tanglewood, played by members of the Boston Symphony Orchestra (George Zazofsky, violin; Joseph de Pasquale, viola; Samuel Mayes, cello). In a perceptive review after the latter event, Jay C. Rosenfeld noted in the *Berkshire Eagle* that the *Fantasia* had received four (?) previous performances that year, and continued: "Fine's trio consists of a very rhythmical and energetic scherzo between slow and maturely introspective movements in which the composer shows a keen insight into the best registers and textures of the instruments he employs. He writes long, tenuous, melodic lines for the slow movements, and assigns the introductory ones in both instances to the viola. Double stops near the end of the third movement are deeply impressive. A profoundly felt emotional content covers his consistent but, at previous times, more apparent erudition." After a 1959 performance of the *Fantasia* in Boston by the Walden Quartet, a critic termed the music "mature and somewhat stylized," finding the effect "reflective [and] impressive in its texture of thoughtfulness." Another writer subsequently cited the work for "the patrician sweetness of the discourse."

The *Fantasia* would have several performances in the next few years, including one by members of the Juilliard Quartet in February 1958. The score was published in 1959, by Mills Music (the August 23 issue of *Cashbox* magazine carried an article, "Mills Music Signs Irving Fine," referring to an exclusive publishing contract probably arranged by his friend Arthur Cohn, who was director of symphonic music at Mills), and that November Fine wrote to Paul Fromm, "It is extremely gratifying to see that the *Fantasia* is getting around."

Decades later, Richard Wernick reminisced: "When Irving first showed me the score of the *Fantasia*, he asked, what do you think? I said, 'Well, it's Beethoven with wrong notes.' He was pleased and replied, 'That's what it's supposed to be!'[1] The *Fantasia* was a move into a wider, more dissonant harmonic field, and, as Copland said, it gave him 'more chords'. Irving never used that expression, but I think that is what he was after, because he was always conscious of the dynamism of harmony." Even though the *Fantasia* has a duration of only fourteen minutes, "He always felt that it was a larger-scale piece than his previous neoclassical music."

In January 1956, during the semester break, Irving, Verna and their two eldest daughters vacationed in Miami. Fine had to leave at the end of the month to resume duties at wintry Brandeis, and on February 2 he wrote to his wife: "I hope you and the kids are storing up on sunshine vitamins. Accumulate a substantial reserve. You will need it for the foul climate." He added, "It is discouraging to see how quickly a tan dissipates—mine is just about gone already."

Fine had arrived back in time to hear performances of one of Copland's most ambitious and little-known scores, the *Symphonic Ode*, played by the Boston Symphony under Charles Munch. This grandiose, dissonant, somewhat bombastic neo-Mahlerian work had been written for Koussevitzky in the late 1920s. Employing a large orchestra with an augmented brass section, it sank without trace after its premiere. Copland, who always considered the *Ode* to be perhaps his most important symphonic piece, had recently revised it for the Boston Symphony's seventy-fifth anniversary, reducing the brass and transposing down the ending, with the aim of making the music more easily playable. On February 6, Fine wrote Copland, who had attended only the Friday performance on the third, his appraisal, which is worth quoting in full. "The Saturday reception of the Ode was somewhat better than Friday's, and (without being able to refer to the score)

---

1. The opening of the *Fantasia* is obviously intended as a homage to the opening of Beethoven's *String Quartet in C-sharp Minor*, Op. 131.

the performance seemed to have more zip. The performing time was reduced by one minute and the ending was much improved.

"I like the piece very much—so much that I immediately began to feel dissatisfied with the conventional attractiveness of the material I have lately been mulling over. If the Ode fails to make its point with the audience and the critics it is possibly as much because of the form as because of the idiom. Even the most intelligent listeners such as Walter [Piston], Harold [Shapero], Arthur [Berger] felt that the ending did not come off. Harold thought it ended in the wrong key. My own feeling is that this is unmistakably intentional but I am inclined to agree with Walter that it comes too late.

"As for the idiom—people will get used to that and even admire it for its cocky forthrightness. I also see what you mean by the tragic elements. As Arthur says—it's sad city music.

"The reviews are awful.[2] Of course the uncomplimentary notices have only served to get Munch's dander up. I suspect he will play it better and better and very often."

That didn't happen. After a further Munch Boston Symphony performance in New York at Carnegie Hall on February 8, Copland wrote to the Fines: "I'm sorry to say the N.Y. performance of the piece was sort of stiff and unconvincing. I guess Munch got self-conscious. Oh well—publication is assured, so it's in the hands of the gods. But I sure do wish I could hear it conducted by an American." The *Symphonic Ode* disappeared once again, to be revived only occasionally when the composer himself conducted it.

The winter of 1955-1956 was a low time, psychologically, for Fine. Despite regular analytic sessions with Dr. Nemiah, he suffered frequent depressions. Although in January 1956, he was offered a commission for a hymn to be included in New York University's publication *American Hymnbook*, he

---

2. On February 4, Cyrus Durgin wrote in the *Boston Globe*: "Mr. Copland was present to hear [the] first performance of the revision yesterday and he seemed pleased. That was more than some of the audience felt, for few new works this season have prompted so much resentment." Durgin observed that despite Copland's obvious skill, the *Symphonic Ode* "is ponderous and cold; professorial, in a way rhetorical and almost de-humanized."

felt unable to take it on. Not only could he not compose, but his career seemed stalled. In a February 22 letter, he went so far as to ask his friend Leonard Bernstein for counsel. "Because of your many past kindnesses to me, I hesitate to impose upon you again for advice on how I can get my music performed and recorded. But if you do have any ideas as to what I might do or whom I might see about getting the Songs and the Notturno done, I should be most grateful." Despondently, he added: "Tough luck that the tape of your wonderful performance at Brandeis of the Notturno was completely flubbed. It leaves me without a satisfactory record to show around."

On May 23, Fine's *Sonata for Violin and Piano* finally had its European premiere, in London at the Royal Festival Hall, played by Yfrah Neaman and Paul Hamburger. The press reception for this early work was not overly enthusiastic. The *London Times* noted that "Irving Fine's sonata drops its Stravinskish postures and grimaces in the middle movement, a lyrical set of variations." The *Jewish Chronicle* thought it "a restless work, built up of short phrases and rather fidgety rhythms."

That June, Fine received a prestigious commission. Harold Spivacke, Chief of the Music Division of the Library of Congress, offered a fee of $750, through the Elizabeth Sprague Coolidge Foundation, for a chamber work. However, because of his worsening writer's block, Fine would not be able to provide such a piece until three years later.

Meanwhile, there was Tanglewood. As Copland recalled in his autobiography, "I still stayed in the [rented] barn in Richmond [Massachusetts] and had my meals with Verna and Irving Fine and their three girls." As an adjunct to his teaching schedule, on July 9 Fine was the pianist in Stravinsky's *Duo Concertant*, with violinist Ruth Posselt. At the same concert, Copland played the piano part in his Jewish-inspired trio, *Vitebsk*. The following month, Fine was gratified to hear that his song-cycle *Mutability* had been presented at the Aspen Festival in Colorado, by Eunice Alberts and Brooks Smith. That October, five of the six songs of his other cycle, *Childhood Fables for Grownups*, were performed in Washington, D.C. at the Library of Congress under the title *Children's Songs for Grownups*, by baritone Martial Singher with the composer at the piano.

234

The year ended with Fine participating in a Harvard Law School Forum on December 6, with Copland and Otto Luening, and Arthur Berger as moderator. The subject was "The Contemporary Composer and His Public." Copland lamented "ancestor worship" among fans of modern music, finding the public's quest for "certified" musical masterpieces a sign of cultural immaturity. "Those who want only masterworks," he declared, "wouldn't know the best music if they heard it." He urged music lovers to interest themselves in living composers, because "each one contributes something unique and vital, which not even such exalted figures as Beethoven or Sibelius could duplicate."

Fine described how serious music had become more and more individualized, noting disapprovingly that "many composers are writing highly private music to be played by public-oriented extrovert virtuosi." He blamed the great popularity of the new long-playing record format for aggravating the problem by concentrating on music of the past. "The advent of the LP has increased the number of dead composers that the contemporary composer must compete with." Composers, he said, "have always been aware of the cultural lag between themselves and their audiences. The truly creative artist is continually in advance of his audience—no matter how enlightened it be." Still, "the composer has too often locked himself off from his public—in a private tone world." Fine could state with authority that "in those cases where the composer himself is actively involved in the performance of his own music, he soon discovers that he is writing for a public; and his music is bound to be affected thereby." He concluded his remarks by shifting focus to musical education in the United States, applauding "fruitful and inspired teaching in the colleges" while regretting a prevailing conservative tendency.

Early in February 1957, even as his creative constipation intensified, Fine cannot have been pleased to receive a grousing letter from Gertrude Norman. The publisher of the score of their collaborative songs wanted a final title and Norman had become impatient. "I do hope your head-shrinking efforts (why, by the way, isn't it head-enlarging?) have now reached a pass where you can make a quick decision about such trivia instead of stewing."

Then, on April 7, Fine, as Chairman of the Brandeis School of Creative Arts, had to speak at the dedication program of the new Slosberg Music Center. Leon Kirchner recalled that at such formal occasions, when distinguished people were present, "Irving had a different persona. He would be a little distant and there would be a slight pompousness about him."

This was to be the last year that Fine taught at Tanglewood, for Brandeis would open a summer school in 1958. He also felt he was being badly underpaid, and was fed up with that aspect of Tanglewood. In his autobiography, Copland remembered the "hectic" atmosphere there during the summer of 1957, and observed: "Irving helped plan and execute a complicated curriculum, reminding me all along that he had not been given a raise since 1948."

Fine's dissatisfaction with the situation at Tanglewood had emerged in a March 28 letter to Copland. "Too bad Lukas can't come; it will be terribly lonesome without him, Lenny and Ingolf [Dahl]. Needless to say you can count on my assistance in discussing plans for the Fromm [Foundation] project. It is difficult for me [to] say whether I can or ought to go along with it (beyond the actual composition teaching) unless I know something about these ideas. You can understand my disinclination to take on additional as well as substantially different duties for the same compensation that has been in effect since 1948." Fine said that he wasn't going "to bargain with the management over salary" but would rather keep the financial arrangements as they were and be allowed to commute to Tanglewood every week from Natick. "It would be infinitely more comfortable for all of us here to have the kids in day camp for six weeks and then depart *en famille* for the seashore for a real vacation together." Perhaps most important, "I should like to be able to work at home away from the distractions of Tanglewood for a continuous period each week." Matters were satisfactorily settled, and on June 18 Copland wrote asking him to decide what scores should be ordered to illustrate his two lectures scheduled for the second and the sixth weeks of classes. The Fromm players, consisting of five winds, five strings, piano and soprano, were set to perform excerpts from whatever works Fine chose.

"Am a commuter this year at Tanglew. by virtue of the new toll road," Fine informed Leonard Bernstein on August 3. "The place seems quieter in many ways—no opera dept., fewer students, no Bernsteins, Fosses, Dahls, Goldovskys, etc. We really miss you and Felicia very much, even though you figure less prominently in my analytical work [psychoanalysis] these days." After congratulating Bernstein on receiving an honorary degree, he noted: "We are all jealous, but Harold [Shapero] is more jealous of your ASCAP rating."

That year, Milton Babbitt taught composition at Tanglewood. He remembered that "Irving and I spent all of our time together talking. This was a transition period for him musically, and he got angry with Copland because Aaron did not want to listen to people who were talking analytically about music, about tonal analysis. That upset Irving, so he and Aaron didn't see much of each other. They didn't seem at all close that summer. And Irving was aware that at Brandeis most of the students were not very interested in Aaron's music." According to Babbitt, Fine's attitude toward Bernstein was also being revised. "He had very mixed feelings about Lenny, and that had an effect on his life. On the one hand, Irving felt he didn't have the kind of skill Lenny had, yet he felt very superior morally." One incident rankled. "He told me the thing that brought him to his senses about Bernstein. Irving was at Harold Shapero's house one day and Lenny walked in. There was some honky-tonk sheet music on the piano, and Lenny was not the kind of musician who could sit down and pick up pop tunes. Lenny asked if he could borrow the music, kept it for the week, and Saturday when there was a party he sat down and played it as if he had just picked it up by ear. That had stuck with Irving. And we all knew that Lenny was vulgar and irresponsible, and lied about people."

Fine's first Tanglewood talk was entitled "Music of the Twenties: Neoclassic Phase," and covered Stravinsky, Hindemith, Albert Roussel and Manuel de Falla. Himself an exhausted neoclassicist, Fine declared: "At this date, it is difficult to bring anything fresh to a discussion of a movement which has been seemingly moribund or on the wane for a number of years." However, he noted that French neoclassicism, especially, "concentrates on elegance and taste as well as craftsmanship" and is "an aristocratic art."

His perceptive analytic mind was more to the fore in his second lecture, "Contemporary Americans, Older Generation," which encompassed Piston, Roy Harris, Howard Hanson, Schuman, Copland, Samuel Barber and Roger Sessions. As an introduction, he observed that Piston, Sessions and Barber "are composers who relate to a more international tradition" than Copland, but that "Piston has retorted that American is more than cowboys, Broadway and New England meeting houses, baseball, etc.; that there is a long and respectable tradition for cosmopolitanism in American life." He said that his former teacher "has been called an American Hindemith, but this is an injustice to both. Piston is at once more elegant and less lyrical, has less vigor." Although Piston had begun as a modernist, "he no longer offers us any surprises. One symphony is pretty much alike another, basically, in essential subject matter and ingredients. What are different are the events within each work. It is as though we had a series of novels involving the same personalities or characters, but in different situations. His orchestration is a model of clarity. The harmonic idiom is essentially tonal with modal inflections, free use of chromatics and contrapuntal dissonance. The melodic idiom is freely chromatic and sharply motivated. The forms are all Classical, [with] transitions apt to be academic [but displaying] masterful control. There is a kind of subjective almost elegiac romanticism in the slow movements which sound more personal, but also more old-fashioned—a kind of academic romanticism."

Fine was especially discerning on the subject of Roy Harris, pointing out his "spectacular" rise to fame and the fact that Nadia Boulanger, his teacher, had "concluded sadly that he never acquired the craft and mastery of traditional techniques" to develop his extraordinary talent. Harris' music was "American in buoyance, momentum, expansiveness and mainly strength. Its epic quality suggests the vastness of the prairies." Fine quoted Harold Shapero, who termed Harris "our outstanding rural composer." Further: "The music is spontaneous, lyrical and not a little awkward. He uses no traditional shapes such as sonata form, but he does favor fugue, passacaglia, etc., which are the means of organizing texture rather than form-shapes. His rhythm is free and basically nonmetrical. His melody derives its character in large measure from the avoidance of those devices which shape and normally give coherence to melody; the ideal is free, unfettered song. The triad is the basis of his harmony, either singly or in bitonal combinations. He uses all twelve tones, but a microscopic inspection of his music reveals a mosaic of small diatonic fragments. The intensity of Harris' music does not grow out of the harmony; it is essentially lyric."

The arch-conservative Howard Hanson got short shrift, although Fine cited his achievement "as propagandist and performer of American music." Hanson's own music was "traditional and eclectic, opposed to the Stravinskyan aesthetic [of music] as an abstract play of forms."

Fine stated that William Schuman had studied with Harris "and superficially resembles him greatly," though his music is "more intense, energetic and jazzy. He is musically more sophisticated." He described Schuman's melody as a "long, swinging line accompanied by non-tonal sequences of triads and inversions," and his energy as "taut and nervous" with "the excitement of a Broadway musical." Then came another quote from Shapero: Schuman was "the vitamin kid of American composers," due to, as Copland had put it, "those nervous, skittery rhythms." Returning to melody, Fine noted that it "has considerable variety. It can be free and declamatory and somewhat improvisatory; it can be long-breathed and intensely singing; it can be jazzy or folksy." But, he concluded, "it is Schuman's rhythmic sense that is completely original and refreshing."

As for Copland, Fine traced his influences: "Stravinsky, Mahler (grandiosity), Satie, Thomson." He noted that his proto-serial *Piano Variations* of 1930 "endeared him momentarily to the dodecaphonists, horrified the academicians and delighted those other members who grew up in the Boulanger/Stravinsky school." Taking heed of the contrast between Copland's so-called simple and severe styles, he asked, "How can a composer who ostensibly composes in so many styles have a real personality or be sincere?" answering that "it is important to note that with Copland, as with Stravinsky, and Picasso, style is subject matter as well as manner, language or rhetoric. In this sense, Copland's works are expressions about something external—or personal associations to a style or event. This is what gives Copland's music a sense of objectivity as well as personal quality." Scores such as the *Piano Variations, Short Symphony, Symphonic Ode* and *Statements for Orchestra* "are a series of abstract, highly dissonant music which is more constructivist than earlier works. They are severe, a little distant in mood but very dynamic in rhythm," and "even in the most constructivist music there is the most jealous care taken of [its] sound, spacing and sonorous impact." (Addressing the populist Copland in a 1954 record review of the ballet suite from *Billy the Kid*, Fine had deplored the fact that "there is often a tendency to minimize Copland's achievement [in *Billy*]. I suppose this is because it is such a delight to hear and because it is written in a language that communicates to unspoiled minds so easily. It is a common enough failing to distrust what one readily understands.")

Fine classified Samuel Barber with Piston as one of the "elegant traditionalists among our serious composers," reflecting that "one is reminded of the elegant sentiment of Mendelssohn or at times of Brahms or even of Chopin, the most Classical of the romanticists." Stylistically, Barber "has incorporated neoclassical elements derived from Stravinsky and has also used a modified form of serial technique in the piano sonata and *The Prayers of Kierkegaard* [for chorus and orchestra]." He concluded: "Barber's approach to modern idioms is to normalize them and to make them compatible with a style that is essentially neoromantic in feeling and elegantly Classical in technique." Although he began as a conservative, he "gives every indication of continuing to develop and change"—the converse of the Piston case.[3]

Roger Sessions was pronounced "one of our ablest writers and profoundest thinkers on music," a composer who "remains far short of the radical wing of twelve-tone music." Generally speaking, "his music seems to have strong tonal moorings and a very careful concern for harmony. It is powerful music, undoubtedly music of great integrity, but terribly serious at all times and lacking in immediate charm and grace." Sessions' harmony was termed "uncompromisingly

---

3. On a personal level, Verna recalled: "I think Irving felt Sam Barber was too ritzy for him. We got introduced all the time at functions, but Barber never seemed to remember who he was."

dissonant," but the music "possesses a kind of Beethovenian power and profundity." (Interestingly, there is no indication here that Fine found Sessions' music at all likeable, only that it could be esteemed, which was very similar to Copland's private view. In a Tanglewood lecture given a decade before, in 1947, he had been more candid. Noting that Sessions' art had "positive qualities that must command the respect of all serious musicians," he continued: "And yet, I cannot truthfully say that I like this music. Technically, I have certain reservations—chiefly about the density of the writing." He termed the music "over-written, complicated rather than complex—too much is going on all the time," citing "its tortuously complicated thought" and expressing himself as being "distressed by the complete absence of brilliance and charm, of grace, [and] by the impression that I receive that Sessions is trying so hard to write masterpieces." Most damning of all: "Perhaps what I miss most is the feeling of being in the presence of genuine musicality.")

On July 28 an article by Howard Taubman entitled "Neglect of Youth—New Native Composers Are Largely Unplayed" had appeared in the *New York Times*. More than a dozen "well-established" American composers, including Fine, had been queried on the subject. All but one agreed that in the United States young composers were being shamefully ignored. The exception was the composer and administrator William Schuman, whose well-known, politically motivated bonhomie eschewed pessimism[4] No "outstandingly convincing" younger composer had yet appeared, he said, which in his mind nullified the whole issue. Schuman was blissfully convinced that no "young composer, or older, for that matter, of recognizable gifts is neglected." Others strenuously disagreed. Otto Luening, also an educator, thought that after young composers finished school and were awarded a fellowship or two, their careers had nowhere to go; the blame lay with performers, critics and "the music business." Milton Babbitt felt that several factors were involved, including the lack of a con-

---

4. Verna remembered that "Irving liked Bill Schuman. They were both choral conductors and Irving thought Bill was a brilliant administrator at Juilliard. He would also say he was a great operator, but he admired that."

temporary-music magazine and the shortsightedness of critics. "The complex of social and economic factors that conspires against the composition and performance of 'difficult, advanced' music," he said, is "contributing to the submergence of our serious music."

Fine joined the lament, agreeing that "the situation of the young composer is more precarious today than it has ever been." He continued: "Hundreds of them are being turned out by the colleges and conservatories, many with talent and admirable technical equipment, but having little or no opportunity to get a hearing beyond the confines of their schools." In a letter to Copland earlier that year, he had addressed the issue on a broader front. "Modern music is in the same position today that poetry has been for centuries. Somebody told me the other day that Chaucer wrote for an audience of no more than 200 readers (probably far less) in the whole of England and that Wordsworth reached a handful until the universities discovered him some decades after he [had] done his best work." He thought that a situation where composers wrote primarily for their colleagues at universities was hermetic and unhealthy: "For me, it is a rather sad prospect. I'm not yet prepared to grant that the conventions of our university intellectuals are necessarily superior because they are entertained by fewer people." Further, in a Tanglewood lecture that summer he stated: "The universities, even the great ones, are not necessarily the best places to develop a truly cosmopolitan point of view. I had a college classmate from Manhattan who told me with great pride that he had been to Europe twenty times but never had been to Brooklyn." Fine warned that this sort of "inverted parochialism" was dangerous to American "neoclassic or international" composers, the danger being that "of inhabiting the isolated outposts of a more or less remote culture, of being regarded at once as country cousins of continental European composers and as outlanders in their own country."

Upon completing his final stint at Tanglewood, Fine drove to Cape Cod with Verna and the children, to spend the second half of August 1957 enjoying the sun and sea. But before that, at home in Natick on August 3, he wrote to Bernstein, who had recently been appointed music director of the New York Philharmonic. For Fine, who was the antithesis of the "pushy" composer, the letter began in a singular manner. "Sonny S. mentioned his call from you today and asked me whether I had also heard from you anything further about the 'Boston composer' program you had thought you might do with the N.Y. Phil. Since I seem to be temporarily less bashful these days [perhaps due to psychoanalysis], I've decided to write you punkt and ask you whether you have a copy of my Louisville piece (the string orchestra Lament) and whether you are still interested in doing it during the coming season." He returned to the subject in a postscript: "Hope you can do the Lament. Its official name is 'Serious Song' (for Canzona Seria). Isn't that awful!" The reminder proved effective. As previously noted, Bernstein programmed *Serious Song* during the 1958-1959 season, and even announced to the radio audience that it was his favorite music by Fine.

Come September, Brandeis beckoned as always. The fall semester promised to be more problematic than usual, because one of the music department's mainstays, Erwin Bodky, was recovering from major surgery. As Fine wrote Copland on October 30, "There is some question as to whether he'll be able to resume his entire program when he returns in about three weeks. In the meanwhile, Titcomb, [Kenneth] Levy and I are carrying his courses." There was, however, a silver lining to this academic cloud. "My assignment has been the Collegium Musicum—in effect, a little Baroque, early-Classical orchestra. It is fun to make music again, even with a group made up largely of the most limited amateurs." But: "I wish there [were] some modern music besides Hindemith that they could play."

In the same letter, Fine spoke of trying to decide on a new car "that we want to buy in Europe next year." This was a reference to a second Guggenheim Fellowship he had received, for work in Italy during 1958-1959. He noted wryly that Verna "inclines to the Fiat 6-passenger multiple because it's funny looking and practical. What does that mean?"

Copland's most ambitious keyboard work, the *Piano Fantasy*,[5] had recently been premiered in New York, at Juilliard by William Masselos, and Fine was greatly disappointed

---

5. While writing it, Copland had described it to Fine as "a monster that must be tamed."

to miss it. "Up to five o'clock on Friday afternoon, Arthur and I had a glimmering hope that we might make it by plane down to N.Y. for your big shindig. But we had two meetings that afternoon, the last of which dragged on until about six-thirty. I had tried to hint to the Dean that he didn't really need my presence (which turned out to be quite true) but he did not take kindly to the suggestion." Fine added: "I imagine you must have mixed feelings about being referred to [in a newspaper review] as the grand old master who can show those young whippersnaps a thing or two." He indicated he would like to have the *Piano Fantasy* performed at Brandeis at the new Slosberg center, but "our hall is booked just about solidly until Christmas. Everybody in the University wants to use it."

That October thirtieth letter contains the only mention of a new choral work, eventually to be called *McCord's Menagerie*. "Just knocked off a couple of trivia for the Harvard Glee Club's hundredth anniversary," Fine wrote. "They wanted a pair of short, light pieces and they're getting them with a vengeance. The texts by David McCord are somewhat arch things entitled 'The Mole' and 'The Clam.' The settings are really short and as vulgar as I could make them—alas, not vulgar enough to be interesting." To McCord himself, he observed: "They are, of course, the kind of verses to which I respond immediately, though I must say that they scarcely need the addition of music to delight anybody."

David T.W. McCord, who lived to the ripe old age of ninety-nine (1897-1997), was, of course, Fine's Boston poet-friend who had previously supplied texts for the Koussevitzky tribute *In Grato Jubilo* and the "Pianola d'Amore" number from *The Choral New Yorker*. He specialized in light verse, much of it aimed at children, and wrote or edited more than fifty books. His nearly two dozen volumes of poetry include *Floodgate, The Crows, Far and Few, A Star by Day, Bay Window Ballads,* and *Twelve Verses XII Night.* McCord also published books of essays (*Oddly Enough, The Camp at Lockjaw, The Fabrick of Man,* among them) and *About Boston,* a cultural and historical guide illustrated with his own drawings.[6]

6. Caldwell Titcomb, who knew McCord well, mentioned

By the end of the year, Fine had set two additional McCord poems, 'Vultur Gryphus' and 'Jerboa,' to make a set of four choral miniatures (duration: five-and-one-half minutes). He wanted to add a fifth song, and wrote to McCord on March 13, 1958 that "what we need now is a really riproaring finale for the set. A fast and furiously funny piece that should last about two or three minutes at the most." Evidently such a poem was not forthcoming. (The four poems that Fine did use had been published in 1954 in McCord's book *Odds Without Ends*, where the original title of "The Clam" was "Who's Ooze.")

*McCord's Menagerie* is cast in a harmonically conventional style, primarily diatonic and triadic. The comic verses provoked music that often verges on the vulgar but is quite effective nonetheless, music in traditional college-singing mode with popular overtones. "Arch" is in fact the right word not only for the poems but for Fine's expert if rather self-consciously cute settings. None of his stylistic fingerprints are found, for this is the sort of pop-inflected, cosmopolitan, impersonal music that he could write practically on autopilot.

The first song, "Vultur Gryphus" (*Allegro moderato*) begins with a jazzy syncopation, the basses repeatedly intoning the sound "loo," over which the tenors sing, "Let us ponder the condor." Musical-comedy style is evident here, especially when two alternating tenors sing "Any on view in the U.S.A." "Yes, a few."

"Jerboa" (there is no tempo mark in the published score, but some kind of allegro is clearly intended) begins with rhythmic declamation on the word "*Jaculus,*" the Latin genus of this small leaping rodent with oversized hind legs, resident in the North African desert. "Front legs too short, hind legs too long. All rather wrong." "Small kangaroo, but not for the zoo."

"Mole" (*Allegro maestoso*) is the shortest of these trifles, lasting just under one minute and employing diatonic college-anthem style. "Man has an oversoul, but not the mole. What the mole has is not clear, but it's an undersoul, I fear" is the entire text.

---

that one of his favorite poems was the witty "Epitaph for a Waiter," which read in its entirety: "Bye and bye/God caught his eye."

The final song, "Clam" (*Alla Marcia*) is a jolly syncopated march set to a recurring, rhythmically varied ostinato in the lower basses on the sound "bng." "I came from the clammy cold sea, same as he. My chassis is classic. His is Jurassic. So I don't give a damn about the clam!" are some of the lines. It begins and ends quietly.

*McCord's Menagerie*, subtitled "Four Vivariations for Male Voices," was the only composition Fine completed in 1957. It had its first hearing at a tryout performance at the Harvard Club of Boston on March 2, 1958, by the Harvard Glee Club conducted by G. Wallace Woodworth; and its official premiere three months later, on June 9, at Sanders Theatre, Cambridge, Massachusetts, by the same forces. The score was published by Mills Music in 1959. Reviewing a subsequent recording, Arthur Cohn termed the songs "light humor, of course, but sophisticated" and cited "the matching of the poet's wit in Fine's clever, fluidly capricious music."

# Chapter 17

■ NINETEEN FIFTY-SEVEN HAD CLOSED with two performances in December of the *"Alice in Wonderland" Suite* for chorus and orchestra in New York, at City College. At the end of the following February and the beginning of March, Fine was again in New York, to attend the local premiere of the *Fantasia for String Trio* by members of the Juilliard Quartet at the Juilliard School, and to hear it played by the Walden Quartet a few days later on a Composers Showcase program, where he and Gunther Schuller were the featured composers. At the latter concert, Fine accompanied Alice Howland in *Mutability*, and Edward Downes noted in the *New York Times* that "Mr. Fine showed himself a sensitive pianist," continuing: "His Fantasia for String Trio was warmly applauded, [but] although it is obviously the work of a skilled and gifted man, it left this reporter cold."

*Mutability* surfaced again on April 27, at Brandeis University, where it was performed by Eunice Alberts and Martin Boykan. On March 23, Fine conducted the first Boston performance of his *Serious Song*; then, on May 13, his *String Quartet* was presented in Geneva, Switzerland, and on June 9 he attended the premiere of *McCord's Menagerie* at Harvard. Verna recalled, "Irving never had trouble getting performances. Somebody wanted every piece he wrote. He never had anything rejected. Of course, he was in academia and had connections, and he never rubbed people the wrong way. Others wanted to promote his music, so he didn't have to do it himself. He was always lucky that way, and he felt more at ease promoting other composers' music than his own."

In the middle of April, Fine managed to escape his teaching duties for a quick, four-day trip to Dallas and New Orleans with Verna. He did Brandeis business in Dallas and gave a lecture at Temple Emanu-El. On the way back, they spent a day in New Orleans, where they so enjoyed a gourmet dinner at the venerable (founded 1840) Restaurant Antoine that they swiped a menu as an *aide-mémoire*. He had arranged a one-year sabbatical from Brandeis to take advantage of his second Guggenheim grant, leaving Harold Shapero in charge of the new summer music session, so in July the entire Fine family went to Rockport, Massachusetts for a brief vacation at the seashore before leaving for Europe in the middle of August.

On July 24, Fine wrote to Leonard Bernstein, thanking him for scheduling performances of *Serious Song* with the New York Philharmonic during the following season. ("Of course the Serious Song is on for next season," Bernstein had informed him in a May twenty-ninth in-flight letter from South America. He mentioned that he had encountered Verna's brother Spencer Rudnick the night before in a Buenos Aires restaurant: "It's a short world, as a Mexican friend of mine used to say.") The Fines ("all five of us, no less") were excitedly preparing for the big trip. "We have rented our house in your favorite town of 'East Nedick' and are leaving our dog with the tenants; we sold our Plymouth, or rather traded it in for a Ford Consul convertible which we are taking abroad with us."

Fine had elected to spend his Guggenheim year in the place he liked best during his 1949 Fulbright grant: Rome. "We have taken, sight-unseen but highly recommended, an outrageously expensive apartment," he told Bernstein. "The whole venture seems fairly idiotic, but is supposed to be a kind of celebration—sabbatical leave from Brandeis, graduation from analysis, Guggenheim fellowship, etc." Regarding the Rome flat, he said that if Bernstein and his wife came for a visit, "we apparently have room in which to put you. Our landlord wrote there was a telephone in each room. This sounds rather bizarre. Do you suppose he meant something else—like hot and cold running water in each room?"

Fine hoped that the atmosphere of the Eternal City would help clear his composing block. He was to be bitterly disappointed.

Irving, Verna, Claudia, Emily and Joanna Fine sailed from New York on August 13, 1958, on the S.S. Independence. They were seen off by the entire Fine clan—George and Lotte, Audrey and Barbara. The ship would make several ports of call before docking at Naples: Casablanca, Barcelona, Mallorca, Genoa, Cannes. Upon landing in Italy, they would drive to Sorrento.

From Sorrento, Fine wrote to his parents. "Casablanca was fascinating [although] a visit to the new and old Medinas made one want to scour oneself." He noted that the city had about 5,000 Jews, and that the family had visited the *mellah*, or Jewish quarter. "Both Verna and I were terribly moved. For me it was like seeing a miniature version of the Market Street or East Boston schules. Why Verna's eyes filled up I do not know—I guess it was homesickness." They entered a synagogue, and "the shamas and the assistant rabbi showed us through and then I followed the cab driver (also a Jew) to the ark to kiss the Torah." The rabbi's twelve-year-old son sang a blessing. "He could have been any little kid in a Winthrop or Dorchester chedar. But most of the Jews live in the same kind of poverty as the Arabs and are indistinguishable from them except that the women wear no veils."

Fine found Barcelona "a fascinating and bustling big city that made all of us want to spend more time in Spain. It was also gratifying to encounter a friendly people who are not out to steal the fillings from your mouth or hold you up at every turn." They went to the obligatory bullfight, and to that Fine had a one-word reaction: "Ugh!"

As for Mallorca: "If I were sure there were decent doctors and medicine on the island, that's where I'd want to live for the year." Then came the first of several recurring references to Papa George's favorite topic, money. "It used to be fantastically cheap. But now it has the most elegant hotels you ever saw. Even at that, you can live at the very best for $10 a day, meals included." In a subsequent postcard, he described Palma Majorca as "the place to retire." Genoa was "beautiful" and Cannes was "beautifully situated with regard to mountains, cliffs and sea, but almost like Revere Beach [Boston] in congestion."

On the ship, they had experienced "perfect hot weather" since leaving New York. The cabins were air-conditioned, but after several days "many of the passengers began to develop minor respiratory complaints. The day before we landed at Casablanca Emily had a sore throat with a temperature [but] was completely recovered by the time we reached Cannes." Little Joanna, nicknamed Jojo, "was the darling of the boat" and Claudia "struck up a passionate friendship with a New Yorker named Harley Arnold," who disembarked at Algeciras, Spain.

In Sorrento, they settled into the Hotel Tramontano for a few days before driving on to Rome. "Everybody seems to love the Tramontano, but I don't particularly like the feeling of being caught between the mountains and the sea." There was sightseeing, although "the days are really too hot for much—one feels like taking a siesta after every meal." One day, Fine and Claudia went to Pompeii. "It was hot as hell and even with a guide, two and a half hours were enough—too *much* for Claudia. I hadn't realized what a big city Pompeii was—in its day it had 20,000 inhabitants." Another time, they took the "spectacular" Amalfi drive, "which I do not recommend for apprehensive souls. The more I see of Italian roads in this part of the country, the less I care to drive." So alarming was the outing that "I needed a strong drink when we got back. Verna and I had highballs—scotch is not expensive here but rye is a bit higher in cost than at home." At the hotel, "Emily seems to be conducting a romance with half of the guests."

Italy, said Fine, "has become terribly expensive—just as New York. They say that London costs are about half those here. Our mastery of the Italian language has not developed one iota. Instead I find that my French improves daily—especially as a result of speaking to French guests here." He signed off thus: "Hope that Mesabi is behaving to your satisfaction."

On September 8, there was another "Dear Folks" letter, but this one gave depressing news. "We have been in Rome for a week now and are still far from settled. The glamorous apartment we had rented [at No. 5 Via del Parco Pepoli] turned out to be something along the lines of 22 Avenue Lowendahl [their unsatisfactory Paris flat in 1949]—only far dirtier." Fine described the neighborhood as one of the city's most elegant. "Our place is next to the Dutch legation to the Vatican. Through our window we can see their beautiful garden and swimming pool." There was also an attractive garden at the rear of their building, but it was accessible only to the tenant on the first floor. The apartment had "three handsome rooms," living room, dining room and study, "but the furniture is in an indescribably bad condition—filthy and broken down." The kitchen was "too disgusting even for our Roman maid, who is no paragon of cleanliness," and the children's bedrooms were "too primitive to describe." A vacuum cleaner was non-functional. "I am doing all right, and am quite capable of adjusting to the disappointment over the apartment, but it has got Verna down—especially when on Sunday she attempted to prepare dinner in a kitchen crawling with ants from every nook & cranny." Never one to keep her feelings to herself, Verna complained loudly, and often. It was hardly an atmosphere conducive to creative work.

Their villainous landlord had made promises—new furniture, new beds, a new stove, "and above all a general house cleaning," but had provided only the stove. "We have been told by the owner of the other apartment in the building that we can expect little or nothing unless we keep after our landlord incessantly, which is impossible since he is out of town and besides speaks no English." As no lease had been signed, Irving and Verna decided to look for another apartment, only to find that "rent for furnished places is astronomically high. But everything is expensive here except help and sightseeing—and with the help you really get what you pay for."

Despite the domestic problems, Fine had not lost his affection for Rome. "It's a fabulous city and a pleasure to be about in it. We are adjacent to the Baths of Caracalla, which are an awe-inspiring sight, and we go around the Coliseum at least 4 times a day and through or past the Forum whenever we come & go from the center of the town." But Rome was not all ancient ruins and filthy lodgings in picturesque areas. "There is a fabulous building boom on around the city, bigger than anything I have seen in the States. Literally thousands of vulgar Bronx or Miami type apartment buildings—though we do them much better."

He noted in disappointment that most of the Romans involved in the arts were still on summer vacation and that the concert and opera season would not begin for another month. He had unsuccessfully tried to visit an acquaintance, the Italian composer Goffredo Petrassi, who was not expected back for another week. But Alexei Haieff was there and "has been a perfectly marvelous friend—greeted us with 3 bottles of Bourbon, Gin & Vermouth and acted as interpreter to our landlord." Meanwhile, Copland had sent a postcard from London, where he was settled into a Mayfair apartment-hotel, intending to use it as a base for conducting orchestras in Europe until December.

The neighbors, a German-Jewish couple, were pleasant.

"The husband works for the U.N. Food & Agric. organization; the wife is a pediatrician. Jojo has a crush on her and wants to visit her every five minutes." And: "As Claudia puts it—and quite correctly—it's so wonderful to do things together as a family—even to eat breakfast together over the same fly-infested Italian renaissance table." Finally: "Saw in the Tribune that Mesabi was holding up well."

On September 20, Fine reported that the children were adjusting satisfactorily both to Rome and to school. Joanna, he said, was a difficult eater: "As far as Roman pasta is concerned she'll have none of it"; while Emily "is rounder than ever & more and more of a clown." The situation with the apartment remained "obscure—or rather completely frustrating. We thought last week we should be able to make a go of it here, but our landlord is a slippery one—after promising everything, or rather our minimal needs, he then begins to hedge & wants $750 in advance. Even then he doesn't promise to do anything before Oct. 15 and adds moreover, 'if nothing unforeseen intervenes'." Increasingly discouraged, Fine confided that they were contemplating cutting short their stay in Rome, and doing "one of two or three things—stay for a few months until Christmas recess or midterm, and travel to the French Riviera, to England afterwards and thence home. Or even limit our travel to Italy & the Mediterranean and thence first to Boston & possibly to Florida." Nevertheless, "Rome *is* a fabulous city, even if it seems terribly unhygienic and inefficient."

He had rented a piano (his studio was "the nicest room we have") and had "begun making music." This was perhaps a reference to the *Romanza for Wind Quintet*, not to be completed until the next year. No "Roman opera or symphony" was yet on the way, he confessed.

Fine told his parents that he himself felt well, but that his wife was a little under the weather. "Wish Verna were able to sleep better and gain a little weight. The bug she got in Sorrento left her somewhat under par and, as she says, not her usually peppy self." It turned out that Verna's "bug" was in reality the beginning of an attack of severe colitis. Along with the wretched living conditions, this signaled the end of Fine's Roman idyll: that change of scene he had hoped, somewhat desperately, would rid him of his writer's block.

252

At the time, the American composer Jack Beeson had a Guggenheim fellowship at the American Academy in Rome, and he occasionally saw the Fines. "I never got to know Irving well, but I admired his music, especially the *Serious Song*. Several years later, in New York, Verna and I became good friends, and I appreciated her intelligence and musical instincts. In Rome, my wife and I had acquaintances who lived in their building, and they told us a story which I presume is true. It had to do with the fact that Verna didn't care for Rome for lots of reasons, perhaps because she was a dyed-in-the-wool Bostonian. One day, the Fines had plumbers working in the bathroom and, Italian plumbers being Italian plumbers, they mixed up the hot-water pipe with the cold. That night, Verna went to the toilet, and when she flushed it she was suddenly transformed into the Cumaen Sibyl, surrounded by clouds of steam—a highly operatic scene, I thought. According to the story, Verna came out of the bathroom screeching, presumably to her husband. Shortly thereafter, the family disappeared from Rome, and it was said that Verna had taken them back to Boston where they belonged and could be happy."

Many years later, Claudia Fine recalled sadly: "They had planned this sabbatical in Italy, where he was going to be composing for a year. My parents were all psyched up about it and rented this supposedly beautiful apartment in Rome. But it did not meet my mother's standards. In her mind, it was dirty and awful, although I don't think my father cared as much about that as she did." Emily Fine remembered that "she was just miserable. The next thing we knew, they said, 'We're going to cut this year short, but we can't go back to Natick because the house is rented.'"

"They looked all over Rome for another apartment without success," said Claudia. "I remember that one day my father was lying on the bed in their room, talking to his mother on the telephone, trying to figure out what to do. 'It's just not working,' he told her. 'We're going to have to come home.' Tears were rolling down his face. It was the first time I saw him cry."

At the beginning of October, the family returned to Boston, where Verna was hospitalized for a short period with colitis. For Fine, it was a great defeat.

On October 3, 1958, Fine—understandably in a discontented mood—wrote Bernstein a stern yet sensible letter. The subject was the conductor's dubious proposal to program Debussy's orchestral triptych *Images* with the New York Philharmonic in a revised sequence. Displaying as it does Fine's severe integrity in musical matters, this letter bears quotation. The salutation is more formal than usual—"Dear Leonard" instead of "Dear Lenny"—and the letter is grouped into several points of objection, briefly stated. "The only conclusion can be (whatever incidental reasonings may be offered) is that you are seeking a 'wow' finish with 'Iberia.' ["Iberia," which itself consists of three movements, forms the middle part of *Images*.] Debussy lived for several years after completing 'Images.' He could have chosen any sequence other than the one he did. You are putting yourself in the position of being a better judge of the material than the man who created it. As Music Director of the Philharmonic, this sets a precedent for other conductors to rearrange, eliminate, alter or otherwise falsify the intent of those whose works provide them with the means for functioning. This may have implications you haven't considered. It is an inartistic and questionable procedure."

Because the lease on the Natick house couldn't be broken, the children were sent to their Aunt Audrey in Fall River, Massachusetts, while Fine stayed with his parents in Brookline. When Verna was released from hospital, her brother Spencer telephoned from Florida. Emily recalled that "he said that there was a house in Miami Shores, just around the corner from his, that the owner wants to sublet. 'If Irving just needs a place to compose, the weather is beautiful and your kids can go to school here.' At that point, I think Daddy said, 'It shouldn't really matter where I live. I should be able to go down there and compose'." They departed for Florida in mid-November.

"My father was very angry, although perhaps not consciously," said Claudia, "because his whole plan had gone to pieces. But he was the kind of person who wanted everyone to love him, so he didn't express anger well." The house in Miami Shores was small, dark and unattractive. Fine rented a piano but found it difficult to work. In Claudia's opinion, "he

254

had a major clinical depression in Florida. He was non-functional. He sat in that bedroom for four months and had trouble even walking out of the house. I was eleven years old, old enough to know things were bad." Absurdly, Verna told Claudia that Fine couldn't compose "because there is no culture here in Florida."

As if things were not bad enough, Fine's mother now became a problem. Emily noted that "I think what pushed my father over the edge was his parents. We always knew that they had a horrible marriage, that Papa George used to hit Nanalotte and that she should have left him years ago." Not long after the Fines had settled in Miami Shores, Lotte telephoned hysterically to say that George had beaten her again. Her son, exasperated but concerned, invited her to live with them for a while. She arrived around Christmas and stayed for much of the time they were there, which put considerable pressure on both Verna and Irving. "Mom's point of view," said Emily, "was that Nanalotte was enough to drive you crazy because she was so passive-aggressive." Claudia felt that "it was hard on her, having her mother-in-law there in that small house." It was also hard on Fine, because Lotte slept on a daybed in the extra room where he had his piano. "It was a terrible time," said Claudia. "Remember, this was a parent who never understood why her son did what he did, and his relationship with her was a little ambivalent."

In only a few months, Fine had seen his dream-year dissolve as if cursed. Wrenched from the splendor of Rome, he found himself adrift in a tacky suburb of Miami. Perhaps most frustrating of all was the fact that the blame for his appalling situation fell squarely on the two women he most loved, his wife and his mother, and he felt unable to express resentment.

According to Claudia, Fine began putting on weight, another source of friction between him and Verna, "although he wasn't as fat as my mother thought he was." Naturally, Fine's ongoing major blackie affected his family. Joanna remembered that "he was clearly depressed—roaming about the house unable to compose—and that depression would emanate into us. When children sense tension from above they get anxious about their own welfare. As a result, Emily and I and Claudia would fight more than usual. Occasionally

255

my father had a bad temper. I recall that one time I bit my sister and he angrily called the doctor and said I was going to be taken to the pound because I had acted like a dog."

Both Emily and Joanna vividly recollected another occasion when Fine lost his temper. "Once," said Joanna, "he impulsively whipped us into the car to go shopping. It seemed compulsive, something he needed to do. We drove to a strip mall and he bought Emily and me a set of matched dolls, exactly the same except that one was dressed in yellow and the other in blue. He said, 'Now, you girls decide which one you want'." Emily: "I picked one and Joanna picked the other, and then she immediately wanted mine. So I switched dolls with her, and then she started whining about wanting the other one. I could see that my father was getting upset." Joanna: "He was miserable. Here he had done this very nice thing. He blew up in the parking lot and slapped me in the face." Emily: "He took her doll and yelled, 'You're not getting anything! What's wrong with you? Stop competing with Emily!'"

Sometime in March 1959, Fine decided he had had all he could take, and the family left Florida to return to Boston. "Daddy was really at the edge," remembered Claudia. "He could not stay there." He rented a house not far from Brandeis University, on Route 16 in Wellesley Hills, until the summer. The only good news during Fine's sabotaged sabbatical came at the end of May, when the family was settled back at home in Natick. A letter from Charles Munch, the conductor of the Boston Symphony Orchestra, proposed a fee of $1,000 for an orchestral work for the 1959-1960 season. It was to have a duration of between ten to twenty minutes. The money came from the Ford Foundation, which would sponsor performances with four other major symphony orchestras. This was Fine's most important commission to date, but he must have wondered at that point whether he could fulfill it.

In a January 13, 1959 letter, Gian Carlo Menotti, who had recently founded the Spoleto Festival in Italy, offered Fine $100 for a short vocal duet, trio or brief operatic scene, with either piano or chamber-orchestra accompaniment. This came to nothing, however, as a depressed Fine felt unable to comply with such a request.

That same month, there were performances of *Serious*

*Song* in Philadelphia and Baltimore by Eugene Ormandy and the Philadelphia Orchestra, which must have somewhat relieved Fine's Florida gloom. The same score had four performances in April in New York at Carnegie Hall, by Leonard Bernstein and the New York Philharmonic, which certainly boosted his spirits even more.[1] On the twenty-third, Fine wrote Bernstein to say how "deeply moved" he had been by those performances. "They were the most passionate, insightful, in short, the best I have ever had." He concluded: "Thanks a million—and thanks as much for the extraordinary personal warmth and kindness you showed to Verna and me. I have always known that, in addition to being a great musician, you were the rarest of friends and a thoroughly lovable person." Perhaps as reward for a friendship valuable personally and otherwise, that June, Fine arranged an honorary degree for Bernstein at the eighth Brandeis commencement.

Meanwhile, there had been "another one of our '58-'59 crises." Soon after returning from New York in April, Verna was rushed to the hospital to be treated for "an excruciatingly painful" bursitis. Fortunately, she recovered enough to be able to attend two Passover seders on the twenty-second, one of them at George and Lotte's.

If 1958 had been compositionally barren, during the next year Fine emerged from his creative doldrums to the extent of being able to complete four short works: a two-page piano piece, a march for Brandeis University, music for a television documentary and the *Romanza for Wind Quintet*. He also composed at least one vocal number for a never-to-be-finished musical.

The *Arioso for Piano*, written in Miami Shores and dated January 8, 1959, was subsequently orchestrated and incorporated into the suite *Diversions*, with the new title "Koko's Lullaby." It will be discussed later in that context.

The *Romanza for Wind Quintet* was probably begun late in 1958, but whether in Rome, Natick or Florida is unknown. The completion date is also uncertain, although Verna, to

---

1. This was part of a venturesome program wherein the first half was devoted to new American music. Along with the Fine, Bernstein conducted the premieres of Ned Rorem's *Symphony No. 3* and William Russo's *Symphony No. 2*.

whom the score is dedicated, remembered that it was some-time in 1959. She recalled that "the *Romanza* was originally going to be in two movements, but then it came to be in only one." As noted, the work had been commissioned by the Elizabeth Coolidge Foundation at the Library of Congress back in 1956.

One of Fine's least-known works, the *Romanza* stands as a small (duration, nine minutes), perfectly balanced chamber-music masterpiece. The idiom is neoclassically tinged tonal serialism, replete with very free twelve-tone writing. Overall, the music is lyric, somewhat rarified, introspective and emotionally cool, but with occasional touches of humor. Although there are momentary suggestions of Hindemith and Stravinsky, they strike the ear merely as intriguing echoes rather than actual derivations. This is one of Fine's most mature and personal scores: concise and unified, ingratiatingly melodic and (perhaps the most formidable task facing a composer) carefully controlled yet radiating spontaneity.

The form is rhapsodic and not easy to define, though variation procedure is often in play. It exemplifies British critic Christopher Palmer's approving dictum about "the anti-intellectual tendency to rhapsodize and fantasize" in Fine's serial pieces. Unity is achieved by melodic and melody-cell linkage, by the basic *moderato* tempo that prevails with only slight modifications and by the constant interplay of 6/8 and 9/8 meters. A sense of contrast is cleverly purveyed by strategically placed changes of motion within the predominating tempo, which lend a stimulating impression of fluidity. Textures and chord spacing are extremely clear throughout, and great care has been taken with every detail, whether melodic, harmonic, polyphonic or rhythmic.

The opening is clearly preludial. Lyric and slightly mordant, it contains an alert rhythmic cell (two sixteenth notes followed by an eighth) that will periodically be prominent in sportive passages. This is followed by a fleetly elegant *più mosso* of running sixteenth notes that leads to a section of *fugato* writing begun by the horn and founded on a three-note inversion of the work's initial three bars. After contrasts between meditative music and playful (flutter-tonguing in the flute) music, and an exquisite flute *arioso*, an abrupt *fortissimo* declamation heralds a flourish of scherzo music (*poco più ani-*

*mato*) in the full complement that suddenly resolves to a lyrical *meno mosso* tellingly punctuated by inert, Stravinskian chords. The final section, which begins with ostinato motion, functions as a coda where all of the essential materials are smoothly recapitulated, its two parts separated by a pause featuring a mocking clarinet solo based on the pervasive rhythmic cell. The conclusion invests the opening materials with enhanced poise and elegance, and in the remote-sounding closing chords is heard the shade of Stravinsky.

Fine was never to hear a public performance of his *Romanza*, although it is possible that he arranged a private reading with instrumentalists at Brandeis, so as to make final adjustments. Why it took the Library of Congress nearly four years to present the premiere of a work it had commissioned is unknown, but the first performance was not given until February 1, 1963, several months after the composer's death, played by one of his favorite groups, the New York Wind Quintet. The score was published that same year by Mills.

Reviewing a recording, Arthur Cohn wrote that the *Romanza* "has an engaging sonority plan, set as it is in a syntax whereby the intervallic elements of twelve-tone technique are reconciled to quasi-tonality. A fresh approach, this, with a refreshing aural result." Another critic, the composer William Flanagan, noted: "The *Romanza* is neoclassic in stylistic commitment, delicate and sensitive in lyric shape, perfectionist in musical detail. It is a lovely, graceful work."

At Natick on August 16, 1959, Fine completed a three-minute march for Brandeis University to mark the beginning of that year's football season. The piece was performed in the fall at a dedicatory banquet for a new athletic center at Brandeis, preceding an address by President Sachar, under the title *The Blue and the White (Brandeis Marching Song)*. The scoring was for solo voice, chorus and piano. Harold Shapero remembered being amused by it. "Irving was so ambitious he wanted to write the Brandeis national anthem. I don't know whether he volunteered or was asked, but it was a good idea."[2]

According to Richard Wernick, Fine liked to joke about his rousing, populist march. "That was a lark. He always

---

2. There are also four pages of undated pencil sketches marked "Hymns for Brandeis."

referred to it as 'Hats *on*, Brandeis.' When you go into a synagogue you put your hat on, and Brandeis was, of course, a Jewish school. That was the pun. He used to kid about it. He actually wanted to subtitle it 'Hats On, Brandeis'."

Fine seems subsequently to have retitled the work *Blue Castle March*. Then, during the winter, he arranged it for full orchestra as *The Blue and White March* (blue and white being the Brandeis colors) and that final version was premiered on May 31, 1960, at Symphony Hall, Boston, by the Boston Pops Orchestra conducted by Arthur Fiedler. When the full score was published by Mills in 1961, however, he changed the title again, to *Blue Towers for Orchestra*. The dedication read: "To Brandeis University and its President Abram Sachar." In its orchestral garb, this charming, effective but little-known occasional piece makes passing references to Copland's open-prairie style, especially as heard in the pop-concert suite *The Red Pony*. The instrumentation is for standard symphony orchestra with optional saxophones and piano.

*One, Two, Buckle My Shoe* was composed during the summer of 1959 as music for a television documentary. "It was commissioned," said Verna, "by Samuel and Helen Slosberg, close friends of ours who owned the Green Shoe Company in Boston, which made Stride-Right Shoes for children. They were multimillionaires who gave the money for the Slosberg Music and Arts Center at Brandeis, and were great patrons of new music and contemporary art." The film showed how the shoes were manufactured; its original purpose had been for marketing and promotion by salesmen. On November 3, 1959, it aired on public television in Boston.

Because of its novel origin and function, *One, Two, Buckle My Shoe* is unlike other Fine chamber works: completely tonal (G major), lighthearted, quite impersonal music in Americana-populist style. As Verna wrote in a program note, it is similar to much of his vocal music in that it is "lively, dance-like and conveys a distinctly jolly mood." Lasting about five minutes, this piece constitutes an odd and decidedly minor entry in Fine's catalogue. It is cast in two parts and has two themes, the first rhythmic, the second lyric (unexpectedly in G minor). The formal setup is simple, the second section mostly a reiteration of the first, except for variation of the rhythmic theme. Throughout, the tempo is *allegro*. The score was published posthumously in 1990, by Boosey and Hawkes.

Aside from the *Romanza*, 1959 had been Fine's *Gebrauchsmusik* year, a period when he concentrated on functional pieces imbued with the common touch. Aware of the looming shadow of serialism, he worried that his music had become too intellectualized. Ned Rorem noted: "Everybody in the 1950s, including Copland and Stravinsky himself, was a little cowed by the serial method. It was in the air." Fine's compulsion to compose in a completely accessible idiom was intensifying and would more fully manifest itself the following year.

Meanwhile, after Fine had returned to his Brandeis duties in the fall, some gratifying performances spiced up the academic grind. On November 23, the Walden Quartet played the *Fantasia for String Trio* on campus. More important, that season the Juilliard Quartet added the *String Quartet* to their tour repertory, presenting it at Yale University and in Mississippi in November, in New York in December and February, in Denver in January and at Cornell University and in North Carolina in March.

The Fines were the guests of Aaron Copland, on Saturday evening, November 14, at a festive Soviet-American concert given by the Boston Symphony to honor a group of visiting Russian composers. The intriguing program included Fekret Amirov's *Kyurdi-ovshari Mugami*, Dmitri Kabalevsky's *Cello Concerto No. 1* and Tikhon Khrennikov's *Symphony No. 1*, along with Copland's *Suite from "The Tender Land"*, the last conducted by Copland. Fine's reactions to the unfamiliar Slavic fare have gone unrecorded. But at a post-concert reception, he and his wife were pleased to meet the featured composers, with the thrilling addition of the renowned Dmitri Shostakovich, all of whom signed their program book. Fine was photographed with Kabalevsky, who, charmed by the vivacious Verna, wrote a letter to her in Cyrillic upon his return to Russia.

On December third, Fine turned forty-five. Middle age was upon him.

# Chapter 18

■ FINE'S DESIRE TO COMPOSE EASYGOING populist pieces alongside challenging modernist scores surely was stimulated by Copland's example: the famous simple-versus-severe division in his friend's output. And, of course, Bernstein had enjoyed phenomenal success with his jazzy and tuneful ballets and musicals.

Richard Wernick recalled that "Irving had this rather crazy notion that he was going to become a popular composer. He thought *Diversions* was going to be his pop number, in the same way Mahler thought his fourth symphony would be his *musique légère* [light music]. He wanted to write important music and he also wanted to write music that would be successful." *Diversions* was designed to break out of the controlled music he was accustomed to compose. "I think it's a little more free-flowing than usual. Irving had this yen to be more spontaneous, and *Diversions* came out of that impulse." Regarding Bernstein, Wernick mused: "It's true that Irving was envious of Lenny. But this is the funny thing: Lenny wanted to be acknowledged as a serious composer, and I know he was jealous of Irving, because Irving could write real concert music and Lenny couldn't."

*Diversions for Orchestra* comprises four succinct movements with a duration of approximately nine minutes. This suite of miniatures is an orchestration, finished in the spring of 1960, of unpublished piano pieces dating from the 1940s and 1950s. The first performance was given on November 5, 1960, at Symphony Hall, Boston, during a Boston Symphony Youth Concert. Harry Ellis Dickson, a violinist from the orchestra, conducted the Boston Pops Orchestra (called the Boston Youth Orchestra for the occasion). The program described Fine's work as "an orchestration of piano sketches from his portfolio." A newspaper review two days later noted that the *Diversions* was "filled with whimsies" and had been greeted by warm applause.

The score, dedicated to the composer's three daughters, was published posthumously in 1963 by Mills, but it had been approved by Fine the year before. On July 19, 1962, he wrote to an academic colleague: "How did you ever hear about Diversions for Orchestra? I have just finished correcting the printed proofs and hope not to see the piece again for a long time."[1]

The first piece, "Little Toccata" (*Vivace*), dates from 1958 and was composed for a painter friend who had given Fine one of her canvases. Sensitively scored, and riding on brisk ostinato motion, it has a delicate if bland harmonic sweetness. The overall impression is impersonal. More effective is the original piano version, which has some bite and dash.

"Flamingo Polka" (*Moderato*) derives from Fine's 1942 incidental music to *Alice in Wonderland,* where it was called "Flamingo Dance" and depicted a mad game of croquet in which the birds were used as mallets. The style of this amusing trifle is essentially that of much nineteenth-century ballet music, but drolly spiced with a few wrong notes à la early Prokofiev and some raucous trombone *glissandi.*

"Koko's Lullaby" (*Andante*) was composed in January 1959. Although Verna stated that it was written "expressly for Irving's beloved, oversized, devoted, sensitive, sweet, white, Royal French poodle with apricot ears and a pedigree, named Koko," the original title, *Arioso for Piano,* would seem to indicate that any canine connection was an afterthought. (The author remembers Verna Fine's laughing references to Koko, who, she said, was decidedly male and overly fond of her. "He was always grabbing my leg, trying to make love.")

The music is refined, lyric and reflective, notable for elegant grace-notes and the special sound of the English horn in harmonic recitative. The chordal ending in the strings, with thirty-second-note quintuplets, shows imagination. It is interesting that the orchestral and piano versions of this piece seem

---

1. Three of the movements ("Little Toccata," "Flamingo Polka," "Koko's Lullaby") were subsequently recorded by Robert Whitney and the Louisville Orchestra; the first recording of the full set was issued in 1993, performed by Joel Spiegelman and the Moscow Radio Symphony.

almost like different music, the piano being more *secco* and far less atmospheric. The last movement follows without pause.

"The Red Queen's Gavotte," like "Flamingo Polka," was originally part of the *Alice* music. There, it was titled "Measuring Music" and illustrated the Red Queen's belligerent bossiness as she measured the ground while Alice glumly munched a dry biscuit. This ingratiating finale, which is not unlike the gavotte from Prokofiev's *Classical Symphony*, has a jolly tune that carries it, with declamatory brass and decorative bells, along to a decisive and festive ending. The original piano piece is also attractive, perhaps sounding a more light-hearted note but necessarily lacking the resonant last bars of the orchestration.

Ned Rorem thought the *Diversions* charming. "The *chutzpah* is that they are certainly not trying to make a great statement. They make campy, skillfully childlike statements, so I like them."

When the full score was eventually issued,[2] the inside front cover boasted a commentary by none other than Leonard Bernstein, dated March 11, 1963. "It is all too easy," he wrote, "to speak glibly of Irving Fine's *Diversions* as a 'charming' piece, and let it go at that. But in fact true charm is one of the most difficult things to achieve musically; and Fine has achieved it by simply and honestly revealing the man in the music. In these four brief pieces we can behold a personality: tender without being coy, witty without being vulgar, appealing without being banal and utterly sweet without ever being cloying. Such a man (and such a work) is rare enough to cause rejoicing." Despite this praise, Bernstein never performed Fine's *Diversions*.

It is easy to see why. For all its charm and often-elegant instrumentation, *Diversions* is a somewhat pallid exercise in eclectic populism. Consequently, it never entered the pop-concert repertory and is today seldom heard. Verna noted that "Irving would have liked to have written Americana music, but Aaron thought of it first. He felt that if he also did that, his music would be too imitative." Fine certainly did not try

---

2. In 1997, Boosey and Hawkes published the original piano version as *Diversions for Piano*. This had been premiered on March 22, 1987, in New York, by Bennett Lerner.

to copy the folksy style of Copland's vernacular pieces in *Diversions*. But when this music is compared with such vivid (and admittedly far more ambitious) works as *Rodeo* and *Billy the Kid* or, for that matter, Bernstein's musical, *On the Town*, it becomes apparent that Fine's pandering instincts were simply too low-keyed to produce successful light pieces. As Verna put it, "He always said that music should be uplifting. The other thing he said was that art is the only place where you can see perfection." Fine was a serious composer, period.

If Fine's foray into the populist field proved less than a resounding triumph, the first half of 1960 had seen numerous performances of his concert works. In January the *String Quartet* had its Parisian debut, by the Quartet Parrenin. The following month the *Sonata for Violin and Piano* was played at Brandeis, by Yfrah Neaman and John Buttrick, and *Serious Song* in Tel Aviv, by the Ramat-Gan Chamber Orchestra on an all-American program that included works by Bernstein and Schuman. (The *Jerusalem Post* termed Fine's score "a lyric work of a certain beauty, although its originality is not striking.") In March, there were two important performances: the violin sonata at the National Gallery of Art in Washington, D.C. (Helmut Braunlich and Robert Parris) and the *String Quartet* at Jordan Hall, Boston (Claremont Quartet). *Blue Towers* was premiered in May by Arthur Fiedler and the Boston Pops. Other highlights of the year included further performances of the *String Quartet*, in Los Angeles in July (Feld Quartet) and in Basel, Switzerland in September (Juilliard Quartet), and a performance of the *Fantasia for String Trio* in Cleveland in October (Concord Trio).

The long Brandeis academic term, with the newly instituted summer session, ran smoothly. In addition to overseeing all three of the Creative Arts departments, Fine taught several classes at both the undergraduate and graduate levels, including Advanced Harmony, Principles of Counterpoint and Composition in the Homophonic Forms. After the University closed for the late-summer break, the entire family left for a lengthy vacation during August, in the White Mountains of New Hampshire and in Quebec.

Mesabi Iron stock hit the jackpot that year, and at last Papa George's dream came true: he was a rich man. That wealth spread into his family. The Fines had always lived well: Verna became independently wealthy after the death of her mother and Fine had a more-than-adequate Brandeis salary, at least in his last years. But now there was money to spare. "Verna and Irving were both rich," said Arthur Berger. According to Wernick, money was never an issue with Fine, which tempts speculation as to whether he might have been more ambitious careerwise and written more music if, like most composers, he had had to struggle financially early on. "Irving knew that was the case. I remember he used the expression 'to rub against life.' He felt he hadn't had to rub against life the way other people did, and that doing so would build character and translate into music. That's a very idealistic attitude and not the way things work most of the time, but he was conscious of it."

Late in the year, at his son's suggestion, George Fine gave a large sum (a million dollars, said Verna) to Brandeis University to establish a chamber-music fellowship. On December 13, President Sachar wrote to him: "We are delighted that you are starting this fund with the proceeds of 200 shares of Mesabi Iron Company common stock," and thanked him for his "generous support." He continued: "Irving has been the cotterpin of our whole Music Department area. But his contribution to the University is not limited to the Music Department or even to the area of creative arts. We call on him continuously where the total welfare of the University is involved because he has the maturity and the breath of vision which makes him a superb collaborator in our common task." The George and Charlotte Fine Endowment Fund came into existence in 1961. Its purpose, as announced, was "to strengthen the University's concert program in chamber music."

Documentation for the last years of Fine's life is scarce,[3] but 1961 began with an academic elevation. On January 13, an article appeared in the *Christian Science Monitor,* "Fine to Naumburg Chair," announcing that he had been named as the first incumbent of the Walter W. Naumburg Chair in

---

3. For instance, the correspondence between Fine and Copland had virtually ceased; according to Verna the two spoke often on the telephone instead of writing.

Music at Brandeis. Three days later, Bernstein affectionately saluted Fine in a postcard as "Dear Professor."

There were two vacations during the first half of that year. The first began the third week of January, at the Brandeis semester break. This time, instead of sunny Florida the destination was sunny Puerto Rico, and Verna, Irving and all three daughters were to join Beatrice and Richard Wernick in San Juan. Getting there was anything but relaxing, thanks to Verna's last-minute jitters. Claudia and Emily jointly told the story. "We were Bostonians living on a dirt road in the suburbs, and driving to the airport in New York was a big event for us. Dad adored Dick Wernick and we were meeting him and Bee in Puerto Rico. As we neared the airport, we got lost. Mom had the map and she could not deal well with frustration and was shrieking, 'I can't read this map!' We were driving around in circles, and it went on and on. Finally, we pulled over the side of the road and Dad tried to calm her down, but she became hysterical. He grabbed the map and yelled 'Stop screaming!' and she ended up with a black eye. He certainly did not intend to hit her—maybe she had lunged forward for the map—but she had pushed him over the edge." Joanna remembered the unpleasant event differently. "Mom was very hysterical about getting lost and missing the plane and Dad lost his temper and hit her. The car swerved. I remember ducking down in the back seat and crying." In any event, Emily noted: "Mom had to wear sunglasses the whole time in Puerto Rico."

That the Wernicks were able to have that vacation was due to Fine's quiet generosity, for Richard was freelancing in New York as a theater composer and money was tight. The two families had established what Wernick described as "a very warm relationship." Beatrice remembered, "We had decided to get away from New York for a few days and go to Washington, D.C. Irving telephoned and when he heard that he said, 'We had a family conference and you're coming as our guests.' Richard: "If we could pay the plane fare, everything else was on him. My guess is that it was Irving's idea. It was the kind of thing he would think of." Beatrice: "We agreed on the condition that we would pay him back, which we did. Irving was a very considerate man, a real gentleman. An example of his graciousness: he sent Dick a check before we left, so that he could pay for our meals and Irving for his family's. Dick was not made to feel dependent."

The Wernicks mentioned that they seldom saw any display of temper from Fine, and the few times they did, it was directed at his children. Richard: "Irving had a sweet nature, but I remember an incident in Puerto Rico. The girls had squandered too much money on tourist stuff and he chewed them out. He said that just because they had money didn't mean that they should spend it in that way, because it was wasteful."

Rather than temper tantrums, Fine was given to pranks. Beatrice Wernick thought him "a great practical joker." He would occasionally frequent a nearby shop that sold joke items for parties. Richard Wernick noted that "Irving's humor could be a little down-and-dirty, but only in the family." He would sneak into the master bedroom with a piece of rubber vomit and carefully place it on Verna's pillow. "Verna liked to go to bed fairly early and read the newspaper. Irving and I would sit in the living room until we heard her screech, and he would howl with laughter." The children were also targets. "He had a rubber snake and a huge rubber tarantula, and they'd always fall for it."

Emily remembered: "He was quite silly and raunchy—toilet humor. He liked to tease us and used to gross out Mom all the time. One Saturday morning, when I was eight or nine years old, I got up a little late and went downstairs, and I heard him yelling from their bedroom. 'Emily, Emily, come here quick! Help me!' I ran in. They had twin beds next to each other and he was lying on his, moaning: 'I'm sick, and look what I've done to myself.' It was disgusting. There was vomit everywhere. He said, 'Go to the broom closet and get a bucket and a mop.' When I returned, he picked up the vomit with his hand. It was fake! And he started laughing hysterically." Emily recalled that her father seldom sent a conventional postcard. One summer, when she was at camp, he wrote: "Tragedy has struck. Duchess [the family dog] got into Claudia's makeup and urinated all over the living room. I told your mother that it was lemonade." A second card also had his eldest daughter's makeup as its subject. "He was upset about that. It said: 'Claudia is home and what is she doing? She's putting on makeup. And what will she be doing in an hour? She'll be putting on makeup. And what does she look like? A clown'."

In late March and early April, Verna and Irving took an automobile tour of Portugal and Spain. They left their children at the Natick house to be cared for by George and Lotte, and Mercedes, the longtime housekeeper. Their vacation companions were Caroline and Edwin Pettet (Pettet was a professor whom Fine had brought into the Brandeis theater department, and an old friend). In an undated letter from Lisbon's Hotel Eduardo VII addressed to all of his daughters, Fine mentioned "three rather exhausting but very pleasant days in Lisbon and its environs," and gave an amusing description of dining out. "We have just come back from a restaurant which specializes in Alentajano food, singing, decor and furnishings. The waitresses wear gingham pants, high leather boots, dozens of skirts, earrings, shawls wrapped around their heads and under their chins and flat black hats on top of the shawls. After they finish serving, they join about eight young men, also dressed in peasant costumes and about a half a dozen little kids. The whole mob then proceeds to sing loud and long enough so that everybody is driven to drink, and this is how the owner makes enough money to pay this small army of country-folk."

Lisbon was "an immaculate as well as beautiful city, handsomely laid with long wide boulevards, and its old parts very quaint & colorful." He noted the smells: "There is a pervasive odor of dried sardines or fish, chicory, coffee, floral scent and slightly rancid oil," and wrote about one of his preferred topics, food, at some length. Shopping for handicrafts, he discovered "that by the time you add up the freight charges, it would be cheaper to buy them in Boston."

After three days in Portugal, where they visited the fishing village of Cascais (Verna was photographed in profile, looking windblown but determined, and Irving half-smiled into the sun, even on vacation attired in suit and tie) and the castle in the mountain town of Sintra, the group left for Madrid. At the El Washington Hotel, Verna had her picture taken, luxuriously breakfasting in bed. In Spain, the Fines and Pettets also saw the sights of Toledo, Córdoba, Granada and Seville.

Fine wrote two letters from Seville on April 2, Easter Sunday, one to Emily, the other to Joanna. After describing the cathedral and the Alcazar, the palace of the Moorish kings, to Emily, he continued: "From the Alcazar we went through the most beautiful section of any city we have seen on this trip. It was the old Jewish section when the Moors or Arabs ruled the city. Everything is white and spick and span." He noted that "there are lots of poor people who work very hard and make no more than seventy-five cents a day. That's less than I make in ten minutes and less than Papa George makes in five minutes (at least this year)." (Mesabi obviously was holding up well.) In the poor section of recently visited Grenada, many of the people, he said, "are gypsies and believe me, they are not all so pretty. The streets where some of them live are so narrow, only one or two persons can get by at a time. And the smell—pewie. The little donkeys make sissy and dooty all over."

Joanna's letter contained the assurance that "we are having a very long and a very good trip. The auto goes up and down and sideways [on mountain roads] and makes me sick to my tummy." Catholic religious processions were then described in some detail. As to cuisine: "I do not think you would like all of the food we get here. I don't. A lot of it is fried fish and fried mish-mash. Very ooky and gooky. The lobster and the roast beef are very good, and they have the best oranges and nuts you ever saw." He mentioned that they had stayed at "that wonderful hotel near Gibraltar named after Queen Christina," in Algeciras, on the Strait.

The following day, from a town called Valdepeñas, he described their "very modern" motel to Claudia. "Superficially, the rooms look elegant, but upon closer inspection one notices that the linoleum is lifting from the under-flooring, the doors do not close or open, the hot water faucet runs cold and vice-versa, the light fixtures on the wall fall off when you turn on the light, etcetera." For their two nights in Seville, they had stayed at the ritzy Hotel Alfonzo XIII rather than the establishment outside the city where they had made reservations. "The motel we fled from was cold, dirty, damp and had two broken-down cots with headboards which looked as though they had been slept in for several months without anybody's thinking of changing the sheets or covers. The room was heated by a tiny electric heater which blew a fuse as soon as we turned it on." Although Seville's cathedral was "quite overwhelming in grandeur," he thought that "the loveliest section [of the city] was the former Jewish quarter."

The four friends had gone to a flamenco show, which was "real fun, sometimes funny, sometimes make-believe fierce, sometimes dignified and graceful." Fine found himself enthralled by a gypsy woman with a stunning figure—"beautiful in a very exotic way"—who danced "like a combination she-devil and cat." He was also fascinated by a male singer, "a man who could be thought of as a kind of gypsy Louis Armstrong—a fantastically powerful singer who seemed to improvise extraordinary songs almost Arabic in character."

In Córdoba, they had "spent time in the old mosque-cathedral & in the old Jewish and Arab quarters where no longer lives a Jew or Arab. Saw the remains of the old synagogue—as pitiful a place as you can imagine—so tiny compared to any little parish church, let alone the mosque." The mosque itself, in which 100,000 people supposedly could pray at one time, was fantastic, "the damnedest place I ever saw or hope to see. Thousands of columns and zebra-striped arches surrounding a gothic cathedral." The group planned to drive back to Madrid the next day, with a stopover in Toledo. "I must say," Fine concluded, "that I have discovered this hopping about from city to city tiring and confusing."

Upon returning home, Fine noted wryly: "We studied Italian before we left for Italy and promptly forgot it when we returned. We have been half-heartedly studying Spanish since we returned from Spain and since we began to employ Colombian maids."

With the exception of a few modern operas such as Britten's *Peter Grimes* and Blitzstein's *No for an Answer* and *The Cradle Will Rock*, Fine was never vitally interested in the genre. Verna remembered that "he was very opposed to opera as an institution in this country. He felt that something like the Metropolitan Opera should not be supported, because it didn't support American opera and was so expensive that it was only for the elite. He wanted to democratize opera."

Still, in 1954 he told her that he had come across "a nice story by Bret Harte that might make an opera." That same year, his friend Gertrude Norman suggested they collaborate on an opera based on Stephen Crane's late-nineteenth-centu-

ry realist novel about a prostitute, *Maggie: A Girl of the Streets.*
On December 15, she expressed excitement about the idea
and asked Fine to read the book and give her his reaction.
Three months later, Norman remained enthusiastic, seeing
great possibilities in the short novel even without having to
alter the plot. She felt it could be the basis of an intense and
pure opera, even an intimate one, and that the story's tragedy
could be expressed by understatement. In a subsequent letter,
she thought that it might be implausible for the heroine to
perish under an automobile during the 1890s as she and Fine
had discussed, but the problem could be solved by having
Maggie fling herself into a river.

By May, Norman had finished a rough draft of a libretto. There was to be only one set, an alley (known as Blood
Alley, it was located in New York City on the site of the present United Nations building) with tenements in the background that somehow encompassed an apartment interior.
She noted that her draft was somewhat like a play, and that
Maggie's death should provide an impressive ending. She had
changed the sequence of events from that on which she and
Fine had agreed, and she emphasized that major questions
about the libretto remained to be settled.

Sometime in 1955, Fine evidently got cold feet, because
that November Norman described herself as perturbed, not
knowing if the composer, who was undergoing analysis and
seems to have been suffering from anxiety about *Maggie,*
would agree to provide the music. Several months later, she
expressed disappointment that he still had not committed
himself, and asked his permission to show her libretto to two
other composers, William Schuman and Gail Kubik.

Nothing came of the project at that time, but their
friendship survived. In February 1956, Fine wrote to Bernstein expressing concern for Norman, who was "in dire straits,
going completely blind from glaucoma, and without any consistent source of income or moral support." He described her
as "a remarkable person—a writer with a musicological background who did a number of jobs for the government during
the war and shortly after, including a considerable part of the
writing of the Japanese constitution." Not only had she provided the texts for his *Childhood Fables,* but she also compiled
and edited an anthology of letters by composers, which had

been published by Knopf. He mentioned that "she'd like to do more musical collaboration."

In late 1959, Fine was again in correspondence with the New York-based Norman about *Maggie*. He had proposed to Brandeis officials that the University give a commission for creating a musical, rather than an opera, out of Crane's book, to be produced by Brandeis. Further, he wanted to compose the score jointly with his close friend and former student Richard Wernick. "Brandeis commissioned only the first act," Wernick recalled. "They were hedging their bets." The plan was for each composer to write separate numbers and then get together and make suggestions to each other. Wernick thought the collaboration a bizarre idea, but during 1960 and 1961 they worked sporadically at it. "The thing that was crazy was that I was trying to write a more serious kind of music and Irving was trying to write show music. He had a feeling that I understood theater better than he did because I had worked in the theater and had played jazz as a kid. He said, 'I can't do this myself, but why don't we work on it together?' He and I used to talk a lot about show music, about Cole Porter, Jerome Kern, Richard Rodgers, George Gershwin, and one of the things he most admired about those guys was the fact that, as he saw it, they were completely uninhibited. They just let it go. He felt that was a real problem with his own music: that it was too inhibited, too controlled."

Beatrice Wernick observed that "Irving pushed *Maggie* at Brandeis so we could have some money, because we were struggling, almost destitute in New York. He was trying to find ways of getting Dick something to live on, and he got us $400 or $500, which was a lot then. I have a feeling that all the money from Brandeis went to us, because Irving didn't need it." She remembered that "they worked on *Maggie* for more than six months, but there were such problems with Gertrude Norman that they dropped it. And Irving was in the midst of composing his symphony at that time."

Wernick said that there were severe problems concerning the libretto. "We couldn't get this woman off square one. We didn't even get a scene finished, much less the first act, because working with her was such a nightmare." As a result, very little was written. Wernick completed one song, "The Moon Looks Like Hell," Fine two: "I Wonder" and "Tell It to the Worms." Not unexpectedly, as Howard Pollack noted, the general style of Fine's songs showed similarities to those of Kurt Weill and Marc Blitzstein. Although there is nothing wrong with them technically, the music is too ordinary to be of interest except as a curiosity. And, as Pollack rightly put it, "a major problem was in writing a convincing book, for *Maggie* was, ironically, a study in tragic inarticulateness: Maggie herself rarely speaks in the novella, and the other characters mostly just curse." Eventually, the Brandeis administration lost patience and cancelled the commission.

*Maggie* may not have been the only intended large-scale work that did not get written in the 1960-1961 period. There was also an orchestral piece entitled *Partita on an Israeli Theme*. According to Verna, her husband labored at this during 1961, a time when he was deeply involved with his symphony for the Boston Symphony Orchestra. Perhaps he planned an alternate, less ambitious symphonic piece to fulfill that commission in case the symphony spluttered out. In any case, no fewer than ninety-four pages of the partita exist. For the most part, these consist of fragmentary sketches, but there are a few pages of full short score, though with only occasional indications of instrumentation.

The music starts quietly with a semi-serial ostinato played *pizzicato* by the lower strings ("quasi 12-tone" accompaniment, as Fine wrote later in the score). In the fourth bar, the Israeli theme begins, stated by a solo trumpet. What music there is constitutes a slightly odd melding of oriental melisma (dictated by the modal character of the tune) with tonal chord progressions (some dissonant, some conventional) and modulations that at times co-exist within a serially inflected décor. Overall, this material seems rather unpromising, which is doubtless the reason it was abandoned.

On the cover-page, Fine gave a formal plan for the work, which was to be in five movements and scored for standard symphony orchestra with coloristic percussion to suggest exoticism (cymbals, tambourine, triangle, glockenspiel and possible xylophone). It read as follows: "I Theme, alla Marcia (andante con moto); II Scherzo 6/8 molto vivace; III Poco adagio (2 variations); IV Rondo (several short variations), fragmentary in character; V [left blank]."

Verna noted that although Fine was well versed in Jewish history, he never felt the need for the social aspects of joining a temple and didn't actively celebrate the Jewish holidays. "But I remember that he and a few other professors at Brandeis got involved in organizing a Sunday School in West Newton, which was run by young Israelis, and he let our children go to that." Perhaps those Israelis managed to intrigue Fine with their songs. As for the State of Israel itself, he seems not to have shown much interest in it and never visited it. Wernick stated: "I cannot recall a single conversation about Israel. Between its establishment in 1948 and the 1967 war, there was a good deal of ambivalence in the American Jewish community. While I don't think Irving took Judaism very seriously, he never belittled it." Wernick was surprised to learn of the sketches for the *Partita on an Israeli Theme.* "I can't believe I wouldn't have known about it if it were written in the timeframe in which it is being claimed," he said. "After I graduated in 1955, we kept in very close touch and I always knew what he was working on." Harold Shapero was also unaware of the partita.[4] "I don't think Irving ever did a 'Jewish' piece. The things he liked in music were not Judaic, not the augmented-second, 'Eli-Eli' stuff like Bloch's *Schelomo*." Further: "I doubt he was particularly interested in Jewishness. I remember that he often used to laugh and quote one of his cousins hollering at a kid—'Stanley, Stanley, didn't I told you you'd fell?'—as an example of the American-Jewish way of ruining the English language."

Interestingly enough, at some earlier point in his career,

---

4. It should be noted that although, as usual, this material is undated, the manuscript paper is very similar to that used in 1952 for the abortive *Orchestral Preludes* and slightly dissimilar to that in which the symphony was sketched in short score—although the brand is the same in all three cases. This raises the possibility that the *Partita on an Israeli Theme* might have been another attempt to execute the earlier Boston Symphony commission. Considering Fine's mixture, during his last decade, of melodic, tonal music with serial elements, it is impossible to date the partita with confidence on the basis of style. But the suspicion arises, given both Wernick's and Shapero's ignorance of the project, along with the fact that Fine was composing his symphony during 1960-1962, that Verna Fine may have misremembered the period of this unfinished work.

Fine had explored the other side of the Middle East question musically. In his archive there is an unpublished, undated, three-page piece for piano, four hands (fifty-five bars, with repeats; tempo, *Allegro vivace*) titled *Kakha-Kakha* and marked "based on Palestinian Folk Song." This is a lively and amusing work, with a far more striking theme than that of the Israeli partita.

In late March 1961, Fine received a letter from Paul Fromm which keenly interested him. The wealthy Chicago patron of contemporary music had decided to finance a new magazine, a semi-annual periodical serving as "a forum for the serious American composer, which would parallel the independence and quality of such journals as the English *Score* and the old *Modern Music*." He noted that the *Musical Quarterly* still had high standards but was aimed primarily at musicologists. Fromm stressed the idea of autonomy, stating that a publication connected to any university music department inevitably "stands between the dual dangers of academicism and parochiality." The first issue was planned for 1962, and although a university press would be found to print and distribute the magazine, "it will be directly identified as a publication of the Fromm Music Foundation, to emphasize its total independence."

Fromm invited Fine to join his editorial board as an advisor on policy and content, and he agreed without hesitation. Subsequently, more than a dozen other respected composers were asked, and his friend Arthur Berger was appointed Editor-in-Chief. The journal's tentative title, which Fromm thought "rather stilted and pedantic," was *Annals of New Music*, and he solicited suggestions for a better one, observing: "Of course, we are far more concerned about what goes inside than what appears on the cover."

The magazine was eventually called *Perspectives of New Music*. In September 1961, a major article in the *New York Times*, "The World of Music, A Composers' Magazine for Informed Public," announced the project. It quoted Fromm saying that "our idea is to present the composer seriously to an enlightened public, with dignity and on a mature level." The editors reportedly were concerned with "communication between composer and performer as well as between composer and public" and wished eventually to reach a European readership. *Perspectives* aimed high. There would be no room in its pages for propaganda, vendettas or partisanship, and every article considered was to be read by three persons "chosen on the basis of their authority in the particular subject involved." The majority of the articles would be by composers, aimed not only at the musician but also the informed layman, "because the editors feel that there is a large group of literate people who are closely concerned with modern literature and art but are woefully ignorant of recent musical developments."

The editorial board comprised Berger, Benjamin Boretz (as associate editor), Elliott Carter, Babbitt, Fine, Foss, Kirchner and Schuller, among others. An advisory committee consisted of Copland, Piston, Sessions, Stravinsky and Ernst Krenek. Looking back, Berger reflected that "Irving was very caring about his friends and their happiness. When my first wife died in 1960, he was concerned about me and thought it would be good if I had something interesting to do. So he pushed me into editing *Perspectives.*"

There were high hopes in the American musical community when *Perspectives* began publication in 1962, but in some circles they faded after a few issues. Berger functioned as editor for only one year, although he remained on the Board. With the ascendancy of Boretz, a former Fine student, the magazine became more and more the realm of theorists than of musicians. The author remembers Aaron Copland, who was never a fan of academic analysis, shaking his head while examining a copy of the magazine in the early 1970s and saying, "This is ghastly, a disaster. What's it got to do with music?" He felt the focus was on music as mathematics, which made it unreadable. To Copland and to others, the contents did not seem intended for musicians, much less laymen, informed or otherwise.

Leon Kirchner was even more adamantly against *Perspectives*, describing many of those who wrote for it as "intellectual misfits. They were certainly not musical, and a lot of what they produced was indecipherable trash." He deplored Fine's interest in the journal. "Irving took it seriously to some extent, because *Perspectives* was 'respectable.' I thought that beneath him." He said that Fine was "sort of leaning toward composers like Boulez and Stockhausen. I don't know whether he was actually interested in them, but it had a lot to do with the influence of that terrible magazine. He was afraid he was missing something."[5]

With *Perspectives of New Music* safely in the hands of Berger, it seemed, in 1961, an ideal situation to Fine. He would not live long enough for disillusionment to set in.

---

5. Milton Babbitt recalled that Fine "felt very drawn to the students at Brandeis. They were interested in the more avant-garde music and he came to that music as an outsider. He was much intimidated, for instance, by Stockhausen, although he didn't feel any affinity for that music."

# Chapter 19

■ "I AM STUCK AT THE BEGINNING of the last movement of my orchestral piece and wish you were here to help," Fine wrote to Copland on January 11, 1961. The reference was to his final and most ambitious score, *Symphony (1962)*.

The work had been commissioned by Charles Munch for the Boston Symphony Orchestra as a part of the American Music Center's Commissioning Series, with a grant from the Ford Foundation, and was dedicated to Munch and the Orchestra. Verna Fine noted that commissioning her husband might have been either Munch's idea or could have been suggested to the conductor by Fine's close friend Leonard Burkat, who was Munch's assistant. "Though he was French, Munch was interested in American music," Verna said. "We spent summers together at Tanglewood, so he knew Irving. It was always understood that he would conduct the premiere."

Richard Wernick recalled that Fine received the commission "a long, long time before he wrote a single note. Finally, they made a serious deadline, and he kept worrying about it." The symphony was begun in the middle of 1960 and finished in February 1962, only a month before the premiere. "He was never a fast worker," Verna noted.[1] In a mild panic, Fine engaged Wernick to copy and edit the score, "to do the dogsbody work," as Wernick put it. "I had to correct mistakes in notation, because there is a good deal of complex musical language in that piece, so that, as in the printed score of the Mahler ninth symphony for instance, you might find a doubling of the bass-line where the basses have an A-sharp

---

1. The end of the pencil manuscript of the full score is marked "2:40 A.M. Feb. 17, 1962," but orchestration details were not complete until three days later. "It was a very dramatic day," recalled Verna, "the day that Colonel Glenn the astronaut went up. Irving was trying to finish everything before he orbited down. 'Gotta beat Glenn!' he said."

and the contrabassoon a B-flat. Irving knew that with his deadline he was never going to have time to go back and fix that kind of thing, so the idea was that as he was composing and orchestrating I would get all the notation to conform." Wernick also copied the orchestral parts.[2]

Fine originally planned his symphony to be cast in the standard four movements, but eventually settled on a three-movement form. The first movement, *Intrada,* was initially the slow movement and bore the not-inappropriate title *Eclogue,* meaning a short pastoral or idyllic poem with elements of dialogue. Verna remembered that "Irving talked about writing another opening movement because he was a little hesitant about that opening in the bassoons in the *Intrada.*" Fifty-one bars in short-score exist of such an attempt at a first movement. Although there is no tempo mark, an *allegro moderato* is suggested by the music, which begins dramatically with two dissonant *fortissimo* chords in the full orchestra that contain all twelve notes of the scale (five in the first chord, seven in the second). In the third bar, a three-note, rising whole-tone motto (B-flat, C, D) is declaimed by the four horns, to be subsequently used in both ascending and descending forms, accompanied by tonal ostinatos. The meter is regular, moving in quarters, so that, unusually for Fine, the rhythmic element is absent. This is mildly discordant but tonally based "grey" music of little affect which was quickly rejected as unworthy.

There are also short-score sketches of the beginnings of two other abandoned movements: a slightly more promising scherzo marked *Molto allegro* that is harmonically neoclassical rather than serial; and what was intended as the third, slow, movement of the symphony, marked *Lento,* commencing

---

2. When Wernick finished the editorial work on the symphony, his last payment of $300 was due. Fine gave him cash and remarked: "I mentioned to my father that I owed you this money and he told me to buy you a hundred shares of Canadian Javelin stock, because it's $3 a share and is going to go through the roof." But Fine felt he couldn't speculate with Wernick's money and knew he needed it immediately. Wernick reflected: "He should have listened to Papa. In one week that stock went from $3 to $27 a share. I would have been rich."

with *pizzicato* strings in dialogue with rhapsodic bassoon triplets, leading to a near-hymnlike progression in trumpets and trombones—dark-hued, tonal expression revolving around another three-note motto comprising a rising semitone and an octave leap. As music, these sketches are of only academic interest, but they do illustrate the composer's uncompromisingly critical attitude to his own work. According to Arthur Cohn, the symphony had "three major recastings" before it went to the publisher.

Aside from the work's aesthetic value, the most telling aspect of Fine's *Symphony (1962)*[3] is that it represents an original and for the most part successful fusion of Stravinskian neoclassicism and Fine's own tonal romanticism with the method, though not the rhetoric, of Schoenbergian serialism. It is clearly intended as an important statement, a score encompassing an expanded mode of expression involving all that Fine had learned concerning the inflection of his preferred style with what was fundamentally an alien technique. Here, he was challenging his audience rather than, as in much of his previous music, charming it.

"There are tons of Stravinskian gestures in the symphony," noted Wernick. "But they are filtered through a different style and through a different set of harmonic ears." Oddly enough, for all its impressive features and perhaps because of its far larger range and restless, sometimes declamatory, rhetoric, stylistically the symphony seems a slightly less assimilated work than the little *Romanza for Wind Quintet*. Even though the dodecaphonic technique is non-dogmatically applied throughout, it stands as the defining element of this score. That is a factor which could not be expected to appeal to everyone. David Diamond pronounced the symphony "forced," and felt that "using the twelve-tone technique seemed unnatural" for Fine, although "the workmanship is absolutely first-rate and it is orchestrated very well indeed. The piece has a kind of glued-together solidity." He recalled

---

3. Fine wanted the year included in the work's title, according to Verna. "He thought that it was better to know when it was written rather than if it was a 'Symphony No. 1'." She remembered he had reflected that perhaps he would never write another symphony—as in fact he didn't.

that "Munch said to me that he thought there was a certain kind of Stravinsky influence but he found Irving's use of serial techniques more interesting than most other composers'. He felt the symphony was a very strong work, if a little too formulated and self-conscious."

Ned Rorem observed: "I think Fine doffs his hat at early Stravinsky at the end of the symphony, where there are *Sacre*-like wallops in the orchestra. I can get a little irritated by that sort of thing. Virgil Thomson once wrote about Copland's third symphony and titled his essay 'Aaron Copland as Great Man,' and this symphony seemed a little bit Irving Fine as Great Man. He is saying, 'I'm writing something important now,' and a composer can't make that decision himself." He concluded that "it is in the last movement where I feel I don't know where he's going or what he's trying to say. The symphony ends, I think, with a sort of question mark."

Conversely, Leon Kirchner remembered: "I was so surprised by that last work, for it had come out of nowhere. It seemed like a new Irving. It was extraordinary, because you don't often see that kind of thing happen, and I was impressed. I was really interested to see what the next work would bring, and when I told him that he received it well. He felt he was on to something and he was aware something had changed. For the first time, he was on the course one takes when one becomes a master." Jack Gottlieb recalled, "I didn't like the symphony the first time I heard it, but I must say it makes quite a splash the second time around. I think it is a wonderful first attempt in a new language." Lukas Foss termed the symphony "a very important work," while Harold Shapero enigmatically described the piece as "modest and successful and quite accessible." He pointed out "a very striking resurrection motive at the end. Perhaps because Irving died, I thought of it as a resurrection."

Aaron Copland, who, at the same time Fine was working on his symphony was composing his aggressively serial and grandiose *Connotations for Orchestra*, took a middle position in an essay written after Fine's death.[4] "Special reference

---

4. Comparing *Connotations* to the Fine symphony, David Diamond said laughingly: "And that was Aaron being perverse. The piece went on for so long, driving everybody nuts."

should be made to the symphony, partly because it represents the composer in his final phase and partly because it demonstrates a reaching out toward new and more adventurous experiences, in certain ways experiences outside the frame of reference of most of Fine's music. It is strongly dramatic, almost operatic in gesture, with a restless and somewhat strained atmosphere that is part of its essential quality." He concluded: "It is saddening to think that Fine was not fated to carry through to full fruition the new directions clearly inherent in the best pages of the symphony."

While the primary and often the subsidiary materials of each movement are demonstrably the result of dodecaphonic thinking, the system is so freely applied that the melodies and harmonies flow in a manner rare in strict serial music, or, as here, in serially derived music. Milton Babbitt noted that "Irving liked to think he had written a piece in which the twelve-tone aspect was not obvious, never on the surface. And it's true that it is much deeper in the symphony than in the quartet, because in the symphony it has a structural effect. We talked about how serialism can function as a referential norm without ever appearing on the surface of a piece. And we discussed issues involving questions of continuity." In this score there are only occasional distant allusions to sonata form. As always, Fine had taken Stravinsky as his model, specifically the sort of structural rhythm evident in the hyper-serial *Movements for Piano and Orchestra*, where all the materials are immediately presented and then quickly disappear into the interior of the music—in Babbitt's words, "the relation of the explicit to the latent."

The two tone-rows on which much, though not all, of the work is loosely based were cleverly designed to provide maximum contrast in the chords and melodic material they generate. Row 1, built on two hexachords (D, B, E-flat, A, G, F; B-flat, A-flat, G-flat, D-flat, E-natural, C), has suggestions of a whole-tone scale; while Row 2 (D-flat, C, A-flat, E-flat, B-natural, D-natural, A-natural, E-natural, B-flat, F, F-sharp, G) is far more chromatic. The interval of the augmented fourth, or tritone, which is a prominent element in this symphony, is found once in each row. Technically speaking, the first movement begins with Row 1 in the bassoons, sly-sounding music about which Verna remembered Fine had doubts as being appropriate for the opening of a symphony; Row 2 is prevalent in the movement's middle part. The ostinato-driven scherzo is the least bound to the rows, although some of the chords are related to Row 1. Both rows are present in the last movement, though Row 2 predominates. The work as a whole is constantly inventive, in the sense that there is little direct repetition. The slow-fast-slow layout is reminiscent of the serially inflected *Fantasia for String Trio,* though on a considerably broader scale. Some derivations are evident: intimations of Stravinsky's *Symphony in Three Movements* in movement one, Copland's *Music for the Theatre* and *Short Symphony* in movement two and Stravinsky's *Symphony of Psalms* in the third movement's closing peroration of static nobility. These are, however, so convincingly integrated that they strike the ear as being intrinsic to this fascinating and rather magnificent score.[5]

Fine's *Symphony (1962)* is scored for a standard-sized orchestra consisting of piccolo, two each of flutes, oboes, clarinets and bassoons; English horn, bass clarinet, contrabassoon, four horns, three trumpets, three trombones, tuba, piano, celesta, harp, timpani, an augmented percussion section (timpano piccolo, snare drum, bass drum, tambourine, crash and suspended cymbals, wood block, triangle, gong, xylophone, glockenspiel, antique cymbals, tubular bells) and strings. It has a duration of approximately twenty-three minutes.

For the premiere, by the Boston Symphony conducted by Charles Munch,[6] on March 23, 1962 at Symphony Hall,

---

5. Concerning the matter of unconscious influences, Wernick had an amusing anecdote. "Irving and I were working together on the second movement of the symphony, and when I saw bar 214 and on I went to the piano and played something similar from the Prokofiev fifth symphony. He yelled: 'You son-of-a-bitch! You've just ruined the whole movement! No matter how you try, it's impossible to be original!' But, actually, he thought it was funny." Wernick also mentioned that he had directed Fine's attention to a repeated-note piano figure reminiscent of Stravinsky's *Petrushka.* "We talked about that. He said, 'No, it may sound like Stravinsky but it comes from me.' He had a good sense of himself." And, after all, nothing is *sui generis.*

6. Wernick stated: "Although the piece was a Boston Symphony commission, I understood it was not absolutely tied to

Boston, Fine provided a brief commentary (dated March 13, 1962) that is an essential guide to the work. Perhaps for fear of alarming his audience, he carefully avoided mention of one of the symphony's most salient elements, serial technique. The following program note includes material from the first typed draft, dated March 6, that was excised, probably because of space requirements, from the version printed in the Boston Symphony program book. Such material is enclosed in square brackets.

"The composition was begun about a year and a half ago. I was applying the finishing touches to the orchestration on February 20, 1962, nervously watching the television set out of the corner of one eye when the news of Colonel Glenn's return from outer space was announced.

["The subtitles, *Intrada*, *Capriccio* and *Ode*, were added to the score after its completion. By employing them, I hope to prepare the listener for a somewhat different kind of continuity than that normally associated with the classical symphony or its descendents."]

"The first movement, *Intrada: Andante quasi allegretto*, suggests a kind of choreographic action in which characters enter, depart, and reappear altered and in different groupings—all of this serving as background for a lyrical and at times pastoral narrative. The music begins quietly in the bassoons and low strings, and passes through a number of episodes in which other instrumental groupings are featured.[7] After reaching a strong but essentially lyrical climax for full orchestra, it subsides gradually into a kind of night music for English horn, other solo woodwinds, harp, celesta, and muted strings. [My visual and literary associations to this movement are with the early Italian Renaissance rather than with classical antiquity.]

---

Munch. I remember Irving saying that if he had his druthers the conductor for the premiere would be Arthur Fiedler." As for the first performance, "Irving felt it was okay, but he was not entirely satisfied. Munch didn't have a complete handle on it."

7. In the manuscript short-score, one of these episodes (building in the full orchestra from bar 74) is marked "Keep it loud! And tough!" That of course was Copland's maxim, and the listener may note that this agitated *tutti* section is decidedly Coplandesque (*Music for the Theatre*).

"Although the second movement, *Capriccio: Allegro con spirito*, occasionally has overtones of the orchestral concerto, it is essentially an extended scherzo in which 4/4 meter predominates and in which the customary contrasting trio has been replaced by a series of connecting episodes. The first of these is playful and soloistic in character; the second, with its alternating and syncopated massed sonorities featuring the brass, is more sardonic and aggressive. In the last episode, beginning with solo bassoons, accompanied by percussion and low chords in the piano and strings, the meter shifts into a 6/8 *burletta*.[8] Materials from the first part of this movement reappear either in varied form or in altered order in the brief final section and coda.

"The last movement, *Ode: Grave*, is essentially a dithyrambic fantasia with a concluding recessional-like epilogue. In the fantasia much of the material employed in the symphony recurs highly metamorphosed in fragmentary statements or outbursts, in brief dramatic canons, or in static ruminating passages with florid figuration. The prevailing mood is darker than in the first two movements. The tempo begins *Grave*, and picks up considerable momentum as it passes through an agitated and highly syncopated section in which the brass toss around a five-note motto related to the

---

8. Wernick remembered that this third episode (beginning at bar 171) originally had a clarinet passage accompanying the bassoons. "When Irving talked about William Schuman's music, he said that one of the things you find there all the time is that when he writes a melody or motif then he's got to write a countermelody or countermotif. He said that was one of the problems with his own music: that he always put those things in. That's why he removed that clarinet *obbligato*. He pointed to that passage and said, 'Those clarinets are wrong because they just clutter up the music'." A few bars on, at 176, there is a bit of a mystery. In Fine's own August 1962 Tanglewood performance of the symphony and Joel Spiegelman's 1993 recording, a striking horn solo soars over the chattering bassoons. This, however, was not played at the premiere under Munch or in a 1966 performance by Leonard Bernstein and the New York Philharmonic; nor does it appear in the published score, though it perhaps exists in a horn part. Fortunately both the Fine and Spiegelman performances are available on commercial recordings.

opening theme of the symphony. Both motto and theme occupy the center of the stage from this point to the end [, first in a broad canonic climax for full orchestra in the original tempo, then through a quiet lyrical episode of more soloistic character,[9] past fragmentary reminiscences of the beginning, to the final epilogue. In this last (a kind of solemn recessional beginning *piano, marcato* and concluding triple *forte*), bell-like quasi-canonic statements of the principal theme are heard in the brass and upper strings against ostinatos in the piano, harp, timpani and low strings.]"

The Boston Symphony gave three performances of Fine's *Symphony (1962)* during March 1962: the premiere on Friday afternoon, the twenty-third, a repeat performance on Saturday evening, and a final performance the following Tuesday evening at Sanders Theatre in Cambridge which was televised live by WGBH in Boston. Verna remembered that Fine had attended all of the rehearsals and Munch had consulted with him before they began. "He was a charming man, not a prima donna at all, very easy to get along with. Munch worked hard with the orchestra and Irving was very pleased with the performances. It was a great orchestra, but he always worried that things could go wrong." Wernick recalled an incident from a rehearsal. "Munch consistently took the apotheosis at the end of the symphony [from bar 80] too fast, and Irving kept telling him, 'No, no, Maestro. Slower, please.' But Munch didn't get it until finally Irving called out, '*Maestoso!*' and Munch said, 'Ah!' It had to be characterized."

Fine surely knew he had written an ambitious work in an idiom that a general audience would find difficult to digest. Thus, he must have been gratified by the surprisingly good, though hardly ecstatic, applause that a tape recording of the symphony's premiere reveals.[10] Verna observed: "To me, the

---

9. Verna reflected that "Irving felt very emotionally involved with the symphony. There is a place in the third movement where the oboe comes in plaintively [bars 105-111]. I remember him playing it for me on the piano, saying, 'You know, Verna, my *guts* are in this'."

10. Although the symphony was listed by its correct title in the Orchestra's program, the announcer for the broadcast referred

first and second movements never sounded too difficult. I thought the third movement was the questionable one. But the mood and drama carry it, and it went over very well at the premiere."

Both of Fine's sisters and their husbands attended that performance. Audrey vividly recalled an incident during the applause. "I was just palpitating because my brother's music was being exposed to the world, and my sister was also agitated and nervous. At the end, we were sitting there hoping and praying that everyone would applaud and stomp their feet. But there was only moderate applause. Then we heard some woman behind us ask, 'What kind of music is *that?*' Barbara and I were so offended that we got up and said to her: 'You are talking about our brother's music!' She collapsed."

The newspaper reviews were mixed. Cyrus Durgin noted in the *Boston Globe* that "although the Friday audience gave Mr. Fine a courteous hand as he bowed from the stage, it displayed no real enthusiasm for this large and recondite score [of] elaborate organization and uncompromising modernity [and] pure abstraction." Still, he termed it "real music," adding, "for all its complexity and sometimes fierce dissonance, this is a work that lives, breathes and moves [and] is not ingrown [or] withdrawn. One cannot fail to recognize its animation, passion and sense of life." Durgin cited the metrical changes and rhythmic subdivisions and thought the music was often "mechanistic in its ejaculation of short, forceful rhythmic and melodic fragments." To some extent, Fine's symphony impressed him as being "theoretical and cerebral" and he drew attention to the "chunkily scored and screechingly dissonant Ode which is the finale," adding: "The shell

---

to it as "Symphony No. 1." The concert itself was a strange and challenging compendium, clearly intended to stretch the ears of the famously conservative Boston Symphony subscribers. Fine's symphony was followed by Prokofiev's then-little-known *Piano Concerto No. 2*, an extended, barbarically discordant score played by the young French pianist Nicole Henriot-Schweitzer (rumored to be Munch's mistress). Then, instead of the expected sop of a Brahms or Tchaikovsky symphony, the second half consisted of Richard Strauss's extravagantly vulgar, hyper-Teutonic tone poem *Tod und Verklärung* (Death and Transfiguration).

on this nut is very hard." Munch was praised for giving an impressive performance.

The *Boston Herald*'s headline was "New Work Is Big, Hortatory, Serious," and its critic, Robert Taylor, thought the symphony "a work of moderately impressive substance" but termed problematic "the vehemence and magnitude of the composer's statement and the exceedingly difficult nature of his idiom." Noting the wit, grace and "eloquent emotional understatement" of much of Fine's previous music, he felt that the "eminently serious" context of this work was "not particularly congenial to Mr. Fine's talents." Taylor then made a literary analogy. "It is rather as though an immensely gifted writer of well-wrought short stories had decided to produce a novel on the scale of Dostoyevsky." He did, however, praise the score for its "fastidious sense of form," describing the first movement as "slow and pastoral," the second as "capering" and bristling "with crisp vigor" and the last movement as "a solemn fantasia with a succeeding epilogue of pomp and circumstances." He concluded: "Mr. Fine has apparently chosen to adopt the prevailing international mode of Stravinskian neoclassicism with a Schoenberg punctuation."

In the *Jewish Advocate,* the reviewer—whose name, amusingly enough considering the context, was Sanford R. Gifford—described Fine's work as "short, vigorous, succinct and almost continuously interesting." It gave the impression of "a brisk, self-assured professionalism, supremely easy to listen to, like a thoroughly readable novel by an established writer [who] controls his material with perfect confidence." He found any influences "thoroughly assimilated" and cited the score as "rich and sometimes dramatic, singularly free of pomposity and pretension."

The most severe reaction came from Harold Rogers in the *Christian Science Monitor,* who wrote: "It is usually a cause for rejoicing when a new work by Irving Fine is announced. There was not much rejoicing, however, when his new symphony was heard in its first performance." Rogers admitted that the Boston Symphony's Friday afternoon audience was highly conservative, but added, "yet one cannot help feeling that the fault in this case is Mr. Fine's [because] the work has apparently departed from [his] finely chiseled methods and has splattered itself across the score paper in a kind of formless array." On one hearing, he had the impression it was "composed in a kind of stream-of-consciousness fragmentation," and could discern no sense of form or "recognizable architecture" in this "extremely busy music." The critic railed, with some exaggeration, against the Stravinskian influence. "These are the hard facts: there were Stravinskian rhythms, Stravinskian timbres, Stravinskian expostulations. At the same time the score is wanting in Stravinskian economy." Fine, he scolded, "should be singing with a voice of his own."

Four years later, at the time of performances of *Symphony (1962)* by the New York Philharmonic in October 1966, Leonard Bernstein discussed the work during a radio interview. It should be mentioned that Bernstein believed firmly in tonality and had a generally negative attitude toward atonal and serial music. The following is excerpted from a transcription of his comments.

"With the gradual dissolution of tonality, from Wagner on, the idea of the symphony becomes less and less viable. In the symphony by Irving Fine, this problem is very apparent. It's almost at its clearest, because here is a beautiful work by an extremely talented young American composer which aims to be a symphony in the, let's say, Stravinsky tradition, which implies some kind of neoclassic thought. It has echoes of the Stravinsky *Symphony in Three Movements*, it has some echoes of the *Sacre* and other works by Stravinsky, but it is also conceived in terms of twelve-tone rows and twelve-tone technique. That is, in atonal terms. And even Stravinsky himself never tried to write a symphony in those terms."

Fine, said Bernstein, was involved in the problem of "writing a symphony in terms of this tonal crisis." Bernstein understandably but erroneously declared that Fine "had decided to abandon tonality," which Bernstein considered the basic ingredient of a symphony. Nonetheless, he acknowledged that "the great tribute to Fine's talent, which was enormous and if he had been spared in his life would have increased enormously, is that the piece is so good in spite of this dilemma." Then came another questionable statement: "It was a kind of self-contradictory situation of having a symphonic work without tonal poles."[11]

---

11. Harold Shapero reacted acidly to Bernstein's appraisal of

Bernstein was, however, perceptive when he spoke of his friend's personality in relation to this music. He noted that Fine "wasn't very serene on the inside. He was rather a tragic person inside, but he never bothered anybody with those problems of his. He very rarely expressed any of that conflict or inner turmoil in his music, and one of the things that makes this symphony so remarkable is that it does that. As though all of this broke out of him for the first time in the symphony. It is a symphony of anguish and conflict, and yet great beauty, and it achieves an apotheosis at the end of great majesty and serenity. In that sense, it is a wonderful piece for him to have written just before his death."

---

the Fine symphony. "That's not really a twelve-tone piece," he said. "It's not even all that chromatic. But Lenny always wanted to whip his audience into a frenzy and had to have an orgasm at every concert. You can do that with Tchaikovsky. But Lenny was at his absolute worst when intellectual music was involved."

# Chapter 20

■ FINE COULDN'T HAVE KNOWN IT AT THE TIME, but his symphony had been his supreme—and final—artistic achievement. Not long after the premiere, he was pleased to be offered a $3,000 commission from the Ford Foundation, which had instituted an unusual program in which performers were encouraged to play new music by selecting composers from whom they would like to have a work. Fine had been chosen by a young New Yorker, Berl Senofsky, the first American violinist to win the prestigious Queen Elizabeth of Belgium contest. On May 4, 1962, Fine responded, expressing interest in the project. The Ford Foundation replied with a request for a score for violin and piano with a duration of between seventeen and twenty-five minutes, to be introduced during the 1963-64 season. On June 20, the commission became official and was announced that day by the *Boston Globe*. According to Verna, her husband immediately received half the fee.

Fine was so enthusiastic that, after making a few sketches for a sonata, he decided instead to write a concerto. Richard Wernick observed: "Irving felt he was on a kind of a roll with the orchestra. He had never felt secure in that area, but after the symphony and the *Diversions* he was much more comfortable. I recall him using the expression, 'I'll really give them their money's worth.' After the March premiere of the symphony, he had said he was going to write another big piece."

Verna remembered that Fine planned a large-scale score for chorus and orchestra using Biblical texts, but nothing came of it. The violin concerto was the last music on which he worked.

In late 1962, Fine's composer-colleague at Brandeis, Martin Boykan, wrote a reminiscence that included this passage: "Conversations I had with him during the course of last year suggested that the symphony was meant to be the last in [his] series of twelve-tone works. He felt that he had said all he could with the serial technique, and in the early part of the summer he began work on a violin sonata in a free chromatic idiom. It is likely that he was reaching out toward a new style, and if so, this represents a tragic loss for American music." Boykan quite rightly concluded that Fine "remained an explorer until the end—open to all that was being written, and at the same time faithful to his own roots."

Concerning the projected violin concerto, Wernick echoed Boykan, wondering whether it would have been a twelve-tone work. "I remember the title-page: *Concerto in G Minor*—and there were two flats in the signature. I imagine what Irving was moving toward was to try to write music without the crutch of the rows. I think he felt he had reached that plateau with the symphony."

Fine left fragmentary sketches for all three movements of the concerto, along with row charts. Most, though not all, of these sketches do in fact show serial derivation. Approximately forty bars of the first movement exist in short score, amounting to a dramatic *fortissimo* orchestral introduction, dissonant and rather promising. The melody and harmony in the first seven bars emerge strictly from the work's basic row, which rises sequentially, contains two tritones and has strong tonal implications. One of the third-movement themes contains eleven notes of the scale, while another soars lyrically in the violin's high register and is freely chromatic. A brief sketch of a progression of dissonant, ear-catching, three-note chords that are directly generated by Set 2 of the row (semitone-upward transposition) is marked "for use in 3rd movet." These scraps are intriguing, but it is impossible to have any idea about what kind of work would have resulted from their use.

"As far as serial writing," said Wernick, "I'm interested in what might have been. Irving might have abandoned the whole thing, but I don't think so. It was giving him new material. If he had continued in that line the method might have become so absorbed into his musical psyche that he wouldn't have pre-composed with row charts. But he may not have gotten to that point." Further: "I think the problem in Irving's music is that he didn't live long enough to develop fully what he was working towards, which was expanding his vocabulary and style. Of course, it's only a matter of speculation where that might have gone. It might have gone no place. His symphony might have been like Harold Shapero's symphony: one big outburst and that's the end. But I suspect that, with Irving, it would not have been the end, because of the way he worked and because of his innate musicality."

During the early part of 1962, two events especially gratified Fine. The first was a performance in January of his *Partita for Wind Quintet* at the University of Chicago by one of his favorite chamber groups, the New York Woodwind Quintet. The second occurred on April 7 in New York at Carnegie Recital Hall: a Composers Forum entirely of his own music (*Fantasia for String Trio, Childhood Fables, String Quartet*) with a question-and-answer period following the performances. Later that month, he must have been amused to receive a postcard from Rome informing him that his *Music for Piano* had been broadcast on the radio—played on the harpsichord. Fine was now at the apex of his prestige and power at Brandeis University, yet Harold and Esther Shapero remembered a disturbing occasion. "Irving was giving a talk at Brandeis," said Harold, "and suddenly, in the middle of it, he started rambling on in an irrational way about his Harvard rejection. It was shocking." Esther thought that "it was totally out of context. I'll never forget it. All of Irving's suffering over that rejection came out in public."

That spring, the matter of the Harvard rejection recurred, in a trenchant essay Fine provided for the Harvard University alumni report observing the twenty-fifth anniversary of the class of 1937—a summarizing article that contains his final words on his career as a musician and educator. Some excerpts follow.

"My commitment to Brandeis has been a strong one. It is almost possible for me to be grateful to the Harvard Music Department for having demonstrated what I then thought was questionable judgement in not recommending my promotion. Actually, that decision was not without justification.[1] More questionable have been (until very recently) the Har-

_____

1. As Fine was known to have been bitter all his life about that decision, this stiff-upper-lip statement (in his best Saint Irving manner) was certainly a gesture of Boston gentleman's-club etiquette.

vard Music Department's conservatism in matters of faculty recruitment and its failure, in spite of substantial financial resources, to stimulate and attract creativity and to provide imaginative and vigorous leadership of the musical life in the university community.

"At Brandeis, I have had many satisfactions, a fair amount of frustration and one unique opportunity, as chairman of the School of Creative Arts, to collaborate in the creation of entire departments of music, fine arts and theater. Our Music Department is regarded very well nationally, though I doubt whether we have any giants on the staff.

"Whatever frustrations I have had at Brandeis were at least in part due to my own lack of professional experience and contacts outside my own field and in part the natural consequence of building a school and attempting to establish its reputation. I might have wished at times that our administration were less impressed with yesterday's headlines; that our publicity were better informed; that art and music historians in general were less concerned with academic responsibility.

"But the satisfactions at Brandeis have far outweighed the minor annoyances. I have enjoyed teaching and even administering, as well as building. Beyond this, I have had the delicious experience of playing the role of impresario at the rather splashy Festivals of Creative Arts we produced until 1957. Perhaps too much of my creative energy has gone into activities which are essentially peripheral to my career as composer. In spite of this, I have had the satisfaction of having works of mine performed by such major orchestras as those of Boston, New York and Philadelphia, and have had the pleasure of knowing that my chamber music is frequently performed and well received both here and abroad. In a less diverting, irritating and challenging environment than that of Brandeis, I might have composed and perhaps performed more, but what a chilling idea!"

Chilling is a word that could apply to an incident in 1961 involving Shapero and Fine. That fall, Shapero began a sabbatical to take advantage of a Fulbright fellowship. Just before he left for Italy, he approached Fine with a request. "I said to him, 'I've been an associate professor at Brandeis for a long time. Arthur Berger is a professor. How about making me a professor when I return next year?' Then Irving said something I can't believe I actually heard. I couldn't believe my ears. He replied: 'Well, you're a better composer than I am, but as long as I'm chairman of this department you'll never be a full professor.' I imagine he was serious. I was astonished. It rankled. I never saw him again after that."

During the first part of July 1962, Fine was busy correcting publishers' proofs of the *Diversions for Orchestra,* an onerous if necessary task he disliked almost as much as he disliked copying music. "Irving got very bored with copying," said Verna. "In those days, before the computer age, it was india ink on onion-skin transparencies. If you wanted to make a correction, you cut a hole and pasted it over. The score he copied of the string quartet looks like swiss cheese. But Dick Wernick took Irving's messy manuscript of the symphony and made a neat copy, and that made Irving very happy."

That summer, Fine looked forward to another performance of *Symphony (1962)* by Munch and the Boston Symphony, this time at Tanglewood. It was scheduled for Sunday afternoon, August 12, and would be recorded live for broadcast by the Boston radio station WGBH. In a singular stroke of bad programming, the other major work was to be Tchaikovsky's overwrought *Pathétique* symphony.

Meanwhile, Emily Fine had written *Life* magazine, which had published a two-page piano piece of notable simplicity by Copland earlier in the year, to tell the editors about *Victory March of the Elephants* and *Lullaby for a Baby Panda.* On August 3, *Life*'s Ellen Thompson replied, regretting that the magazine had no plans to publish further pieces for young students. She added a postscript: "In the spring of 1956, when you were very little, I baby-sat for you and your sisters one evening. I was a student at Wellesley at that time [and] I've always wished that I could have a record collection like your father's!"

On Friday, August 10, the *Berkshire Eagle* announced that French conductor Pierre Monteux would substitute for Charles Munch at the Sunday Boston Symphony Tanglewood concert, because "Dr. Munch has been ordered by his physicians to rest over the weekend." Munch had a heart condition and had suffered a painful angina attack. Not mentioned was the fact that Munch had asked Fine, who was already at Tanglewood for rehearsals of his symphony, to conduct the work in his stead. Verna remembered that "when Munch didn't feel well, Irving and I went to his house. Irving wasn't prepared to step in, but Munch gave him lessons in how to conduct his own symphony. He was in pajamas. It was very charming." As a guest conductor, Fine was to be paid a fee of $200 for the performance and rehearsals, including one open to the public on the morning of the eleventh.

Naturally, he was nervous about the unwonted assignment, for he had far more experience conducting choruses than orchestras. But as Monteux could hardly be expected to learn a complicated and unfamiliar score in a mere three days, there was no alternative except cancelling the performance. A revealing photograph taken on the lawn at Tanglewood that Friday afternoon shows the composer seated on a folding chair. He is informally dressed in short-sleeved shirt, bermuda shorts and tennis shoes, intently studying the score of his symphony propped on his crossed leg, while beating time in the air with his right hand. Leon Kirchner recalled that "when Munch became ill, I asked Irving when he had last conducted a major orchestra. He was always intensely nervous under stresses of that kind. I worried about him. I said, are you sure you want to do this?"

If Fine was nervous, he also felt excited. He had conducted the Boston Symphony only once before, way back in 1948, in his *Toccata Concertante*,[2] but it was by far his favorite orchestra. ("When you're brought up in Boston, it's the Boston Red Sox and the Boston Symphony," said Verna.) From his years of teaching at Tanglewood, he knew many of the players personally. "Irving was this gracious, gentlemanly person, a fixture at Tanglewood," Wernick observed. "Everyone liked him, so he had the good will of the orchestra. At rehearsals, they kept telling him, 'Irving, don't worry about it.

---

2. Harold Shapero remembered Fine's reaction to that event. "He was talking about the sensitivity of the orchestra. He said, 'They're unbelievable. If you give just a little wiggle with the baton, they make a great *crescendo*. They're looking for anything you give them, and they respond instantly with enormous vitality and power.' Irving was very impressed with that."

Just give us downbeats. As long as the downbeats are in place, we'll figure out what to play in the middle'."

Wernick noted that Fine's conducting was similar to Monteux's, "with a minimum of motion and with no histrionics. He had no trouble with the stick. He stood with his feet solidly on the podium and conducted with fairly concise movements. He was not terrifically good at subdividing, although clear, but the orchestra wanted him to subdivide less rather than more anyway." He seemed to recall that the courteous Monteux took only one rehearsal so that Fine could have the rest, which he clearly needed. "I remember there was a complicated passage in the last movement, and Irving was terrified about whether he would be able to keep everything together. But it worked okay, because Irving was, after all, a real conductor."

The night before the concert, Fine's psychiatrist friend and neighbor Arnold Modell dined with the family group, which included George and Lotte. "Irving's parents were ordinary people, not cultured. His father was an insensitive man. They were friends of Leonard Bernstein's parents, whom I once met at the Fine's house, and they were very similar types." That evening, Papa George did not share in the jubilation over the imminent performance of his son's most ambitious piece. Modell recollected that at one point in the supper George glared at Fine and declared: "Irving, you're a master. A master. A masturbator!" "Obviously his father was demeaning him, but I think Irving took it in stride. He was probably used to that kind of interaction with him." Even so, coming at such a time, Papa George's offensive behavior must have irked.

The Sunday afternoon concert in the Shed began at 2:30 with Beethoven's *Leonore Overture No. 3*, conducted by Monteux. Then came Fine's *Symphony (1962)*. In a photograph taken during the performance, Fine stands before the orchestra stiff-backed and majestic, in white tuxedo jacket, both arms raised, baton quivering, a laying-down-the-law grimace on his face. It is impressive, but not nearly so impressive as the performance itself, which was later issued by RCA Records.[3]

---

3. That recording was fully subsidized by Brandeis University, which had been given sufficient funds for the purpose by George Fine. "Papa George wanted to preserve the symphony as conducted

This is a vivid reading with surprisingly few flaws, and it can be considered definitive. As the composer William Flanagan would later write in a record review, "both performance and recorded sound are far better than they have any business being under such conditions." In the words of another reviewer, "It is clear that Fine needed no apologies as a conductor of his own music," and still another: "Fine's conducting is grand, with surely-mapped detail." Decades later, Wernick reflected: "I think Irving felt good about his own performance of his symphony."

"I remember that the audience applauded after the scherzo, they liked it so well," said Verna. "I sat with Aaron, and I thought, well, it's a different audience at Tanglewood. But Irving was probably very annoyed by the interruption."

The following week, Jay C. Rosenfeld noted in the *Berkshire Eagle* that "the Berkshire Music Center considers [Fine] one of its prime exhibits." Fine's symphony "is in three movements in unconventional sequence" and its most notable feature "is its insistence on metrical irregularity." This aspect, he felt, "dominates the composition so that no one is certain what is the measure of progress, including not only the audience but the conductor and the performers," a factor that, he feared, "would affect the future of such a work." Rosenfeld found the opening movement "turgid" but liked better the succeeding movements, especially the scherzo, "which generates excitement."

On Sunday evening, after the Tanglewood concert, the Fine family began a brief vacation and drove to Canada to see the Niagara Falls. Irving, pleased with the way his symphony had been played and received, was in a relaxed mood. In the back seat of the car, his three daughters cavorted, misbehaving as children will on an outing. Suddenly, Joanna uttered piercing screams. Fine turned around smiling. "Stop making so much noise or you'll give me a heart attack," he said. Joanna never forgot that.

Fine was something of a hypochondriac and made fre-

---

by Irving," said Verna. "To fill out the album, RCA got Erich Leinsdorf and the Boston Symphony to make studio recordings of the *Toccata Concertante* and *Serious Song*." The record was issued in 1966, with a liner essay by Aaron Copland.

quent references to his health. "Irving kvetched," said Wernick. "He was convinced that he had some kind of cancer." Because of his periodic headaches, he worried about a brain tumor and once told Claudia that he would probably die from one, like George Gershwin. Verna reflected that "Irving was a very heavy smoker, almost like Lenny Bernstein. Smoking was a part of our culture." Verna used a cigarette holder with a filter, Irving did not, although he began smoking filter cigarettes when they were introduced in the early 1950s. "He smoked three packs a day, until the end of his life, right up to two days before he died." Fine often had severe heartburn and would mention stomach cancer as the probable cause. Claudia and Emily thought their father might have an ulcer because he imbibed so much Gelusil, a liquid antacid. "He was always burping and spitting up," Claudia remembered. "When we'd travel, it would take him five minutes to pack his clothes and two hours to go through the medicine cabinet to be sure he had the right medications for indigestion."

For more than a year, Fine had regularly experienced esophageal spasms, or gastroesophageal reflux, the result of an inflamed esophagus, involving the backward flow of acid and producing chest pains. A comparison of photographs taken between March 1962, at the time of the premiere of the symphony, and on August 10 at Tanglewood and August 13, soon after the Tanglewood concert, reveals that Fine had put on weight during that period—had in fact grown rather tubby—which might have been a factor in his physical ill-being.

At any event, after Niagara Falls the family visited Fine's old Harvard friend Allen Sapp and his pianist wife Norma Bertolami in Buffalo, New York. Emily recalled that her father "was totally drained from having to conduct the Boston Symphony at the last moment." He experienced chest pains, but assumed they were caused by an upset stomach. Claudia noted that "he was always a heartburn-kvetch person and would chew Beeman's gum for indigestion, which my mother hated because she thought he was classy and that to chew gum was cheap."

The trip back to Natick on Saturday, August 18, turned nightmarish. Verna drove, and stopped the car several times when Fine's pain became intense. Emily remembered that he would get out and stand by the roadside, panting for breath.

"We would ask, 'Daddy, are you okay?' and he'd answer, 'It's a horrible heartburn,' swig some Gelusil and say, 'I feel better now.' We would drive for a while and then he'd say, 'I can't stand the pain. Stop the car, Verna,' and he'd get out again." Finally, they arrived home.

The following evening, Verna and Irving gave a small dinner party for Lotte and George and the Wernicks. "It was a typical Fine party," Wernick reminisced. "The grill came out and Irving cooked steaks on the porch. But he wasn't feeling well." Wernick observed Lotte paging through a new South American magazine and discovering a photograph of Leonard Bernstein. "Irving," she complained, "there is a picture of Lenny Bernstein in this magazine. Why isn't your picture in this magazine?" Fine was annoyed. "We went into his studio," said Wernick, "and he bitched about the whole Jewish-mother thing. 'Why do I have to compete with Lenny?' he asked. 'I'm not enough of a success for my mother?'" A snapshot taken on that occasion shows Verna and Irving with Lotte and George on the lawn of the Natick house. Verna and Irving are smiling and Irving has thrown his arm over the shoulder of his grumpy-looking father. As Lotte grimaces in the setting sun, Verna's shadow obscures the lower part of her husband's face. He is decidedly in the background. Ironically, that was the last photograph of Irving Fine.

On Monday morning, August 20, the Wernicks drove back to New York. That afternoon Verna telephoned them to say Irving had had a mild heart attack. Amazingly, it occurred during an electrocardiogram examination at Boston's Beth Israel Hospital, where Fine had gone at the recommendation of his friend Dr. Jack Fine (no relation), the head of surgery. Later that day, Jack Fine came to visit, and said: "Irving, who but you would have a heart attack while in the hospital? You're a lucky man." The luck would not hold.

A relieved Verna informed the Wernicks that Irving had been put in an oxygen tent but, according to the doctors, everything was under control. She laughed because her husband had once again complained about stomach cancer, now that he thought his heart was stable. Still, she had been told that the next seventy-two hours were a critical period, and she recalled Fine's saying to her at one point, "Verna, I don't think I'm going to make it."

In retrospect, Wernick mused: "As far as that first heart attack, I don't think medical technology was advanced enough then for the doctors to know to what extent it might have done an enormous amount of damage. I'm not a cardiologist, but I'm not convinced that the stress leading up to the Tanglewood performance didn't bring it on." Verna disagreed. "I don't think conducting at Tanglewood had anything to do with it. Exercise is good for you. It was something that was brewing—a clot had developed in the heart." Harold Shapero reflected: "Irving went and conducted his symphony and that got him all excited. But, according to the doctors, if you're going to have a heart attack, it's not brought on by something like that. Your arteries are clogged, period."

Fine's sisters visited him on Wednesday afternoon, August 22. "The doctor told us he was going to be okay," said Audrey, "so at about six in the evening we headed home to Fall River, where we both lived. Hours later, the phone rang. Irving had taken a turn for the worse." Shapero recollected Verna's account of that grim night. "As she drove back to the hospital, she kept thinking she should put on the windshield wipers because it was raining. But it wasn't raining. It was the tears rolling down her face."

In the early hours of Thursday, August 23, 1962, Irving Fine suffered a second heart attack. It was massive, and fatal.

# Epilogue

The doctors at Beth Israel Hospital had fought to save Fine, opening his chest to massage the heart. But, as Dr. Jack Fine told Richard Wernick, there was little left to work with because the organ had disintegrated to such an extent that no muscle remained. Irving's sister Barbara remembered that, although her brother was only forty-seven years old when he died, "they said he had the arteries of a ninety-year-old man;" and Esther Shapero noted that "the doctors thought he had lived fifteen years beyond what they would have expected, with those clogged arteries."

The Shaperos were in Rome at the time, and received the tragic news in a cable from Arthur Berger. Esther recalled that "we couldn't believe it was true. It seemed like a hideous black joke." Harold said: "He deserted us all by dying. I didn't cry because I was in shock. Despite the analyst, Irving and I were still buddies." Shapero spoke of "a strong friendship which endured almost twenty-five years, to the day of his death" and stated that "his sudden loss caused me the most profound grief and personal sadness."

Barbara and her husband had the unwelcome task of informing Lotte and George. "That was awful. They were just devastated." Arnold Modell used the same word: "Irving's death was absolutely devastating to me and to anybody who knew him well." Shapero recollected that he had been told that Leon Kirchner "burst into terrible tears when Irving died."

Early in the morning of August 24, at Verna's request, Wernick telephoned Aaron Copland. "I woke him up and he snapped into the phone: 'What is it?' I said, 'Aaron, I'm sorry, but I have bad news. Irving has died.' There was absolute silence. Then he said, 'I'll be up as soon as I can.' He and Lenny Bernstein flew up that morning and Bea and I met them at the airport." Naturally, both men were deeply shocked and grieved, but it was the unsentimental Copland, not given to public displays of emotion, who proved a pillar of strength for Verna at that time, as well as a devoted friend in later years.

The funeral service was held on the Brandeis University campus at the Leah and Mendel Berlin Memorial Chapel, at 1 p.m. on Friday, August 24. Among the notables in attendance were Copland, Bernstein, Kirchner, Randall Thompson, Nicolas Slonimsky and Mrs. Serge Koussevitzky. The music at the service was Haydn's B-flat-major string quartet, Op. 76, No. 4 ("Sunrise"). President Abram L. Sachar delivered the eulogy, from which the following excerpts are taken.

"I join in this service not to attempt any consolation for a bereaved family, for the huge multitude of friends, or for an institution to which Irving Fine gave himself so completely. Irving was the ideal teacher because youngsters consistently brought him back to his own aspiring, groping, developing days, days that won him the respect of Walter Piston and Serge Koussevitzky, who were his own revered mentors and whose patience he repaid many, many times in his own concern for the latest talents that came to him for fruition.

"The cruelty of perfectionism which he would never inflict upon others, he imposed upon himself. It was out of this travail that his compassion for fellow artists emerged. His legion of students in the universities and orchestras of the country are today truly orphaned along with his own family.

"Irving left not only music, but the example of how it completed life with richness and beauty."

Burial took place at 2:15 in Sharon, Massachusetts, at the Sharon Memorial Park. Rabbi Harold Weisberg, chairman of the Brandeis Department of Philosophy, officiated. The pallbearers included Arthur Berger, Aaron Copland, Leon Kirchner, Arnold Modell and Richard Wernick.

Many years later, Verna reminisced. "At the funeral I remember saying to myself, amidst my tears, 'Oh, Irving, if only you were here. Though you didn't feel important or famous, you really are famous.' We had two policemen to escort us to the cemetery, and there were 5,000 people there. But that was part of Irving's problem: he didn't feel important."

The *Boston Herald* thought otherwise. On August 25, it ran an editorial entitled "A First Symphony and an End."

This read, in part: "The loss to music by Irving Fine's death is incalculable. It is particularly sore to his native city, Boston. His efforts in the cause of musical education comprise a dedicated saga in themselves. He was all too often overlooked or omitted by contemporary critical studies. Since he did not write in large forms as a rule, since he did not follow the currently popular inspiration of Schoenberg and von Webern, his musical personality was frequently overshadowed by others. He was a master, nonetheless, of the gift of eloquent understatement. Although he died untimely, Irving Fine created an artist's confirmation of his own immortality. In future years he will be heard."

Telegrams and letters to Verna poured in. "Deeply shocked with your terrible news," said Igor Stravinsky. "Can hardly believe terrible loss," wrote Nadia Boulanger. Darius Milhaud was "terribly shocked by dreadful news," and Charles Munch observed that "we are all poorer today for the loss of a dear friend, a kind man and a most extraordinarily gifted musician." Harold and Esther Shapero were "heartbroken." Walter Piston noted that "the awful news that Irving has gone came as a great shock." Arthur Fiedler lamented: "What a pity to lose him when he was just really getting into his own stride." To Marc Blitzstein, Fine's death was "so useless, such a waste! The symphony was so good, the promise of the next one even better."

Paul Fromm professed himself "shocked and stunned," but predicted that "Irving's work will live on. We loved Irving for being such a good human being. As an educator, he will always be remembered for having been culturally aware, socially responsible and morally inspiring." Max Lerner reminisced: "I need scarcely tell you that he was a delight to me whenever we talked, and added immeasurably to my feeling not only about music but about all the arts, and about the way of life of the artist." Caldwell Titcomb remembered Fine's reliability. "Dozens of times, when difficult problems arose at school, we have said, 'Irving will know what to do.' As the years roll by, rest assured that my love for Irving and my gratitude for all he did for me will not diminish."

Nicolas Slonimsky was clearly distressed. "Aaron said it's unbelievable, but one feels anger instead of sorrow—anger at the gods of biology, at the unfairness of it. It is so true that Irving was—is—loved, and that he was free of envy, of the spirit of competition, of anything petty. And that marvelous mind of his! Those pathetic—sudden—childish cries of the girls dressed in blue at the grave: I never heard anything more heartbreaking."

Jack Gottlieb dedicated a major song-cycle, *Songs of Loneliness,* to Fine's memory. There was even a condolence letter to Verna from Senator Edward M. Kennedy, who had once served on a scholarship committee with her husband.

On the day of the funeral, Lukas Foss added the Coda from the *Partita for Wind Quintet* to a Tanglewood chamber-music concert as a memorial to Fine. A *New York Times* critic noted that "Mr. Foss described the Coda as representing for him all that Mr. Fine had been—lovely, gentle and civilized, to judge by the work." In the same newspaper, on September 2, Arthur Berger paid tribute to his friend as "one of the most eminent composers of his generation and one of the most resourceful and versatile musicians," continuing: "He was not only a creative artist at the height of his powers, from whom many additional significant contributions to American music were to be expected, but he was also a remarkably selfless, generous and responsible person [and] a warm and loving personality."

Aaron Copland provided a tribute for the October 30, 1962 issue of a Brandeis University newspaper entirely devoted to the memory of Irving Fine. Referring to Fine's compositions, it concluded with these words: "The future will decide as to their originality and their staying power. But for us, his friends and colleagues, they have imbedded in them one of the most cherishable musical natures of our time."

October 4, 2001
Tangier

# Acknowledgments

Verna Fine, widow of the composer, commissioned this biography in October 1999. Fortunately I was able to interview her twice before her untimely death on November seventh of that year. Subsequently, Howard Pollack provided me with a copy of his 1982 taped interview with Verna, which proved invaluable. Thanks also are due to Irving Fine's three daughters, Joanna, Emily and Claudia; his two sisters, Barbara Kates and Audrey Salhanick; Milton Babbitt, Jack Beeson, the late Arthur Berger, Martin Bookspan, the late Paul Bowles, Rosalie Calabrese, Mary Daniels, David Diamond, Joseph Disponzio, Benjamin Folkman, Lukas Foss, the late Richard French, Jack Gottlieb, Leon Kirchner, Gavin Lambert, Noël Lee, Arnold Modell, John C. Nemiah, Daniel Pinkham, Ned Rorem, Harold Shapero, Esther Shapero, Joel Spiegelman, Claude Nathalie Thomas, Caldwell Titcomb, Richard Wernick and Beatrice Wernick.

Jon Newsom, Chief of the Music Division of the Library of Congress, was extremely cooperative in all aspects of my work in the Library's excellent and exhaustive Irving Fine Collection. Iris Newsom proved a vigilant and affable editor. Kenneth Lisenbee typed both the initial and the final versions of this book with commendable diligence.

P.R.

# Chronological List of Completed Works

*(With dates and places of premieres)*

1941   *Music for Modern Dance*, Boston, 1941
     (unpublished)

1942   *"Alice in Wonderland"* (Incidental Music*)*, Boston,
     May 22, 1942 (unpublished)
     *Three Choruses from "Alice in Wonderland,"*
     Cambridge, March 4,

1943   *Two Songs from "Doña Rosita,"* Cambridge,
     April 28, 1943

1944   *The Choral New Yorker*, Cambridge, January 25,
     1945
     *Voices of Freedom* (arrangement of "Battle Hymn of
     the Republic" for baritone solo, chorus, organ and
     piano), Boston, 1944 (unpublished)

1945   *A Short Alleluia* for Women's Chorus (premiere
     unknown)

1946   *Sonata for Violin and Piano*, New York, February 9,
     1947

1947   *Toccata Concertante for Orchestra*, Boston, October
     22, 1948
     *Music for Piano*, Boston, November 19, 1948

1948   *Partita for Wind Quintet*, New York, February 19,
     1949

1949   *Hymn* from *In Grato Jubilo* for Women's Voices and
     Small Orchestra, Boston, May 2, 1949
     (unpublished)
     *The Hour Glass* for Chorus, New York, December 3,
     1950
     *"Alice in Wonderland"* Suite for Chorus and
     Orchestra, Worcester, Massachusetts, October
     1949

1951   *Notturno for Strings and Harp*, Boston, March 28,
     1951

1952   *Old American Songs* (choral transcriptions of Aaron
     Copland's solo-voice arrangements of six songs),

Cambridge, November 9, 1951(Nos. 1,2,4,5)

*Mutability*, Six Songs for Mezzo-Soprano and Piano, New York, November 28, 1953

*String Quartet*, Waltham, Massachusetts, December 10, 1952

1953 *An Old Song* for Chorus, Cambridge, March 1954

*Three Choruses from "Alice in Wonderland,"* Second Series, Bradford, Massachusetts, April 1954

1954 *Childhood Fables for Grownups* for Medium Voice and Piano, Set 1, New York, February 20, 1956

1955 *Serious Song, A Lament for String Orchestra*, Louisville, November 16, 1955

*Childhood Fables for Grownups* for Medium Voice and Piano, Set 2

1956 *Victory March of the Elephants* for Beginning Pianist (premiere unknown)

*Lullaby for a Baby Panda* for Beginning Pianist (premiere unknown)

*Homage à Mozart* for Intermediate Pianist (premiere unknown)

1957 *Fantasia for String Trio*, Urbana, Illinois, March 3, 1957

*McCord's Menagerie* for Chorus, Cambridge, June 9, 1958

1959 *Romanza for Wind Quintet*, Washington, D.C., February 1, 1963

*Blue Towers for Orchestra*, Boston, May 31, 1960

*One, Two, Buckle My Shoe* for Oboe, Clarinet, Violin and Cello, WGBH-TV, Boston, November 3, 1959

*Diversions for Piano* (1942-1959; the basis for *Diversions for Orchestra*), New York, March 22, 1987

1960 *Diversions for Orchestra*, Boston, November 5, 1960

1962 *Symphony (1962)* for Orchestra, Boston, March 23, 1962

# Index of Irving Fine's Compositions

# Interviews

Milton Babbitt: October 23, 2000, New York
Jack Beeson: November 17, 2004, New York
Arthur Berger: November 9, 1999, New York; May 1, 2000
(telephone); January 17, 2001 (telephone)
Martin Bookspan: February 28, 2000, New York
David Diamond: December 13 and 14, 1999 (telephone);
January 14 and 24, 2001 (telephone)
Claudia Fine: March 22, 2000, New York
Emily Fine: March 22, 2000, New York
Joanna Fine: March 23, 2000, New York
Verna Fine: October 25 and November 1, 1999, New York;
   May 16, 1982, New York (interviewed by Howard Pollack)
Lukas Foss: November 10, 1999, New York
Richard French: March 22, 2000 (telephone)
Jack Gottlieb: December 9, 1999, New York; January 31,
   2000, New York; January 17, 2001 (telephone)
Barbara Kates: March 22 and 23, 2000 (telephone)
Leon Kirchner: February 4, 2000, Cambridge, Massachusetts
Noel Lee: April 4, 2000 (telephone)
Arnold Modell: March 23, 2000 (telephone)
John C. Nemiah: March 20, 2000 (telephone)
Daniel Pinkham: March 23, 2000 (telephone)
Ned Rorem: March 22, 2000, New York; January 17, 2001
   (telephone)
Audrey Salhanick: March 20, 2000 (telephone)
Harold Shapero: February 5, 2000, Natick, Massachusetts;
   February 24, 2000 (telephone); January 14, 2001
   (telephone)
Esther Shapero: February 5, 2000, Natick, Massachusetts
Joel Spiegelman: January 28, 2000, New York
Claude Nathalie Thomas: September 5, 2001, Tangier,
   Morocco
Caldwell Titcomb: January 31, 2000, New York
Richard Wernick: December 15, 1999, Media, Pennsylvania;

January 14, 2001 (telephone); May 11, 2001, Washington, D.C.
Beatrice Wernick: December 15, 1999, Media, Pennsylvania

# About the Author

**Phillip Ramey** is a composer, pianist and writer. He studied composition with Alexander Tcherepnin at DePaul University in Chicago and at the International Academy of Music in Nice, France; graduate work was with Jack Beeson at Columbia University. His musical output comprises orchestral scores, among them three piano concertos; chamber pieces and a large body of solo-piano works that includes five sonatas and the *Leningrad Rag*, the latter composed for Vladimir Horowitz. Ramey's *Horn Concerto*, commissioned by the New York Philharmonic to celebrate its 150th anniversary, was premiered in 1993, conducted by Leonard Slatkin.

Ramey is the author of several hundred liner notes, many of them for Columbia Masterworks and CBS Records. He has published numerous interviews with American composers and is an authority on the music of Aaron Copland. In 1985, Copland chose him to orchestrate the piano piece *Proclamation*, which had an unusual bicoastal premiere on Copland's eighty-fifth birthday: by Zubin Mehta and the New York Philharmonic during a nationally televised concert, and by Erich Leinsdorf and the Los Angeles Philharmonic. From 1977 to 1993, he held the position of Program Editor of the New York Philharmonic.

# Index

birth of, 3

children born to, 86-87, 178, 200

on choral music, 199

as conductor of his own work, 87, 300-302, 300n

on contemporary composers, 235, 237-42

and Copland, 46-49, 61, 74-75, 136, 200, 232-33

death of, xiv, 305; reaction to, 307-8; tributes to Fine following, 308-10

depressions suffered by, 86, 217-25, 233-34, 255-56

early interest in music, 1, 3-5

early love interest of, 31

early years of, 3-6

eating habits of, 5-6, 209

education of: early, 9; as student at Harvard, 9-16; as student of Boulanger, 18-19, 24-28

engagement and marriage to Verna Rudnick, 31-36

father's ambitions for, 10, 11

father's support of, 27-28, 301-2n

in France on Fulbright, 122-30

on French composers, 127-30, 132

frustrations of as composer, 65-69, 112, 178, 218, 220-21, 223, 233-34, 252, 255-56

grants and awards: Fulbright Fellowship, 121-34; Fulbright grant sought by, 112-13; Guggenheim grant sought by, 112; Guggenheim grants, 134, 158-59, 161, 243, 248-53; Wyman Foundation grant, 19, 27

health concerns of, 302-5

Jewish faith of, 9

and Koussevitzky, 76, 79-82, 87-88, 110-11

and Koussevitzky's death, 176-77

at the MacDowell Colony, 83-86, 121, 183, 187, 190, 195, 204, 205, 223n, 228

during the McCarthy era, 202-3

and Milhaud, 123-25

as music critic, 53-60, 211, 221

on *musique concrète*, 127-28

and the Naval Glee Club, 38-40

in New Orleans, 247-48

parents of, 1-3, 34, 255, 301, 304

photographs of, 141-48

as pianist, 22-23, 37-38, 45, 175, 234

in Portugal, 270

as practical joker, 269-70

in Puerto Rico, 268-69

in Rome on Fulbright, 248-53

sexual interests of, 7, 132-33, 190-93

on Shapero's music, 95-96, 104-5
in Spain, 270-72
and Stravinsky, 29-30
studio of, 135-36
at Tanglewood, 73-74, 75-76, 79-82, 85, 111-12, 115-16,
175-76, 199-200, 231, 236-42, 288n
temper displays of, 256, 268
travels to France as a young man, 21-23
Wernick urged to study with, xi-xii
works of: awards honoring, 139, 186, 196; commissions, 177-79,
187-88, 195, 201, 204, 213, 215, 228, 234, 256, 258, 260, 281,
295; composed for his father, 212; Copland on, xvi; early
compositions, 12-14, 15, 26, 28-29; harmony in, xvi, 182, 232;
neoclassicism of, 50, 237; opera (unfinished), 272-75;
publication of, 43, 63, 71, 93, 108, 115, 134, 139, 206, 215,
231, 246, 259, 264, 265n; recordings of, 108, 185-86, 185-86n,
196, 210, 212, 230, 288n, 301, 301-2n; reviews of, 42-43, 63,
71, 89-91, 93-94, 106, 108, 139-40, 169-70, 184-85, 195-97,
201-2, 209, 215-16, 231, 234, 246, 247, 266, 290-92, 302;
rhythms in, xvi, 43-44; serialism in, xiv, xv, xvii, 95, 179-82,
184-85, 186, 189-90, 207, 228-29, 283, 284, 285-86, 292,
293n, 295-96; Stravinsky as influence on, xvi, 19, 30, 49-51, 69,
84, 88-89, 91, 93-94, 107, 137, 140, 229, 283, 284, 292. *See
also* "Index of Irving Fine's Compositions"
Fine, Jack, 304, 307
Fine, Joanna, 135, 148, 223n, 249, 250, 252, 256, 268
  birth of, 200
  on her father's depression, 218
  recollections of her mother, 34, 191, 209
Fine, Louise, 3
Fine, Nathan, 2
Fine, Verna Rudnick, xii, 5, 7, 21, 37, 46, 143, 144, 148
  daughters' recollections of, 34, 191-92, 209-10
  engagement and marriage to Irving, 31-36
  in France, 122
  friends' impressions of, 33-34
  and Harvard faculty, 102
  health problems of, 252, 253, 257
  and Irving's affair with Irene Orgel, 190-93, 190n
  Irving's sisters' recollections of, 32-33
  in Italy, 249, 251, 252, 253
  musical experience of, 36
Finney, Ross Lee, 209
Flanagan, William, 259, 302
Foote, Arthur, 81n
Forbes, Elliot, 25, 65

*Fantasy and Rondo,* 57
Masselos, William, 243-44
Mayes, Samuel, 231
McCarthy, Joseph R., 202-4
McCord, David, 62, 110, 171, 244-46
McCracken, James, 171
McMeekin, Isabel McLennan, 62
Mellers, Wilfrid, 95, 114, 137
Menasce, Jacques de, 71
Mendelssohn, Felix, 177
Menotti, Gian Carlo, 204, 256
Merrick, Becky, 22
Merritt, Arthur, 12
Merritt, Tillman, 53, 64, 65, 74n, 97, 98-99, 100, 101
Mesabi Iron Company, 212, 266-67
Messiaen, Olivier, 126, 126n, 129, 130
Middlesex University, 153-54
Middleton, Robert: *Madrigal,* 83n
Milhaud, Darius, 80, 126, 145, 146
  at Brandeis, 172
  Fine's article on, 123-25
  works of: *Cantate Nuptiale,* 172; *Les Euménides,* 124; *Les Malheurs d'Orphée,* 124; *Médée,* 124, 172; *Salade,* 172
Mingus, Charles, 173
Modell, Arnold, 103, 191, 191n, 220, 301, 307, 308
*Modern Music,* 53-60
Montealegre, Felicia, 171
Monteux, Pierre, 299, 300
Moreux, Serge, 127
Mozart, Wolfgang Amadeus, 173, 227
Munch, Charles, 147, 175, 256, 281, 299-300, 309
  Copland's *Symphonic Ode* conducted by, 232-33
  Fine's *Symphony* conducted by, 188, 284, 286, 289
*musique concréte,* 127-28, 168, 168n, 169

Neaman, Yfrah, 234, 266
Nemiah, John, 224-25
New Art Quintet, 106, 108
New York Philharmonic, 248
New York Woodwind Quintet, 297
*New Yorker Book of Verse,* 61
Nigg, Serge, 130
Norman, Gertrude, 204-5, 205n, 210-11, 235-36, 272-74

O'Connell, Richard L., 44
Orgel, Irene, 190-93, 195
Ormandy, Eugene, 216, 257

*329*

on Fine's music, 91-92, 96, 265, 284
*Symphony No. 3,* 257n
Rosenfeld, Jay C., 231, 302
Ross, Hugh, 80
Roussel, Albert, 237
Roy, Klaus George, 94, 108, 139-40, 160, 195-96, 197
Rudnick, Carl, 32
Rudnick, Florence, 32, 35, 73, 135, 217
Rudnick, Justine, 209
Rudnick, Spencer, 209, 248, 254
Rudnick, Verna. *See* Fine, Verna Rudnick
Russell, George, 173
Russo, William, 257n

Saarinen, Eliel, 77
Sachar, Abram L.
  eulogy for Fine, 308
  on Fine's talents as administrator, 163-65
  as president of Brandeis, 146, 153, 155, 166, 170, 173, 174, 259,
    260, 267
Sachs, Hans, 219
Sadovnikoff, Mary, 173
Saidenberg, Daniel, 200
Saint-Saëns, Camille, 26
Sapp, Allen, 37-38, 41, 42, 46, 110, 199, 201, 303
Sarfaty, Regina, 208
Satie, Erik, 50
Sauguet, Henri, 91, 126
Schaeffer, Pierre, 127, 128, 129n, 168
Schoenberg, Arnold, xv, 54, 130
Schoenberg, Harold C., 71
Schubart, Mark, 209
Schuller, Gunther, 173, 278
Schuman, William, 156, 177, 184, 204, 238, 239, 241n, 273, 288n
  *Prayer in Time of War,* 53-54
  *Symphony No. 5,* 168
  *Undertow,* 221, 221n
Senofsky, Berl, 295
serialism. *See* twelve-tone music
Sessions, Roger, 81n, 182-83, 238, 240-41, 278
Shanet, Howard, 215
Shapero, Esther, 37, 97, 132, 133, 143, 192, 192-93n, 220, 307
Shapero, Harold, xii, xv, 2, 13, 31, 37, 41, 75, 79, 94, 101-2, 143,
    147, 157, 192, 204, 207, 212, 229, 238, 248, 276, 298-99, 305
  on Bernstein, 292-93n
  on Fine's death, 307, 309
  and Fine's depressions, 217, 218-20, 225

on Fine's music, 91, 107, 214, 227, 284
friendship with Fine, 47-48, 67, 103, 116
at the MacDowell Colony, 85, 86
and Tillman Merritt, 98
and Walter Piston, 98-99n
recollections of Verna Fine, 33
short sonatas of, 94-96
Stravinsky as influence on, 49, 74-75
at Tanglewood, 78
as teacher at Brandeis, 159, 159-60n, 160
travels with Fine in Europe, 131-33
works of: *Credo for Orchestra,* 213, 213n; *Piano Sonata No. 1,* 95-96, 106n, 178; *Symphony for Classical Orchestra,* 95, 104-5, 219; *Two Psalms,* 187; *Variations in C Minor,* 95
Shapiro, Karl, 168
Shaw, Robert, 80
Shostakovich, Dmitri, 79, 261
Shute, Florence, 25
Singher, Martial, 234
Slatkin, Leonard, 84
Slonimsky, Nicolas, 308, 309-10
Slosberg, Helen, 260
Slosberg, Samuel, 260
Smit, Leo, 45, 49, 93, 100
Smith, Brooks, 234
Smith, John Hall, 153, 157
Smith, Warren Storey, 196
Solomon, Izler, 172
Spellman, Francis Cardinal, 154
Spiegelman, Joel, 91, 96, 209n, 221, 264n, 288n
Spies, Claudio, 46, 49, 74, 143
Spivacke, Harold, 234
Starer, Robert, 208
Still, William Grant, 55
Stohl, Phyllis, 41-42
Strauss, Richard, 290n
Stravinsky, Igor, xiv, 26, 237, 278, 309
   Boulanger as admirer of, 18
   Fine's association with, 29-30
   as influence on American composers, 49-51, 74-75
   as influence on Fine's music, xvi, 19, 49-51, 69, 84, 88-89, 91, 93-94, 107
   neoclassic ideals of, 18, 18n, 19, 49-51, 81n
   works of: *Concerto for Two Pianos,* 30; *Dumbarton Oaks Concerto,* 16, 51; *Duo Concertant,* 45, 234; Fine as conductor of, 104; *L'Histoire du Soldat,* 18; *Mass,* 83-84; *Movements for Piano and*